Organizing democracy in eastern Germany
Interest groups in post-communist society

The emergence of interest group politics is one of the decisive factors in democratic transformation in post-communist society. Stephen Padgett argues that evidence from eastern Germany suggests that market transition produces rather open and fluid societies, in which group interests and identities are tenuous. Lacking a supportive social infrastructure, interest groups operate on 'entrepreneurial' lines, a form of associational activity which falls far short of pluralist ideals. With its accelerated transition to a market economy, eastern Germany provides a 'fast-forward' study of an 'advanced post-communist society' that enables us to anticipate the social structures and issues shaping interest group politics in the newly democratizing states of east/central Europe. Examining a number of different interest groups, and comparing a number of countries across east/central Europe, this book may also offer a vision of the future of interest group politics in the west.

STEPHEN PADGETT is Professor of Politics at the University of Liverpool. Formerly Jean Monet Reader in European Politics at the University of Essex, he was founding co-editor of the journal *German Politics*. He is the author of *A History of Social Democracy in Post-War Europe*, and editor or co-editor of *Parties and Party Systems in the New Europe*, *Adenauer to Kohl: The Development of the German Chancellorship*, and *Developments in German Politics*.

Organizing democracy in eastern Germany

Interest groups in post-communist society

Stephen Padgett

CAMBRIDGE
UNIVERSITY PRESS

PUBLISHED BY THE PRESS SYNDICATE OF THE UNIVERSITY OF CAMBRIDGE
The Pitt Building, Trumpington Street, Cambridge, United Kingdom

CAMBRIDGE UNIVERSITY PRESS
The Edinburgh Building, Cambridge, CB2 2RU, UK   http://www.cup.cam.ac.uk
40 West 20th Street, New York, NY 10011–4211, USA   http://www.cup.org
10 Stamford Road, Oakleigh, Melbourne 3166, Australia

First published 1999

Printed in the United Kingdom at the University Press, Cambridge

Typeset in Plantin 10/12pt [VN]

A catalogue record for this book is available from the British Library

Library of Congress Cataloguing in Publication data

Padgett, Stephen, 1951–
   Organizing democracy in eastern Germany : interest groups in
   post-communist society / Stephen Padgett.
       p.   cm.
   ISBN 0 521 65170 0 (hardback); ISBN 0 521 65703 2 (paperback)
   1. pressure groups – Germany (East)   I. Title.
   JN3971.5.A792P765   1999
   324'.4'09431–dc21   99–12130   CIP

ISBN 0 521 65170 0 hardback
ISBN 0 521 65703 2 paperback

The author wishes to acknowledge the support of the Economic and
Social Research Council in the form of a Senior Research Fellowhip
which facilitated the research on which this book is based.

Contents

List of tables *page* vi
List of abbreviations and glossary vii

Introduction 1

1 The emergence of civil society 28

2 Socio-economic foundations 52

3 Organization 73

4 Participation and the logic of collective action 98

5 Group dynamics 126

6 Organized interests, the state and public policy 137

Conclusion 166

References 179
Index 193

Tables

3.1	Trade union membership: Germany and east/central Europe	*page* 78
3.2	Trade union membership: eastern Germany 1991–7	88
3.3	Employers' association membership: eastern Germany 1992–3	92
4.1	Political efficacy in Germany and east/central Europe	101
4.2	Indicators of economic development: Germany and east/central Europe	101
4.3	Economic attitudes: Germany and east/central Europe	102
4.4	Trust in public institutions: Germany and east/central Europe	104
4.5	Evaluations of political and economic systems: eastern Germany and east/central Europe	106
4.6	Adherence to collectively agreed wage rates in eastern Germany	119

Abbreviations and glossary

ATLAS	Ausgesuchte Treuhandsunternehmen vom Land angemeldet zur Sanierung [Treuhand Companies Selected by the State for Stabilization]
BASIS	Beratungsstelle für arbeitsorientierte Strukturentwicklung in Sachsen [Consultancy Bureau for Employment-Oriented Structural Development in Sachsen]
BDA	Bundesvereinigung der Deutschen Arbeitgeberverbände [Confederation of German Employers Associations]
BDI	Bundesverband der Deutschen Industrie [Confederation of German Industry]
BfB	Bundesverband der freien Berufe [Federal Association of the Free Professions]
BVMW	Bundesverband Mittelständische Wirtschaft [Confederation of the Mittelstand Economy]
CDU	Christlich Demokratische Union [Christian Democratic Union]
CITUB	Confederation of Independent Trade Unions of Bulgaria
CMKOS	Czech–Moravian Confederation of Trade Unions
CSKOS	Czech and Slovak Confederation of Trade Unions
DGB	Deutscher Gewerkschaftsbund [Confederation of German Trade Unions]
DIHT	Deutscher Industrie- und Handelstag [German Council of Industry and Commerce]
DPG	Deutsche Postgewerkschaft [German Union of Postal Workers]
FDGB	Freier Deutscher Gewerkschaftsbund [Confederation of Free German Trade Unions (GDR)]
FDP	Freie Demokratische Partei [Free Democratic Party]

FNPR	Federation of Independent Trade Unions of Russia
GdE	Gewerkschaft der Eisenbahner Deutschlands [Union of German Railway Workers]
GdP	Gewerkschaft der Polizei [Police Union]
Gesamtmetall	Gesamtverband der metallindustriellen Arbeitgeberverbände [Federation of Metal and Electrical Industry Employers' Associations]
GEW	Gewerkschaft Erziehung und Wißenschaft [Union of Teaching and Scientific Workers]
Gew. Leder	Gewerkschaft Leder (Union of Leather Workers)
GGLF	Gewerkschaft Gartenbau, Land und Forstwirkschaft [Union of Forestry and Agricultural Workers]
GHK	Gewerkschaft Holz und Kunststoff [Union of Wood and Plastics Workers]
GNGG	Gewerkschaft Nahrung-Genuss-Gaststätten [Union of Food Processing and Catering Workers]
GTB	Gewerkschaft Textil-Bekleidung [Union of Textile and Clothing Workers]
HBV	Gewerkschaft Handel, Banken, Versicherung [Union of Workers in Trade, Banking and Insurance]
ICM	Interessenverband Chemnitzer Maschinenbau [Interest Association of Chemnitz Machine-Builders]
IfEP	Institut für Empirische Psychologie [Institute for Empirical Psychology]
IG Medien	Industriegewerkschaft Medien [Union of Media Employees]
IG Metall	Industriegewerkschaft Metall [Union of Engineering and Electrical Workers]
IGBAU	Industriegewerkschaft Bauen-Agrar-Umwelt [Union of Workers in Construction, Agriculture and the Environment]
IGBE	Industriegewerkschaft Bergbau und Energie [Union of Mining and Energy Workers]
IGBSE	Industriegewerkschaft Bau-Steine-Erden [Union of Construction Workers]
IGCPK	Industriegewerkschaft Chemie, Papier, Keramik [Union of Workers in Chemicals, Paper and Ceramics]
IHK	Industrie- und Handelskammer [Chamber of Industry and Commerce]
IWH	Institut für Wirtschaftsforschung Halle [Institute for Economic Research, Halle]

KdT	Kammer der Technik [Chamber of Technology]
LSI	Landesverband der Sächsischen Industrie [Confederation of Industry in Sachsen]
LVSA	Landesvereinigung der Arbeitgeber- und Wirtschaftsverbände Sachsen-Anhalt [Confederation of Employer and Industry Associations in Sachsen-Anhalt]
MAOSZ	National Confederation of Hungarian Employers
MGYOSZ	Association of Hungarian Manufacturing Industry
MSZOSZ	National Association of Hungarian Trade Unions
NAV	Verband der Niedergelassenen Ärzte [Association of Private Practice Doctors]
OPZZ	All-Poland Alliance of Trade Unions
ÖTV	Gewerkschaft Öffentlichen Dienste, Transport und Verkehr [Union of Workers in the Public Sector]
PDS	Partei des Demokratischen Sozialismus [Party of Democratic Socialism]
Podkrepa	Independent Federation of Labour (Bulgaria)
RUIE	Russian Union of Industrialists and Entrepreneurs
SED	Sozialistische Einheitspartei Deutschlands [Socialist Unity Party of Germany]
SMEs	small and medium-sized enterprises
SPD	Sozialdemokratische Partei Deutschlands [German Social Democratic Party]
SZOT	National Council of Hungarian Trade Unions
UV	Unternehmerverband [Entrepreneur Association]
UVB	Vereinigung der Unternehmerverbände in Berlin und Brandenburg [Confederation of Business Associations, Berlin and Brandenburg]
VAS	Vereinigung der Arbeitgerberverbände in Sachsen [Confederation of Employers' Associations in Sachsen]
VB	Virchow-Bund [East German Doctors' Association (merged with NAV)]
VDI	Verein Deutscher Ingenieure [Association of German Engineers]
VDMA	Verband Deutscher Maschinen- und Anlagenbau [Association of German Machinery and Plant Manufacturers]
VME	Verband der Metall- und Elektroindustrie [Association of the Metal and Electrical Industry]

VOSZ   National Association of Entrepreneurs (Hungary)
VSME   Verband der Sächsischen Metall- und Elektroindustrie
             [Association of the Engineering and Electrical Industry
             in Sachsen]
VWT   Verband der Wirtschaft Thüringen [Association of
             Business in Thüringen]

Introduction

The emergence of interest group politics in post-communist society is one of the decisive issues of democratic transformation. Interest groups occupy a key position in pluralist democracy, aggregating private interests, representing those interests in the public policy process and thereby mediating between society and the state. The free association of individuals in groups formed to promote their common interests is thus an important tributary of the democratic process. Their emergence in the new states of east/central Europe is widely recognized as one of the main preconditions of democratic consolidation. Research suggests, however, that, whilst interest groups have proliferated across the region, they bear little resemblance to the pluralist model. Their predominant characteristics are continuity with the old regime, organizational instability and fragmentation, elite domination and mass passivity, and an outsider status in the public policy process. This book attempts to explain the hesitant emergence of associational activity in post-communist society, and to predict the sort of associational order we might expect to see in the future.

It approaches the question from the perspective of group theory. The theoretical core of the book is provided by the various strands of pluralist theory which identify the source of associational activity in particular patterns of social differentiation and stratification arising out of economic relations of modern society. Economic interests and the resultant interest group configurations, it is argued, are embedded in the structure of capital, employment relations and labour markets, and it is here that I shall seek to identify the source of associational activity in post-communist society. This analysis provides the background to the central hypotheses of the book.

The first hypothesis relates to the socio-economic conditions of interest group formation. Given the suppression of social differences under communism, and in the absence of a fully developed market economy, post-communist societies may be insufficiently differentiated to generate the kind of interest group activity seen in western democracies. The

1

progressive emergence of the market economy, it is argued, can be expected to break up the monolithic structures of communist society, but is unlikely to be accompanied by the sharply defined cleavages and cohesive social formations which gave rise to interest group activity in western democracies. The evidence points instead towards a pervasive process of social dealignment, and to the emergence of rather fluid and atomized societies in which group interests and identities are tenuous, and in which the tendencies identified in 'post-modern' social theory will be unusually pronounced.

A second hypothesis concerns the behavioural dimension of associational activity, addressing the question of why and under what circumstances individuals participate in collective action. Group theory offers a number of approaches to the question. Social psychology links participation to personal security and a sense of competence in the private sphere, contrasting the participant 'democratic personality' with the passivity of the anomic type. A second approach relates participation in associational activity to co-operation and trust in the private sphere that spill over into public life, constituting a form of 'social capital' which sustains associational activity. Finally, rational choice theory explains participation in terms of the incentive structures and organizational resources available to the group.

From all these perspectives, it is hypothesized, the fluidity and atomization of post-communist society militates against participation in associational activity. The evidence suggests that market transition is accompanied by a dual psychological response, either economic individualism or a sense of powerlessness and anomie, neither of which is consistent with participation. The accumulation of social capital, it will be argued, is retarded by social dealignment. The tenuous character of social interaction in a society of free-floating individuals inhibits the formation of those networks of co-operation and trust at the heart of the civic culture. From the rational choice perspective, collective action suffers from a scarcity of organizational resources. In the absence of the supportive social networks and distinctive group identities that provide solidary incentives for participation, group mobilization is overdependent upon individual economic motivations, exacerbating the problems identified in collective action theory.

The behavioural dimension of associational activity cannot but be reflected in the internal dynamics of interest group life. I shall examine group dynamics from two theoretical perspectives. In the pluralist model, interest groups are the product of the autonomous associational activity on the part of the beneficiaries, with a professional staff limited to the function of organizational maintenance. Exchange theory, by contrast, is an offshoot of the rational choice approach. Taking as its starting point the professionalization of group activity, this type of analysis characterizes group leaders as 'political entrepreneurs' offering benefits and services in return for membership, in a form of commercial activity. Lacking a supportive social and cultural infrastructure, it will be hypothesized, interest groups in post-communist society will relate to a loosely constituted and shifting clientele, corresponding to the entrepreneurial model identified in exchange theory.

The final hypothesis concerns the relationship between organized interests, the state and public policy. Pluralism suggests a loose-jointed relationship, with a competitive multiplicity of interest groups jostling for influence whilst the state retains its autonomy. Corporatism, on the other hand, postulates the institutionalization of a bipolar configuration of class interests in the public policy apparatus of the state. A symbiotic relationship between *interest mediation* and *policy-making* – the two faces of corporatism – is the defining characteristic of the genre. In post-communist society, it will be argued, the spectrum of interests is too diffuse to be accommodated in a bipolar system of interest mediation. Moreover, the entrepreneurial interest group is too loosely constituted to be able to bind its members to the terms of corporatist exchange. Thus, without the function of genuine interest mediation, the institutions of corporatist policy-making which have proliferated across eastern and central Europe can be seen as no more than attempts by hard-pressed governments to legitimize the social costs of economic transformation. All of these hypotheses contribute to the central project of the book – predicting the sort of associational order we can expect to see emerging alongside the consolidation of market transitions in post-communist society. Before pursuing these hypotheses further, however, we need to embed them more firmly in theories of associational activity, and it is to these that we now turn.

The idea of association

Associational activity occupies the ground between state and society, mediating the two spheres and thereby resolving the central problematic of democratic theory: the tension between the state as the source of authority and civil society as the embodiment of popular sovereignty. In the Athenian polis or Roman republic, the tension did not arise, since state and society were synonymous. Civil society *was* the political order, based upon the principles of citizenship and law, in which liberty and authority were two sides of a single coin. The distinction between state and society that emerged with the Enlightenment was initially accompanied by a libertarian perception of civil society as guardian against the authoritarian potential of the state. Taking society to be a body of undifferentiated individual citizens, Enlightenment thinkers postulated a synthetic definition of 'the general will', embedded in a unitary conception of civil society, exercising sovereignty over the state.

Changing conceptions of the relationship between state and society reflected the transition of *Gemeinschaft* to *Gesellschaft*. With the progressive dissolution of the organic community in the face of the more differentiated forms of social organization accompanying the market economy, the idea of a *unitary* civil society became unsustainable. Market society was seen as a sphere of competitive individualism, dominated by the pursuit of private interests, its egotistic particularities governable only under the 'higher surveillance' of the state (Keane 1988b: 53). For Hegel, the state was the ultimate instrument of social integration: 'the highest purpose of public life is to generate a rational universal identity that he equates with the patriotic ethos of the state' (Cohen and Arato 1992: 113). Thus, in place of the social restraints exercised by civil society over the state in earlier conceptions, Hegel cast the state in the role of regulator of the egotistical tendencies of civil society.

Others sought to restore the earlier libertarian emphasis in state–society relations by identifying a source of social integration within civil society itself. In de Tocqueville's terminology, 'civil society' was equated with private economic interests. The sphere of civil organization between economy and state, to which others have attached the term, he called 'political society'. It is the function of political society to counteract both the egotism of private interests and the tyrannical potential of the modern state. Democratic revolutions had stimulated a drive for social equality and welfare, in the course of which a panoply of 'public utilities' had been created in the form of an all-pervasive state administration. Unchecked, the state is penetrated by and subordinated to private economic interests, stifling social and political liberties. The tyranny of the state and civil society is prevented by vigilance of the 'independent eye' of political society, the realm of autonomous associational activity comprising local self-government, parties, churches, newspapers and public opinion (Kumar 1993: 382). Thus de Tocqueville sees the 'art of association' as fundamental to the democratic well-being of society (de Tocqueville 1988).

Sociological theory, however, adopted a new perspective on the problematic of social integration. Abandoning the attempt to *overcome* social difference, either through a comprehensive, synthetic definition of the general will or through the universal state, Durkheim's (1964) conception of civil society not only recognized but was rooted in social differentiation. Like his predecessor, his starting point was the division of labour, but instead of taking this to be the source of social fragmentation and conflict, his solution focused on the bonds of interdependence and co-operation engendered by this complex and differentiated form of social organization (Saunders 1993: 70–1). The progenitor of functional representation, Durkheim took the professions as his model, seeing in professional ethics the essence of civil morals and the antidote to the egotism of the marketplace. Simmel had a similar view of group affiliation arising out of social conflict, with society 'binding itself together through its own internal divisions' (Simmel 1955: 17–20), whilst Parsons formulated social relations in terms of a 'societal community' composed of a multiplicity of voluntary associations, in which solidarity is the product of discussion and deliberation between individuals bound together through consensus and common values (Parsons 1969: 11–20).

The idea of association thus arose out of attempts to revive the pre-modern community in the face of the social differentiation and egotism of modern society. Instead of subordinating economic interests to political surveillance, either under the state as in Hegel or through autonomous political activity as in de Tocqueville, the sociological tradition entrenched the idea of association in economic life. The sociological theory of group behaviour thus provided a blueprint for the design of a social order regulating the clash of egotistical private interests and reconciling societal pluralism with social solidarity. Simultaneously, by postulating a pluralistic formula for the aggregation of private interests, it provided the foundations for a 'a system of interest representation . . . linking the associationally organized interests of civil society with the decisional structures of the state' (Schmitter 1979b: 9), the defining characteristic of modern pluralism.

Association in post-communist society

The pluralist conception of civil society had a strong resonance in the context of the transition from state socialism to liberal democracy. Democratic revolution entailed a fundamental re-ordering of the relationship between state and society, which lies at the core of democratic theory. The diverse groups that made up the anti-communist movement in 1980s Poland, Hungary and to a lesser extent Czechoslovakia were conceptualized by dissident intellectuals in terms of the emergence of an autonomous sphere of organizational activity alongside or against the weakening apparatus of the party-state. Part of a long-term strategy geared to the liberalization of the state, civil society was identified both as a force undermining communist regimes, and as the foundation of the new post-communist order (Arato 1981; Arato and Cohen 1984; Pelczynski 1988: 362; Miszlivetz 1997: 31).

The attraction of civil society is its offer of a pluralist model for social integration in societies that had previously known no more than an illusion of politics, representing an alternative to the 'pathological' maladies that threaten post-communist societies: either an anomic 'post-modern' individualism, or fundamentalist forms of collective identity based on nationality or ethnicity (Offe 1992: 2). Thus the emergence of civil society is widely regarded as one of the main preconditions of democratic consolidation in post-communist society.

The fall of communist regimes generated expectations of a rapid outgrowth in associational activity, spilling over from mobilization against the communist regime and augmented by autonomous initiatives expressing the spectrum of views and demands that had been suppressed under socialism (Wiesenthal 1995c: 33). In retrospect, it is easy to see how these expectations were misconceived. Amorphous in composition, brought together only by their reforming mission, the movements that accompanied the breakup of communist regimes lacked social foundations and were unsustainable once their mission was complete. Paradoxically, as we shall see in chapter 1, democratization was accompanied by 'the strange death of civil society' (Lomax 1997). The central question of this book is whether we can expect to see its rebirth, and to answer that question we begin by seeking to identify the social roots of associational activity in group theory.

The social foundations of association

Pluralists and corporatists echo earlier themes in group theory, locating the roots of associational activity in the combination of social differentiation and interdependence generated by economic relations in modern society. Thus, 'the conflict generated by structural differentiation and interdependence serves as the midwife to pluralistic interest formation' (Schmitter 1979a: 78). Interest groups are 'constituted on the basis of their function in the social division of labour' (Cawson 1985a: 4), reflecting the institutionalization of the cleavage structures of capitalist society. At the root of this conception of associational activity is the employment relationship, representing the source of the 'categoric cleavage' between employer and employee, around which economic interests form. Interest organization thus reflects the ordering of exchange between capital and labour in employment relations.

Employment relations and the structure of capital

The pluralist model is characterized by fluidity and decentralization, with a multiplicity of employers and trade unions engaged in competitive relationships which fluctuate between co-operation and confrontation. Employment relations are seen as private economy arrangements, outside the political arena. Order and stability are imparted by a mutual desire to contain conflict within a web of rules – 'a commonly shared body of ideas and beliefs regarding the interaction and roles of actors which helps bind the system together' (Dunlop 1958: 383).

In corporatist theory, by contrast, employment relations are institutionalized in a network of formal structures, either backed by legislation as in Germany, or deriving from historic 'basic' agreements between capital and labour as in the Nordic countries. Weaker forms of corporatism may be based on more voluntary and informal arrangements regulating employment. Common to all these systems, however, is the institutional support given to *collective* forms of organization, either by law or by mutual recognition between employers' associations and trade unions. At its most basic level, this means collective wage-bargaining, but the corporatist model also encompasses the institutionalization of employment rights, labour market regulation, worker participation and vocational training.

Collective action in trade unions is embedded in the labour market, where the common interests and status of union members as employees counteract the more diverse spectrum of interests arising out of occupational hierarchies, as well as those product-market related interests which workers might share with their companies. Trade union solidarity thus goes hand in hand with labour market homogeneity (Streeck 1992b: 97–9). Segmented labour markets, on the other hand, can generate a complex pattern of interest divergence along the lines of earning capacity and skills and qualifications between workers with different types of contract (Baglioni 1990: 8–18), as well as between wage-earners and the unemployed (Offe 1985). Divergent interests also reflect labour market variations between high-technology growth sectors and rust-belt industries, and between sectors exposed to international competition and sheltered sectors (Crouch 1993: 17–20, 242–3).

Associational activity amongst employers also stems from their common interests in labour market relations, but this is by no means the exclusive source of collective identity and action in the business arena. Their interests are defined also in relation to the status of firms as owners of capital and producers. Business organization thus reflects the different configurations of interests arising from the structure of capital, and the complex mixture of competition and co-operation surrounding product markets. Variations in the strength and cohesion of business organization are explained in terms of capital concentration, and the relationship between national and international capital (Atkinson and Coleman 1985: 28; Streeck and Schmitter 1992: 208–14). Particular attention has focused on the configuration of large and small firms in the economy or sector. A continuous and even distribution of firms along the size axis promotes sectoral solidarity and co-operation, whilst polarization between large and small firms gives rise to divergent definitions of collective identity, exacerbating a conflict that is endemic to business associations (Grant and Streeck 1985: 162).

Social dealignment and the dissolution of group interests

A model of associational activity embedded in economic relations is, of course, sensitive to shifts in the mode of production. Pluralist and corporatist conceptions, it has been argued, are derived from a pattern of institutionalized employment relations replicating the mode of standardized mass production in which they were rooted. In the late twentieth century this has been undermined by the related syndromes of economic globalization, accelerated technological change and post-Fordism. The shift from national to transnational capital and the accompanying polarization between multinationals and SMEs are difficult to contain within traditional forms of business organization (Streeck and Schmitter 1992: 212–14; Marginson and Sisson 1994: 46–7). Increasingly competitive, specialized and fast-moving product markets are reflected in a more differentiated and polyvalent labour market (Piore and Sabel 1984), undermining institutionalized systems of employment relations and eroding the organizational foundations of trade unions (Baglioni 1990; Visser 1994: 81; Baglioni and Crouch 1990; Hyman 1994: 109–13). Complexity in production is reflected in consumption, with new technologies of customization and marketing leading to market segmentation and cultural differentiation (Beck 1986: 13).

The effects of these tendencies can be seen in shifting patterns of organizational activity, the order and hierarchy of corporatist systems giving way to 'the mobilization of more and more groups', suggesting a 'less orderly model of the policy process' and 'a move back from the corporatist pluralism of the 1970s to the competitive pluralism of the 1950s' (Jordan 1993: 66–7). This 'de-structuring' of interest group systems is seen by others as the breakdown of pluralist interest representation. Increasingly complex and shifting patterns of social differentiation, it is argued, have eroded the group interests and identities on which pluralist association rests. Private interests 'no longer correspond to stable social groups sharing a definite place in the hierarchy of power and influence' (Melucci 1988: 257). Decoupled from their social foundations, interest groups must relate instead to loosely constituted and shifting clientele (Fuchs 1993) with inevitable effects upon the logic of collective action.

Social structure and group interests in post-communist society

As we have seen, group theory locates the foundations of associational activity in patterns of conflict and interdependence arising in economic relations. Given the suppression of social difference under communism, societies in the early stages of market transition are unlikely to be sufficiently differentiated to generate the socio-economic issues and cleavages around which group interests and identities form (Wiesenthal 1993). 'In a society in which the labour market is unknown . . . the social structure lacks the requisite . . . differentiation of status, interest, and cultural identity that only a developed market society will generate' (Offe 1991: 876–7). Most authors have assumed, however, that, as the market economy expands and the communist legacy recedes, interest group policies will converge with the model with which we are familiar in the west. This book challenges this assumption.

Trajectories of market transition are, of course, subject to cross-national variation. Poland, the Czech Republic and, to a lesser extent, Russia adopted radical strategies of 'shock therapy' involving a rapid divestment of state assets to the private sector through mass privatization. Hungary initially took a more gradualist path, building on market economy developments which had begun under the old regime, but subsequently adopting more radical measures to step up the pace of transition. The Balkan model reflects the continuing exercise of power by communist elites, retaining a large part of the state sector in a mixed economy in which entrepreneurial activity remains restricted and regulated. These different trajectories, however, have been subject to convergence, as radical strategies encountered political obstacles which slowed the pace of privatization. Even in the countries that pursued shock therapy, privatization has failed to penetrate parts of the state sector, a residual core of which continues to coexist with the private sector in a dual-track economy not totally dissimilar from the mixed model which predominates in the Balkan countries.

Market transition, it is argued, is not yet reflected in a consolidated structure of capital ownership, or a fully developed labour market. The predominant mode of mass privatization produces a dispersed distribution of capital and a weak property structure which retards the formation of an entrepreneurial business class. Cross-cutting cleavages between state and private sectors, large and small firms, indigenous and foreign capital, and the liberal and 'nomenklatura bourgeoisie' are replicated in organizational activity, with an anarchic plurality of business circles and entrepreneur clubs. With underdeveloped structures of capital ownership inhibiting role differentiation between managers and employees, employment and labour market relations are ill defined. The dominant trend, however, is towards decentralization and individualization, with little evidence of institutionalized forms of collective bargaining. Across the associational order, then, the inchoate character of economic relations means that associational activity is deprived of the social infrastructures that support collective action in the pluralist model.

Chapter 2 of this book examines the social foundations of interest group politics in post-communist society. It is motivated by one central question: is the emergent market economy likely to generate the cohesive social formations and interdependent interests underpinning the pluralist model of the associational order, or do the indications point instead towards rather fluid and atomized societies in which group interests and identities are tenuous, and in which the tendencies identified in contemporary social theory will be unusually pronounced? With societies still in flux, the countries of eastern and central Europe provide no more than a tentative answer. An accelerated transition to the market economy means that eastern Germany should provide a sharper image of the social structures and cleavages shaping associational activity in an *advanced* post-communist society.

Organizational design

Organizational design occupies a prominent position in corporatist analysis. Corporatist systems make heavy demands upon the associational capacity of their constituent groups, the representation of broadly based class interests through centralized organization being the defining feature of the genre. Centralization is often seen in terms of hierarchical discipline, focusing on the strength of 'peak' confederations at the apex of the system, and the authority that they are able to exert over their constituents (Schmitter 1981: 294). Corporatist systems are monopolistic, with unitary groups dominating their respective interest domains.

Whilst centralization is the dominant form of corporatism, an alternative perspective uses the concept of *articulation* to define its structural prerequisites (Crouch 1993: 54–5). In place of hierarchical discipline, an articulated structure is characterized by strong relations of interdependence between confederation leadership and the organizational base, mediated and co-ordinated at the sectoral level. Co-ordination is most effective in concentrated systems with a limited number of internally cohesive and centralized sector organizations 'in touch with lower levels and also in straightforward communication on a face-to-face basis with leaders at confederal level' (Crouch 1993: 192). A strong tier of organization at the sectoral level thus provides an alternative to centralized confederations as the focus of corporatist systems. Both these variants of the model are monopolistic, however, presupposing that at both confederal and sectoral levels representational activity will culminate in a unitary organization exercising hegemony over its interest domain.

Hierarchy and order are alien to the principles of voluntary association which underlie pluralist theory. Whilst corporatist centralization implies unitary organizations exercising a monopoly over their respective interest domains, pluralist systems are characterized by a multiplicity of voluntary, competitive, non-hierarchically ordered groups (Schmitter 1979b: 15). Thus, in contrast to the concentrated model of corporatist interest representation in which the 'peak' organizations of capital and labour play a key role, pluralist analysis suggests a fragmented system of competing interests. It will be argued in chapter 3 that, in the absence of cohesive social formations, and with its broad and diverse spectrum of interests, post-communist society is likely to gravitate towards the pluralist model of competition and fragmentation rather than the more concentrated and orderly design of corporatist structures.

Participation and the logic of collective action

Classical democratic theory paid little attention to the questions of why and under what circumstances individuals engage in collective action, simply equating participation with citizenship, conceived by Hegel in terms of *Sittligkeit*, the ethical norms of a society's public life (Taylor 1975: 382), or by de Tocqueville as 'the manners of the people . . . habits of the heart . . . character of mind' (de Tocqueville 1988: 244). Pluralism and corporatism also offer little to explain the behavioural and attitudinal dimension of collective action. Associational activity is merely the product of voluntaristic action on the part of individuals brought together by common interests. Groups are constituted around interests, the *individual* pursuit of private interests leading inexorably to the *collective* pursuit of group interests. Social science offers a number of theoretical perspectives on the question of participation. Social psychology provides the first perspective, taking participation to be a property of the 'democratic personality', an outgrowth of a sense of personal competence and security in the private spheres (Lasswell 1948; R. Lane 1959). A second approach is via the concept of social capital. Co-operation in social life generates the interpersonal trust and organizational skills that sustain a participatory political culture (Almond and Verba 1963). Finally, in rational choice theory, participation in collective action is explained in terms of economic incentive structures and resource availability (Olson 1965). Each of these perspectives generates its own expectations about the dynamics of group participation in post-communist society.

Participation and political efficacy

Social psychological explanations take participation to be a property of the democratic personality, in which a sense of security and competence in the private sphere engenders perceptions of efficacy in public life. Thus, 'a general sense of personal effectiveness is intrinsic to democratic participation' (R. Lane 1959: 163; Gabriel 1995: 359). 'It is only when people feel in control of their own lives that they will venture out to play an active role in the wider society' (Saunders 1993: 86). An ability to relate to others and a sense of confidence in the social environment have also been identified as part of 'the democratic character' (Lasswell 1948: 148–73). Conversely, the anomic individual, characterized by a sense of powerlessness and alienation, and with a concomitant sense of mistrust, hostility and cynicism, is much more likely to be a passive citizen (Campbell 1962). Alongside the *internal* dimension, the individual's sense of efficacy is also conditioned by perceptions of the *external* political environment. Orientations towards democratic participation are strengthened by the belief that the political system is responsive to individual intervention.

With its emphasis on personal security as a prerequisite of political engagement, social psychology introduces economic variables into the equation. Inglehart offers a variant of this type of approach, in which political values and behaviour are closely related to the economic environment. His concept of post-materialism is based on a hierarchy of social needs, the most fundamental of which are material and physical security. Only when 'people are safe and they have enough to eat' do they turn their attention to those 'higher' goals which are still in short supply: quality of life, self-expression and personal freedom (Inglehart 1971: 996–7). This re-orientation of objectives goes hand in hand with the intensification of political engagement and the diversification of the repertoire of participatory activity. Characterized by economic insecurity and a preoccupation with basic social needs, post-communist society cannot be expected to support post-materialist value orientations. Indeed, it may not fulfil the prerequisites for the traditional repertory of participation.

In post-communist society, it has been argued, the individual's sense of political efficacy is depressed by the syndrome of 'civilizational incompetence', which has been identified as part of the communist legacy. Powerlessness in the face of the capricious and unresponsive power of the state bred a fatalistic view of the world in which individuals saw little opportunity to control their own lives, and even less influence over public life. Low levels of internal efficacy were compounded by the limitations of the external political environment. Engagement was seen as futile, since 'people were unable to see any way in which it could change anything' (Sztompka 1993: 91). The communist legacy thus stifles the sense of personal competence and efficacy that fosters a readiness to engage in the public sphere. Moreover, if, as social psychology suggests, participation is a correlate of individual security in the private sphere, then post-communist society can be expected to be infertile ground for collective action. Market transition, it will be argued in chapter 4, is accompanied by a combination of opportunities and threats that elicits a dual response: either economic individualism and a syndrome of 'lifeboat economics' in which the pursuit of private solutions is uppermost, or a passive withdrawal into anomie and isolation in the private sphere. Neither of these psychological responses is conducive to participation in collective action.

Participation and social capital

The concept of *social capital* explains cross-national differences in participation with reference to cultural variables. For Almond and Verba, the foundations of the participant or civic culture are located in patterns of interpersonal relations and sociability in which individuals venture forth from the private sphere in a spirit of mutual confidence and trust. Co-operative interaction in social life generates social capital in the form of civic competence which is reinvested in democratic political activity. Indeed, the private and the public are related in a seamless network of interaction linking the individual, civil society and the state.

On this basis, Almond and Verba constructed a threefold typology of political culture. The *parochial* type is associated with pre-modern societies in which life revolves around primary relations in the private sphere, with little or no orientation towards politics. By contrast, the *subject culture* is characteristic of a modern political system, but one in which participation is limited. Individuals have little confidence in their ability to influence politics. Their attitudes towards political institutions are detached or distant, with an instrumental 'output orientation' towards system performance. The third type is the *participant* or civic culture in which an abundance of social capital is reflected in a highly developed sense of personal competence, confidence in individual influence in politics, an activist role in public and political life, and a deep-rooted and generalized attachment to political institutions. Drawing upon this logic, Putnam (1993) has deployed the concept of social capital to explain the relationship between civic traditions and political behaviour in relation to the 'two Italies' – one characterized by democratic participation, the other by parochial and clientelistic clan relations. Democratic participation, he argues, is closely correlated with the existence of a densely organized public sphere of social and cultural activity, in the absence of which the civic community is impoverished and clientelism flourishes.

Social capital is a generalized resource which carries over into democratic allegiance, representing a bedrock of mass support and legitimacy at the foundations of system stability. Contemporary political analysis uses a number of indicators of allegiance to democracy: popular belief in the core principles and values of democracy; satisfaction with democratic regimes (the way democracy works); and attitudes towards political institutions. The relationship between democratic allegiance and economic performance is a common theme in the literature. In the absence of socially rooted allegiance, support for political and social institutions is conditional on satisfaction with performance, and institutions may be overloaded with the burden of expectation.

The emergence of a civic culture in post-communist society might be expected to follow from the democratization of public life, and the acquisition in this arena of the social and organizational skills which constitute social capital. The process may be inhibited, however, by the communist legacy of disjuncture between private and public spheres, preventing the spillover of social capital from interpersonal relations to public life. By restricting public life to the elite, it has been argued, communism prevented the development of the social and organizational skills that constitute social capital, leaving a legacy of 'civilizational incompetence', which is the antithesis of the civic culture. The facility with which individuals in liberal democratic society move between the private and public spheres was alien to communist society. Indeed, the dichotomy between the two spheres was 'the most fundamental . . . cultural code organizing thought and action' under communism. The public sphere was perceived as 'alien and hostile . . . the arena of conspiracy, deceit, cynicism and inefficiency'. Private networks by contrast, at work, among friends or at home, were 'overestimated and idealized' (Sztompka 1993: 90).

The prevalence of interpersonal networks is a common theme in accounts of communist society. Social co-operation replicated the matrix of the family, as 'small groups connected by common interests, views and . . . customs became the fundamental settings of social identification', transforming society into 'an aggregate of primary groups' (Marody 1992: 171–2). Rose draws the analogy of the 'hour-glass society' with a rich social life of interpersonal relations at the base, and a dense web of elite networks at the top of the glass. 'The narrow mid-point of the glass insulated individuals from the influence of the state' (Rose 1995: 35), constricting the interaction between the private and public sphere that is one of the hallmarks of the civic culture. Where the public arena is regarded with suspicion, it has been argued, and emphasis is placed upon the moral superiority of private relations, citizenship is likely to take a more passive form (Turner 1993b: 9).

The expectation that the opening up of the public arena is accompanied by 'social learning' and the accumulation of social capital will be examined in chapter 4. In the countries of east/central Europe, it will be argued, there is little to suggest the emergence of a participant civic culture. Society remains marked by the disjuncture between the private and public spheres, and by a pervasive sense of social mistrust, both of which inhibit the accumulation of social capital. The east German case suggests that, even in an advanced post-communist society, social capital accumulation is retarded by a preoccupation with private concerns, and by a process of social dealignment that accompanies market transition, preventing the formation of those networks of social co-operation and trust that are characteristic of the civic culture.

Incentive structures and organizational resources

Variants of rational choice theory provide a third perspective from which to explain participation in collective action. Challenging the pluralist assumption that groups are constituted around interests, and that the individual pursuit of private interests leads logically to the collective pursuit of shared interests, the exponents of this type of analysis see collective action in terms of cost–benefit calculations and incentive structures. The main conclusion derived from this logic is that collective material interest provides insufficient incentive for group action. Since the benefits of collective interest representation are freely available to members and non-members alike, it is argued, the rational individual will not sacrifice his time and money in the pursuit of common interest, but will stand by as the passive beneficiary of the collective action of others (the 'free-rider' syndrome). Rational individuals will subscribe to collective action only in response to the offer of private economic incentives exclusive to group members. Interest groups derive their strength and support from the provision of selective economic benefits, with representation merely a byproduct of this primary function (Olson 1965).

Criticism of the rational choice model focuses on two main shortcomings of the analysis. First, the model neglects broader strategic considerations. Where collective goods are of strategic importance, and when their supply is insecure, group members may subscribe to the organization even though the benefits are available to outsiders (Kimber 1993: 44–5). Under these circumstances, the decision to join is based on a calculation of the risks of free-riding seen in terms of organizational breakdown and the subsequent loss of benefits. Secondly, the model neglects the 'purposive' political benefits of group membership. This concept introduces a political dimension into the rational actor model: 'members who agree with group goals, especially if motivated by class consciousness and feeling of solidarity, may join and participate because of the expressive benefits gained from doing so' (Moe 1980: 170). This reasoning is carried forward by resource mobilization theory. Concurring with the conclusion that collective material interests *alone* provide insufficient incentives for group formation, this variant of group theory relates the potential for mobilization to the *organizational resources* available to the group. Mobilization is greatly facilitated by two key resources: a distinctive group *identity* providing solidary incentives for participation, and a supportive infrastructure of *interpersonal networks* amongst the potential participants (Jenkins 1983: 538).

One of the central arguments of this book is that incentive structures and organizational resources of collective action are rooted in economic life. In chapter 2 we will see how the post-communist economy generates a fragmented spectrum of interests. The structure of capital, it will be argued, is unconducive to the formation of the intercorporate networks that support the mobilization of business interests. Similarly, the fragmentation of individual and collective interests in the labour market undermines employee solidarity. In the absence of the social infrastructures that the pluralist model takes for granted, interest groups are underendowed with the organizational resources that sustain collective mobilization and are susceptible to the collective action problems identified in rational choice theory. Lacking the supportive social networks and distinctive group identities that provide solidary incentives for participation, group mobilization becomes overdependent on the provision of selective membership incentives. The membership profile of business groups, professional associations and trade unions thus reflects a logic of collective action in which individual economic incentives predominate, with a corresponding weakness in membership ties.

Across east/central Europe, collective action in both trade unions and business circles is heavily concentrated in the state sector, where it draws heavily on organizational resources inherited from the previous regime. In the trade unions, solidary incentives appear to be ineffective, with membership motivations revolving primarily around economic calculations. Similarly in business associations, selective membership incentives predominate, alongside the lure of economic advantage derived from the clientelism and corruption which permeates the associational order. In the German case, where trade unions and employers' associations are institutionalized in industrial relations, incentive structures are inextricably bound up with the dynamics of wage-bargaining.

Towards the post-modern scenario?

As we saw at the end of the last section, the social infrastructures that support associational activity in the pluralist model with which we are familiar in the west have been subject to the related syndromes of globalization, technological change and post-Fordism. Conceptualizing the resultant tendencies towards social dealignment, contemporary social theory postulates a progressive shift away from Almond and Verba's stereotype of 'the civic culture', towards what some have termed a 'democratic pathology', in which a reduced sense of political efficacy is coupled with a corresponding increase in alienation, cynicism and apathy towards politics. An upsurge of individualism is seen in terms of 'a new breed of self-centred and calculating citizens' motivated by the 'costs and benefits of political involvement' and an 'instrumental assessment of political performance'. Negative perceptions of the latter have led to reduced confidence in political institutions and a declining belief in democracy. Less tightly bound to society, individuals become more critical, more demanding and less reliable participants in collective action (Kaase and Newton 1995: 28–37). With little sense of group identity, solidary incentives prove ineffective. Group membership becomes increasingly instrumental and dependent upon the provision of selective incentives (Aarts 1995: 205). In the absence of strong social networks, mobilization lacks the requisite supportive infrastructure.

Whilst the 'black' post-modern scenario identifies social dealignment with democratic decline, others take a more optimistic view, identifying opportunities for the revitalization of democracy. For them, the erosion of institutional politics opens up space for new social movements (Offe 1985: 819–20), substituting 'participation, autonomy and solidarity for consumption, efficiency and growth' (Cohen and Arato 1992: 44). The prescription for the renewal of civil society through social movement politics is formulated in terms of space for individuals to assert their identity in 'public places . . . independent of the institutions of government, party system and state'. Social movements in this formulation serve a dual function, articulating collective demands and at the same time identifying the individual with the 'general interests' of the community (Melucci 1988: 258–9), in a conception of 'the democratization of everyday life' that can be seen as a post-modernist variant of de Tocqueville's notion of self-organization and the art of association.

Does the post-modern scenario provide a convincing template against which to predict the sort of associational order that can be expected to emerge in the countries of east/central Europe? At first sight its use may appear inappropriate. Not yet integrated into the global economy, still technically backward and with industrial relations continuing to exhibit the hallmarks of the communist legacy, post-communist societies remain unexposed to the forces of post-modernism. Yet there are grounds for anticipating developments in this direction. Market transition renders these societies susceptible to the tendencies towards social fragmentation and individualization that underlie the post-modern syndrome. Drawn within the ambit of international capital, and with the acceleration of technological change, we might expect advanced post-communist society to be subject to the forces of social dealignment that have undermined traditional forms of associational activity in the west. It will be argued in this volume that the evidence of eastern Germany's advanced post-communist society already points in this direction.

Group dynamics

If, as rational choice theory suggests, group *membership* is governed by economic self-interest, then it is but a short step to apply a similar perspective to the *leadership*. The classical model of interest groups as solidarity communities implies autonomous organizational activity and a participatory style of decision-making, with a professional leadership restricted to the functions of organizational maintenance and co-ordination. This model has long since ceased to reflect reality. The intensification of relations between interest groups and the state generates a more technical style of interest representation, with increasingly complex organizations subject to the domination of professional specialists and members cast in the role of clients rather than participants in internal organizational life (Etzioni 1961).

Exchange theory takes this reasoning a step further, characterizing the leadership and professional staff of organized interests as 'political entrepreneurs' offering benefits and services at a price in return for membership (Salisbury 1969). From this perspective, 'the founding and running of "voluntary" associations would appear to be a variation of business activities involving the production and merchandising of simply another commodity' (Wiesenthal 1995c: 7). The concept need not be taken literally to imply individual entrepreneurs deriving economic gain or personal political influence from their role in group organization. It can be seen in the broader sense of interest groups dominated by a salaried leadership offering services to a membership of clients and customers in pursuit of organizational goals. The defining characteristic of this mode of organization, however, is the essentially impersonal relationship between the group and its members. It suggests a qualitatively different associational order from the one postulated by classical group theory, replacing co-operation and interdependence with commercial exchange as the medium of organization.

It has been hypothesized above that, lacking supportive social infrastructures, collective action in post-communist society will be characterized by pragmatism and instrumentality in membership motivations. It can be further expected that, where the decision to join is motivated by access to selective economic benefits, the willingness to participate in internal organizational life is likely to be lower than where membership revolves around the solidary incentives associated with group identification. Group dynamics are thus likely to be characterized by mass passivity and professional domination, taking the form of the loosely coupled exchange relationship of entrepreneurial model rather than the pluralist ideal of autonomous associational activity. Contrary to contemporary accounts, the anti-communist movements that accompanied democratic revolution in some eastern and central European countries showed little evidence of autonomous associational activity. As we shall see in chapter 1, mass mobilization was largely orchestrated by elites, and quickly evaporated once its mission was accomplished. It will be argued in chapter 5 that associational activity in post-communist society is similarly dependent on elite orchestration.

Organized interests, the state, and public policy

In contrast to the separation between the public and private spheres in classical democratic theory, both pluralists and corporatists see state and society entwined in a relationship mediated by organized interests. The relationship is conceived, however, in different ways. Corporatism sees a *structured* relationship in which organized socio-economic interests are incorporated into the public policy process and allocated certain functions of economic governance. Structure is alien to the pluralist model:

'almost any structured relationship between associations and government is suspect' (Anderson 1979: 285).

The two faces of corporatism

Schmitter (1979b: 9) has defined corporatism as 'a system of . . . interest representation . . . linking the associationally organized interests of civil society with the decisional structures of the state'. This definition allowed him to distinguish between the two faces of corporatism: the first as a mode of *interest mediation*; the second as a system of *policy-making* (Schmitter 1982: 262–3). Conceived as a mode of interest mediation, corporatism explains the way in which patterns of socio-economic differentiation acquire organizational form. As a mode of policy-making, it signifies a system of public policy formation characterized by exchange between organized interests and the state. Schmitter's distinction underlines the defining feature of the corporatist paradigm as the 'fusion' between interest mediation and policy formation. Corporatism thus purports to resolve the dual problematic of democratic theory, by providing a formula for solving the conflicts generated by social differentiation through an ordered system of interest mediation that at the same time relates social interests to the state (Cawson 1985a: 8; Lehmbruch 1982: 8).

Institutionalizing social cleavages in the policy process, *macro-corporatism* takes the form of co-operative exchange between capital, labour and the state for mutual political benefits. The state undertakes to promote high levels of employment in return for trade union commitments to wage restraint, which provides an incentive for employers to exercise social responsibility in their investment and employment decisions. A crucial variable in this model of generalized political exchange is the role of government as gatekeeper to the entry of organized interests into the political arena. Observers have drawn attention to the function of government as patron of political action in shaping the configuration of interest group systems, 'creating, maintaining and empowering' organized interests. The participation of organized interests in politics has often been taken to reflect the weakness of the state, but the equation may also be reversed. The state must be sufficiently strong to allocate roles, set agendas and induce groups to comply. Thus a strong state is taken to be a prerequisite of corporatist arrangements (Atkinson and Coleman 1985: 29; Hayward 1995: 226–8).

Political parties also play an important role in corporatist systems, legitimizing and mediating the entry of social interests into politics. Corporatism infringes the liberal doctrine of democracy, the incorporation of privileged social interests into the political process posing a challenge to the centrality of parliamentary representation. The gulf between the two systems may be reduced by the linkages that political parties provide between organized interests and the parliamentary arena. The ability of parties to perform this mediating role, however, depends heavily upon their roots in civil society. The traditional type of mass party identified by Neumann (1956) had its foundations in the social collectivities that constituted society, embedded in the 'solidarity communities' of labour movement, entrepreneurial middle class and church. Despite the weakening of class structures in the post-war era, the large parties of western Europe retained an identification with allied social interests. Thus the corporatist bargaining of the 1970s was often brokered by social democratic parties mobilizing their historic affinity with organized labour (Cameron 1984).

In contrast to the class-rooted structures of interest mediation at the macro level, *meso-corporatism* revolves around much narrower sector-specific interests, cutting across the class alignments which prevail at societal level (Cawson 1985a: 12–14). The complexity and variability of state–sector relations precludes a clear-cut definition of meso-corporatism, but in broad terms it is indicative of co-operation between the state and sectoral interests in the formulation and implementation of industry policy. Interlocution tends to be technical in character, conducted through a discourse of specialist expertise rather than political partisanship. A common variant of meso-corporatism occurs in industries in structural decline, in which government and sectoral interests conclude crisis management agreements that serve to defuse the social conflicts attendant upon industrial crisis. The costs of industrial restructuring are distributed between the state, capital and labour, with the state providing subsidies to support corporate restructuring, in return for trade union acceptance of plant closures and redundancies. Not infrequently, such agreements are the result of crisis cartels between unions and management lobbying government for financial support. Where a region's economy is heavily dependent on the declining sector, mutual reinforcement between sectoral and territorial solidarity provides the foundation for regional corporatism.

The rise and decline of corporatism

With its emphasis on stability and order, macro-corporatism was at its most effective in mediating the economic strategies of the 1960s and 1970s. The western European experience suggests a relationship of mutual reinforcement between corporatist policy-making and Keynesian solutions to the problem of reconciling growth, inflation and employment. On the basis of this experience, it was argued that macro-corporatism contributed to stable governance (Schmitter 1981), and enhanced economic performance in terms of employment and inflation (Schmidt 1982). Since the early 1980s, however, the evidence is much less compelling. Corporatist policy-making, it has been argued, has been a 'fair weather creature' (Cawson 1985a: 10), relying heavily on the capacity of the state to reconcile capital accumulation with high levels of employment and welfare. In the face of economic recession, macro-corporatism loses much of its force as capital turns to more flexible accumulation strategies with an emphasis on company initiatives rather than bargaining at the level of the national economy (Crouch 1993: 17).

The decline of corporatist policy-making also reflects decisive changes in the party arena, the mass party giving way to the more loosely constituted Volkspartei, and subsequently to the professional-electoral party (Panebianco 1988). The progressive differentiation of post-modern society has produced a more open political landscape, accompanied by the intensification of party competition, a correspondingly more intensive exploitation of new information and marketing technologies in electoral strategy, and a proliferation of professional technical specialists at the heart of the party apparatus. The loosely coupled and anonymous organizational systems of this type of party are ill adjusted for the performance of the traditional functions of social integration. Increasingly distant from their traditional interest group allies, parties are less able to mediate corporatist relations.

Corporatism in post-communist society

Schmitter's distinction between the two faces of corporatism is a productive one in the context of post-communist society. As a system for reconciling conflicting class interests, corporatist *mediation* depends upon the existence of broadly based social formations, with clearly defined interests and sufficient organizational strength and discipline to bind their members to agreements. Amorphous and atomized, containing a diverse spectrum of interests, and with a low organizational potential, post-communist society is unconducive to interest mediation on these lines. Conceived as a mode of *policy-making*, on the other hand, corporatism has obvious attractions for governments as a means of ordering relations between the state and the economy, and of pre-empting conflict by legitimizing the social costs of economic transformation. It will be argued in chapter 6, however, that the one-dimensional form of tripartism characteristic of the post-communist countries bears little more than a superficial resemblance to the consolidated corporatist arrangements deployed in macro-economic crisis management in western Europe in the 1970s.

The preconditions of macro-corporatist exchange, it will be argued, are almost entirely lacking from post-communist society. First, in the absence of the social infrastructures which underpin collective action in the corporatist model, neither business nor the trade unions possesses the requisite organizational strength to sustain corporatist exchange. Secondly, the ideological bonds between trade unions and parties of the left that sustained the classical model of corporatism are largely absent from the east European variant, which rests for the most part on a tenuous alliance between governments often of the centre-right and trade unions, based on pragmatism and a common commitment to an ill-defined conception of 'economic reform'. Thirdly, undermined by deteriorating economic performance, tripartite bargains are often little more than symbolic gestures on the part of hard-pressed governments, made in return for rhetorical commitments of support by trade unions. Thus the relationship between organized interests and the state in the post-communist societies can be seen as 'tripartism without corporatism', characterized by instability and highly susceptible to breakdown.

Transformation theory and comparative method

Although all the formerly communist countries of east/central Europe have undergone democratic transformations, the region is characterized by a high degree of political diversity, with considerable cross-national variation in the pace and extent of the transformation process. The most developed and consolidated democratic systems, it has been argued, are to be found in Hungary, Poland and the Czech Republic, followed by Slovenia, Slovakia and Bulgaria, with the Balkan countries lagging behind (Lewis 1997: 4–5). Theoretical attempts to explain these differences in the trajectory of democratization have focused first on the wide variations in levels of socio-economic development across the region (Huntington 1991). The equation of stable democracy with economic development has a long pedigree (Bendix 1964; Moore 1966, Lipset 1959, 1994). It provides the foundations for political development theory (Almond and Coleman 1960; Pye and Verba 1965; Pye 1990), in which economic modernization is linked to a growth in the scale and complexity of government, and the accompanying diffusion of political power. This type of theory identifies the factors of change – economic growth, technological advance and the intensification of communications – progressively liberating politics from authoritarianism, bringing in their wake a more open and participatory political style conducive to associational activity.

The theoretical perspective outlined above provides a sharper focus on the relationship between economy and democracy, locating the socio-economic foundations of associational activity in patterns of social stratification generated by market relations. From this perspective, we would expect to find a correlation between pluralist association and the more rapid and thoroughgoing market transitions found in Poland, the Czech Republic and Hungary. Retarded economic transformation in the Balkan countries, by contrast, can be expected to inhibit associational activity on pluralist lines.

A second theoretical perspective has attempted to explain variations in democratic development in terms of different patterns of elite interaction that accompanied regime change (Szablowski and Derlien 1993). Transition from above, as in Russia, leaves economic elites relatively undisturbed, and the associational order is likely to be marked by the persistence of old structures and modes of behaviour. Where regime change was effected through negotiation between communist and counterelites, as in Poland and Hungary, interest group politics can be expected to assume a dual character, with familiar structural and behavioural patterns of association persisting alongside emergent pluralist forms. Where democratic transition followed the collapse of the old regime and involved a radical process of elite turnover, as in Czechoslovakia, we might expect to see a cleaner break with the past. Finally, where regime change and élite interaction is surrounded by ethno-linguistic conflict, as in the Balkans, associational activity on socio-economic lines is likely to be eclipsed by more fundamentalist forms of mobilization.

The utility of elite exchange theory lies in its ability to explain the dynamics of political systems, which are largely unrelated to the social cleavages underlying politics in the west, and which have revolved instead around relations between hardliners and reformists in the old communist elite, interaction between communists and democrats, and conflicts between the advocates and opponents of the market. It may have less utility in explaining the mobilization of collective, social interests in the associational order. Nevertheless, it may help to explain the particular type of interest group which, as suggested above, appears to be characteristic of post-communist society. The *entrepreneurial* interest group is essentially elite-oriented and, where associational activity takes this form, interest group systems may be seen as an extension of the competitive struggle for influence among elites. Competition between reformed communist trade unions and their new union rivals could be seen in these terms. Similarly the competitive mêlée of business groups might be construed in terms of the interaction between a reconstituted communist nomenklatura and newly emerging economic elites. From this perspective, group politics in the post-communist societies can be expected to reflect the different configuration of elites arising out of political and economic transitions rather than the more socially structured model found in the west.

Whilst the analysis in this book is attentive to these comparative questions, however, a comprehensive and systematic cross-national comparison of interest group activity across the region is beyond its scope. Democratic revolutions preceded economic transformation, and, whilst constitutional and institutional arrangements are now sufficiently clearly defined to submit to comparative analysis, the outline of the associational order remains too indistinct for us to be able to identify or explain cross-national patterns of interest group politics. Rather than a comparative study of the diverse characteristics of group activity in different post-communist *societies*, then, the book is first and foremost a study of the dynamics of interest group activity in post-communist *society*, emphasizing common features rather than cross-national differences.

The central focus of the book is interest group politics in the *advanced* post-communist society of eastern Germany. The former GDR is, of course, set apart from the rest of east/central Europe by a unique road to democratic transformation via assimilation with an advanced capitalist economy and a 'ready-made' liberal democratic state. Whilst the singularity of the German case makes comparison hazardous, it does, however, provide valuable insights into the formation of interest group politics in a post-communist society at an advanced stage of economic development. An accelerated transition to the market economy is reflected in ownership relations, capital formation and labour markets, providing a 'fast-forward' study which enables us to anticipate the socio-economic structures, cleavages and issues which might be expected to shape interest group politics in the less developed post-communist societies. It thus allows us to test whether the features identified in interest group politics elsewhere in east/central Europe are merely temporary effects caught in snapshot images of societies in an early stage of democratic transition, or if they are likely to be more permanently embedded in the post-communist political landscape.

Eastern Germany is also unique in respect of a democratization process that took the form of unification with the Federal Republic and an associational order which came ready-furnished by institutional and, in large part, elite transfer from the west. Characterized by 'broadly encompassing, internally homogenous interest organizations' (Streeck 1984: 145), invested with a 'highly developed capacity for generating interest positions' (Deubner 1984: 519) and a 'deep sense of interdependency and social responsibility in the exercise of private economic power' (Dyson 1981: 53–4), the German model incorporates a configuration of structural and normative features that corresponds very closely to the pluralist ideal. By examining the functioning of the model in eastern Germany, we are able to assess the congruence between the pluralist ideal and the realities of post-communist society.

Research

Whilst the analysis of associational activity in east/central Europe relies entirely on secondary sources, the core of the book is based on around forty-five qualitative interviews with interest group officials in eastern Germany, conducted in 1994–5. Whilst most studies of interest group activity focus on a single type of group, or sector, this research spans three types: business and employers' associations, trade unions, and professional groups (in the medical and engineering professions). The scope of the research is thus wide enough to generate broadly generalized conclusions. At the same time, however, the research is confined to economic interests. A more widely inclusive study would be confronted by a bewildering diversity of group types, inevitably reducing the potential for generalization. Interest group officials were targeted as interview subjects because of their strategic overview of activity.

Interviews were semi-structured to focus on the key dimensions of associational activity as identified from group theory. The first part of the interview was concerned with organizational mapping: eliciting information about the strength and depth of group organization in terms of membership density, staffing levels and the extent of its local apparatus. A second set of questions examined the socio-economic foundations of the group, seeking to identify links between underlying patterns of social stratification and the composition of group membership. The purpose of this part of the interview was to assess the organizational resources at the disposal of the group, in terms of the social networks and collective identities that sustain associational activity in resource mobilization theory. This led to a third part of the interview, examining the behavioural and attitudinal dimensions of group activity, with questions derived from the theoretical perspectives of social psychology (orientations to collective action, and perceptions of personal and political efficacy), theories of social capital accumulation (the acquisition of social and organizational skills) and rational choice theory (incentive structures and membership motivations). A fourth part of the interview ranged over group dynamics, assessing the quality of internal group life in terms of levels of member participation and relations between salaried staff, elected officers and the rank and file. The concern here was to locate the group between the pluralist ideal of autonomous organizational activity and the model of the entrepreneurial interest group postulated by exchange theory. Finally, interviews addressed interorganizational relations and the interface between the group and the state apparatus, characterizing relations on the continuum between the institutionalized exchange of the corporatist model and the more limited, ad hoc exchange found in pluralist theory. The resultant data is presented in the book in the form of generalized summaries accompanied by interview citations, or in the form of direct quotes from interview subjects. The objective is to present an analysis of associational activity in an advanced post-communist society derived from group theory and informed by the accounts of key participants.

1   The emergence of civil society

As we saw in the introduction, association was initially ascribed a key role in democratic transition. The rise of Solidarity alongside the crisis of the communist state in Poland in the 1980s and the emergence of undercurrents of opposition elsewhere in east/central Europe fostered a widespread belief in the potential of autonomous associational activity for hastening the demise of communism and creating the conditions for post-communist democracy. This belief was buttressed by changing perceptions of the power structure of the communist state, as the notion of totalitarianism gave way to a more pluralist conception of group interests jostling for influence within a more differentiated political system. Perceptions of oppositional activity as the seedbed of civil society were thus reinforced by a pluralist analysis of group mobilization in the internal dynamics of the regime, fuelling the belief in association as the mainspring of post-communist politics and society.

In retrospect, the belief in opposition movements as the foundation of post-communist civil society can be seen to have been greatly exaggerated. Whilst other revolutions have come about through the mobilization of new social formations, the democratic revolutions in east/central Europe were precipitated by the enfeeblement and collapse of regimes through economic sclerosis. In some countries, democratic revolution was not accompanied by mass mobilization; even where it occurred, it was rarely much more than a sideshow to the main event. The course which the revolutions took, and the outcome, was dictated much more by the interaction of elites. A number of models have been identified (Szablowski and Derlien 1993: 307–10). The opening up of politics and society in the Soviet Union, of course, occurred through reform from above, initiated by the communist elite itself. In the Balkan countries, democratic revolutions took the form of conflict and realignment amongst communist elites. In Poland, political transition was negotiated between the communist government and the Solidarity leadership; in Hungary it was a gradual accommodation between government and emergent democratic party leaders. Czechoslovakia experienced the sharpest break with the past, with a new constitutional order designed by democratic party leaders following the resignation of the communist government. Although democratic elites in Poland, Hungary and Czechoslovakia had the backing of popular movements, the latter were transient actors in the drama, lacking social foundations and destined to break up once their task was completed (Waller 1992).

In this chapter I shall survey the opposition movements that accompanied democratic revolutions in some countries, explaining their incapacity to provide the focus of associational activity in post-communist society. Reflecting the concerns and aspirations of citizens under decaying communist regimes, they were ill adapted to the issue agenda accompanying economic transformation. On the other hand, in the absence of the sharply defined patterns of social differentiation which gave birth to associational collectivism in the west, new configurations of interest group activity were slow to take shape, leaving the associational order of the post-communist societies strongly marked by the legacy of the past. It will be argued, however, that the pluralist analysis of interest mobilization in communist society exaggerated the autonomy of such groups from the state. Thus, whilst business groups and trade unions with antecedents in the old regime are a strong feature of the associational order, when deprived of a supportive state apparatus they lack organizational vigour.

In the German case, the mass mobilization of anti-communist opposition played little role in regime transformation, providing virtually no foundation for the subsequent emergence of associational activity. Opposition emerged late, held back by a combination of repression and, relative to other east European countries, economic privilege. Regime transition was precipitated by the opening of the border between East Germany and Hungary, the resultant mass exodus of East Germans to the Federal Republic via Hungary simultaneously undermining the GDR regime and applying pressure on the West German government to embrace the east in a rapid process of national unification. Mass mobilization took the form of street demonstrations rather than movement formation; the New Forum movement which emerged as the focus of anti-communist opposition was largely restricted to an intellectual elite.

Regime change, of course, occurred through the incorporation of the former GDR into the Federal Republic. Institutional transfer was not confined to the state apparatus, but extended also to the whole spectrum of interest group activity. Thus, although the social foundations were as weak as in other post-communist countries, the institutional apparatus of the associational order was furnished ready-made from the west. Elite exchange was rapid and thoroughgoing. Business organization was initially built out of an alliance between west German groups and the GDR managerial elite, but as privatization took its course the latter quickly disappeared from the corporate landscape. Organization-building initiatives in the trade unions minimized contact with GDR predecessors. Thus the associational order in eastern Germany represented a much cleaner break with the past than that of its eastern neighbours.

Institutional transfer was widely construed by observers as colonization by west Germans, but this conception conceals the weakness of indigenous associational activity, in which respect the GDR resembles other post-communist countries. Confined to a brief interlude between the breakdown of the old regime in October/November 1989 and the acceleration of the unification process in February/March 1990, group formation was singularly lacking in enthusiasm. Once the unification process took off, the opportunity-cost of autonomous organizational activity was prohibitively high in relationship to the low-cost–high-benefit potential of membership in a ready-made system of interest group representation. Only where groups based in the west failed to represent east German interests did indigenous organizations survive. Democratic revolution in eastern Germany then, did as little to catalyse associational activity as it did elsewhere in east/central Europe.

Association and democratic transformation

The attempt to identify pluralist patterns of associational activity behind the monolithic facade of the communist state originated in the 1960s, following the relaxation of Stalinist authoritarianism. It conformed also to the contemporary perception that detected a convergence between liberal democratic and communist systems. Advanced industrial society imposed its own logic on politics. Economic diversity could be expected to lead to political differentiation and the opening up of totalitarian systems. Following this logic, the proponents of the pluralist analysis sought to refocus attention, away from the rigid hierarchy of formal political institutions, and towards the informal relations which took shape around the decision-making process (Skilling and Griffiths 1971). Some went further, arguing that informal elite groups were incorporated into the state apparatus in a form of 'institutionalized pluralism' (Hough 1979), or that the politics of the communist states could be understood as a form of corporatism (Chirot 1980; Staniszkis 1984; Ekiert 1991: 215–20).

This type of analysis was subject to sharp criticism from those who argued that, whilst it was possible to accept the existence of 'opinion groupings', these groups remained dependent upon the state and lacked the defining element of *autonomy* characteristic of pluralist interest representation in the west (Brown 1984). Nevertheless, it served as a useful corrective to the orthodox characterization of communist totalitarianism, showing that communist regimes were less monolithic than previously assumed. Pluralist analysis provides a background to the analysis of interest group activity in post-communist society. Although the liberalizing tendencies of the post-Stalin era did not lead directly to pluralist association, they nevertheless began to generate a more pluralistic style of politics. With the progressive disintegration of the party-state at the end of the 1980s, semi-organized interests began to break out of the straitjacket of the communist system.

These developments can be seen most clearly in Hungary, where liberalization allowed the emergence of private commercial activity alongside the official state apparatus. Struggling to manage this hybrid form of political economy and the conflicting interests which it generated, the state was forced to engage in 'behind-the-scenes interest group politics' characterized by 'client–patron relationships, oligarchic and nepotistic mechanisms, [and] corruption' (Hankiss 1990: 83, 107). The 1980s saw a rapid increase in organizational activity in the private economy sector, with a proliferation of groups sheltering under the legal umbrella of the official chambers of commerce. Associational activity coexisted uneasily with the state socialist system, contributing to the erosion of the latter. Whilst private economy interests remained dependent on the state, their drive to expand the scope of their commercial activities threatened the state sector, provoking a backlash from the managers of state enterprises. By the late 1980s the capacity of the state to balance these conflicting interests was nearing exhaustion, with open struggle within the party elite and an emerging alliance between the new economic interests and re-form-minded elements in the party (Cox and Vass 1994: 156–61).

Hungary was unique amongst the countries of east/central Europe in the scale of economic liberalization and the extent of the accompanying interest formation. Elsewhere, associational activity took the form of *political* mobilization, with subcultural or 'issue' groups providing the foundation for more broadly based opposition movements. These movements had diverse origins, some emanating from the subversion of official, party-controlled mass organizations, others taking a more autonomous form. Oppositional activity can be classified in terms of four main types (Waller 1992). First, environmental protection served as a catalyst to political mobilization. Although activity was spearheaded by the scientific community, it often spread to more broadly based associations like the Danube Circle in Hungary or the Slovak Union for the Protection of the Environment. Regarded as relatively harmless by the authorities, environmental action was a way of registering protest against the regime without confronting it head on. Secondly, there were the libertarian youth movements emerging either from the subversion of official youth organizations, independent student movements or the 'alternative' subculture. A third form of opposition was the peace movement against Warsaw Pact deployment of intermediate-range nuclear weapons in the late 1970s, sometimes succeeding in deflecting the official 'peace committees' from the Soviet line. Fourthly, involved in all these forms of action were the circles of the dissident intelligentsia, who saw independent organizational activity as the stirrings of civil society against the state.

Denied a right to autonomous organization, much of this activity was clandestine, and had 'a twilight samizdat existence of endemic confrontation with the political authorities' (Hayward 1995: 238). Poland provides the only example of a vigorous mass movement of opposition, rooted in a strong sense of national identity and shielded by the influence of the Catholic Church. The emergence of Solidarity provided a focus for political mobilization, bringing together group activity in a broad social movement which transcended its trade union origins in the Baltic coast shipyards. Solidarity largely restricted itself to protest against economic hardship, stopping short of direct political confrontation with the regime. Nevertheless, with a membership of over 10 million, it constituted a de facto challenge to the hegemonic role of the ruling party. Driven underground by the imposition of martial law after 1981, it remained a subversive force undermining the foundations of the regime. Charter 77 played a similar aggregating role in Czechoslovakia. Originating in protest against violations of the Helsinki accords on human rights, the movement subsequently expanded its activities and influence, serving as a vanguard of the opposition. In contrast to Solidarity, however, it remained an elite circle of no more than around 2,500 signatories, and, whilst it commanded broad public sympathy, it could not be said to constitute a mass movement. In Hungary, the restrictions on oppositional activity were progressively relaxed as the dual economy undermined the political foundations of the regime. A gradual transition to democracy in the late 1980s meant that there was little need for the sort of broad anti-communist front which formed in Poland and Czechoslovakia, and the opposition remained diffuse, lacking both a unifying focus and a mass following.

Across the countries of east/central Europe, communist collapse was the result of political rot, economic sclerosis and the withdrawal of the Soviet Union from its role as guarantor of the internal security of its satellite states. Whilst opposition movements were not the primary motivating force behind democratic revolution, however, they nevertheless contributed to its momentum by expanding the scope for autonomous political activity, thereby weakening the hold of state on society. Moreover, the movements which unified the democratic opposition in the final stages of communist collapse in some countries played a crucial role in negotiating the transition to democracy in 'round-table' talks between outgoing communist governments and the forum movements: Solidarity in Poland, Civic Forum (a reincarnation of Charter 77) in the Czech lands, People Against Violence in Slovakia, the Union of Democratic Forces in Bulgaria and New Forum in the GDR.

Widely conceived, as we have seen, as initiatives in self-organization against the communist state, opposition movements were expected to play a central role in the process of democratization, constituting the foundations of post-communist civil society. The decade following the revolutions of 1989–90, however, exposed the flaws in this analysis, the movements proving to be no more than transient actors in the democratic transformation:

It fell to them to see out the old and bring in the new . . . the role they played was powerful but simple; and once they had performed it, they were bound to fall subject to differentiation and transformation. (Waller 1992: 141)

Essentially products of the old order, the movements which bore the democratic revolution were destined to break up once their principal task had been completed. Moreover, the organizational vigour taken by many as evidence of a burgeoning civil society was revealed as an illusory effect of historical circumstance.

There are a number of reasons why the organizational dynamism of the late 1980s was unsustainable. First, broadly based movements of opposition reflected the amorphous character of communist society. Articulating the voice of 'the people' in an anti-communist front transcending sectional interests, they lacked the social foundations for long-term sustainability. Secondly, the capacity of the movements for mass mobilization concealed their elite character. Attention has already been drawn to the narrow base of Charter 77. The underground existence of Solidarity meant that it relied heavily upon the prominence of top leaders to hold it together. In Hungary, a gradual transition to democracy occurred through elite accommodation: 'all types of mass mobilization were led and controlled by the old and new elites', and popular political activity was of only marginal importance (Szabó 1991: 310–14). As we shall see in the following chapter, organizational activity in post-communist society is strongly marked by the legacy of elite dominance.

This leads to a third reason for scepticism over the equation of opposition movements with an emergent civil society. Elite dominance left the movements vulnerable to 'colonization' or absorption into the political arena, as associational activity succumbed to an electoral process which 'structured political action in a different way' (Wiesenthal 1995c: 33). The 'pull' of *parliamentary* as against *functional* representation stimulates party formation and sustains a system of governance with authoritative decision-making powers, whilst emergent parties provide career opportunities that meet the aspirations of individuals looking for influence and recognition. Thus, as associational activity was subordinated to parliamentarism, civil society was 'looted' by the process of party formation (Miszlivetz 1997: 32; Lomax 1997: 51). Entering the political arena, Solidarity fragmented along lines of ideological and factional division previously obscured by the common anti-communist cause, greatly weakening the trade union wing of the movement. In the Czech Republic and Slovakia, Civic Forum and People Against Violence experienced a similar breakup. Already pluralist in composition, the Hungarian opposition constituted a ready-made multiparty system, whilst in the GDR New Forum simply evaporated in the face of an emergent party system replicating the template of the Federal Republic.

Robbed of much of its organizational strength by the process of party formation, civil society nevertheless began to reconstitute itself through a profusion of associational activity accompanying democratization. Some 6,000 civil associations were registered in Hungary by 1992. Although the majority of these were in the nature of cultural, sporting or leisure groups, around 1,000 were representative of economic or professional interests (Cox and Vass 1994: 155). Here, as in other countries, however, such groups were characterized by a high degree of continuity with the old regime.

Nowhere was continuity more apparent than in the trade unions, where the official trade unions or their successors retained their hegemony over worker organization. Although they remained passive in the process of democratic transformation, the old trade unions were nevertheless successful in adapting to system change, distancing themselves from their former masters in the party-state. Reform meant decentralization, as sectoral and occupational unions asserted their autonomy from all-embracing national confederations. Reformed or reconstituted along more pluralist lines, however, the old unions still retained much of their former apparatus and personnel. The inheritance of property holdings from their predecessors, and their continuing role in the administration of state welfare benefits gave them a crucial advantage over the new unions emerging from independent initiatives accompanying regime change. Grassroots revitalization thus proved abortive, and the trade unions of the past successfully survived system change.

In Hungary, a pluralist structure began to emerge in 1988 with the fragmentation of the nineteen sectoral federations constituting the central trade union council (SZOT) into more than 140 occupational unions. Most of these retained their affiliation to the central council, which was reconstituted in 1990 in the form of the more loosely confederated National Association of Hungarian Trade Unions (MSZOSZ). Alongside this survivor of the old regime, a plethora of newly emerging unions formed rival confederations, the largest of which were the League of Independent Trade Unions and the National Alliance of Workers' Councils. Despite the proliferation of independent unions, however, the MSZOSZ remained dominant, polling over 70 per cent of votes in the first works council elections (Cox and Vass 1994: 157, 165–9).

In Poland, also, the official communist trade union remained dominant. Incorporation into the political arena as a party of government prevented Solidarity from reasserting its former role as an independent trade union. Weakened by internal divisions and breakaway initiatives, it was unable to regain its mass membership of 1980–1, remaining in the shadow of the All-Poland Alliance of Trade Unions (OPZZ) that had been formed by the state in the early 1980s to counter the attraction of Solidarity. Similarly in Bulgaria, Podkrepa was unable to sustain its challenge to the old guard trade union confederation CITUB.

The Czechoslovakian trade unions took a different road to democratic reformation. Here an opposition labour movement emerged in the late stages of regime collapse, taking the form of workers' committees orchestrating the protest strikes of November 1989. Lacking an organizational infrastructure of their own, committee activists positioned themselves strategically to take over the assets of the official trade unions by infiltrating the old structures, gaining a majority in the reconstituted Czech and Slovak Confederation of Trade Unions (CSKOS) early in 1990. Whilst accommodation between old and new elements eliminated the competition that divided the trade unions elsewhere in east/central Europe, it meant that the CSKOS apparatus was strongly marked by the legacy of the past (Myant 1994: 61–2).

Entangled with the breakup of the Soviet Union and the accompanying conflicts over political and economic reform, the emergence of trade unions in post-communist Russia took a tortuous road. The All-Union Central Council of Trade Unions asserted its independence from party and state from 1987, articulating a conservative voice against Gorbachev's reform initiatives. Moves towards republican autonomy began in 1990 with the formation of the Federation of Independent Trade Unions of Russia (FNPR), which became the centrepiece of attempts to reconstitute the official union apparatus from the wreckage of the Soviet Union. The FNPR inherited its predecessor's conservatism, mobilizing protest against Yeltsin's 'shock therapy' programme of economic reform.

Independent trade unions, on the other hand, were generally supportive of government reform initiatives. The incorporation of their leaders into the Yeltsin administration compromised their independence, reducing their capacity for mass mobilization and their ability to challenge old unions which, despite organizational atrophy, retained their dominance in the workplace. New unionism in Russia is thus confined largely to strategically placed groups of workers like miners and air traffic controllers.

Associational activity in business circles was also strongly marked by the legacy of the past. Economic transformation lagged behind political change. As we shall see in the next chapter, privatization often meant little more than the 'commercialization' of state enterprises, leaving existing management structures intact and allowing old managerial elites to re-group in the form of a 'nomenklatura bourgeoisie'. An entrepreneurial class with its roots in the old regime inevitably inherited modes of associational activity based on personal networking, clientelism and corruption characteristic of interest mobilization in communist society (Lomax 1997: 49). Many of the business associations which proliferated in east/central Europe have antecedents in the old regime. Thus the Russian Union of Industrialists and Entrepreneurs (RUIE) had its origins in the 'science and industry group' of the USSR Supreme Soviet, which brought together the directors of the mega-enterprises which dominated the Soviet economy. Of the nine business associations in post-communist Hungary, six can be traced to roots in the old regime (Cox and Vass 1994: 170). Associational activity amongst the new generation of private entrepreneurs was slow to emerge, since most of these tended to be self-employed rather than employers and saw little need for collective action (Héthy 1991: 351).

Emergent business organizations often conformed closely to the entrepreneurial model of interest representation, in which individuals initiate organizations for commercial profit or to provide themselves with the backing to launch political careers. Opportunities for this form of organization were particularly plentiful amidst the chaos of economic transformation. Groups like the RUIE in Russia and the National Association of Entrepreneurs in Hungary were thus subordinated to the political ambitions of their leaders. Entering the electoral arena and acquiring the characteristics of political parties, these groups tended to put the 'logic of influence' before the 'logic of membership', militating against the consolidation of a mass membership base.

The expectation that democratization would be accompanied or even driven by the forces of a dynamic civil society thus proved illusory. The illusion was based on three misconceptions of the character of associational activity in communist and post-communist society. First, it was rooted in an exaggerated perception of the scope for autonomous association in a state-managed society under communism. Although the liberalizing tendencies of the post-Stalin era generated a more pluralistic style of politics, the articulation and mediation of economic interests were confined largely to internal relations within the state bureaucracy. Even in those countries where a second economy was tolerated, private economic interests were absorbed into the state apparatus through 'clientelistic networks . . . distributing privileges and resources in exchange for political compliance' (Ekiert 1991: 226). Private economic interests remained dependent on the state, and lacking in the element of autonomy essential to pluralist interest representation.

A second source of the 'civil society illusion' was a misconception of the opposition movements of the late 1970s and 1980s. Transcending socio-economic interests, the social movements which made up the opposition in Hungary, Poland and Czechoslovakia were too amorphous to constitute the foundations of a post-communist civil society. Moreover, broad public backing disguised the elite orientation of opposition groups, which made them susceptible to absorption into politics following democratization. A third misconception arises from an underestimation of continuity amidst change, and the capacity of old elites to reconstitute themselves in the post-communist environment. Both trade unions and business associations emerged from the democratic transformation indelibly marked by the legacy of the past, and correspondingly ill equipped to ply their allotted role in a pluralist civil society.

Civil society by institutional transfer: the German case

Germany stands out as a special case of post-communist transformation. The 'German question' shaped the character of the communist regime, the forms of opposition to it and, most decisively of all, the dynamics of the transformation process. The existence of the Federal Republic as an alternative German state meant that the GDR lacked the force of national identification that buttressed the legitimacy and stability of communist states elsewhere in east/central Europe. The insecurity of the GDR's national identity placed a premium on political stability, maintained by repressive social control through an all-pervasive apparatus of internal security combined with an implicit social contract in which consent was based on a subsidized economy and a relatively generous welfare state. Political reform was seen as inherently destabilizing; only by retaining its rigidly socialist character could the GDR remain distinct from its West German neighbour. Thus, lacking the catalyst of acute economic deprivation, and without the political opportunities of liberalization, opposition was limited in scale and intensity. Although the Protestant churches provided a roof for a constellation of opposition groups similar to that in other communist states, it was not until September 1989 that a concerted democratic movement emerged, led by New Forum. Even then, it was the exodus of migrants to the west, combined with spontaneous mass protest in the streets of Leipzig, that played the decisive role in bringing down the regime. As in the other countries of east/central Europe, opposition movements rapidly disintegrated, torn amongst conflicting visions of the future, undermined by the logic of unification and subsequently marginalized by an emerging party system with its roots in the west. In the GDR, then, the foundations of civil society were singularly shallow.

The associational order which emerged in 1989–90 can be traced to three sources. First, there were some rare cases of GDR organizations that succeeded in adapting to the liberal democratic arena, finding a niche in the associational order by establishing themselves as a reference point for those interests threatened by socio-economic change. A second type of organization was that emerging from indigenous initiatives in the first stirrings of associational activity in 1989–90. For the most part, however, indigenous initiatives were quickly overtaken by interest groups expanding eastwards from their base in the Federal Republic. This third type of organization rapidly established its hegemony in the associational order of eastern Germany.

With the progressive disintegration of the GDR in autumn 1989, the previously closed sphere of civil society was opened up. Associational activity, however, was characterized by hesitancy and disorientation, reflecting the uncertainty which surrounded the future of the regime. Whilst the old political and economic structures were fatally undermined, the outline of the new order was as yet unclear, with ill-defined conceptions of internal reform coexisting with aspirations towards confederation or unification between the two German states. Thus, whilst democratization and economic liberalization were on the agenda, there was no clear sense of the institutional forms which either would assume. Poised between state socialism and capitalist liberal democracy, the political and economic order provided no orientational reference points for organizational activity.

With the future for the GDR in the balance, there remained some scope for the reform of old institutions like the trade unions, and for new forms of indigenous associational activity. With the rapid acceleration of the unification process in February/March 1990, however, these initiatives were overtaken by events. Unification through institutional transfer – the extension of the constitutional, political and socio-economic institutions of the Federal Republic to the so-called new German *Länder* – under-mined initiatives geared to the creation of a separate system of interest representation for eastern Germany. Subordinated to the logic of unifica-tion, attempts to reform GDR institutions or to establish independent initiatives were abandoned, their adherents increasingly attracted by the organizational strength of their western counterparts. Indigenous organ-izations either were assimilated into the organizational life of the Federal Republic or struggled to compete. For their part, West German interest groups intensified their activity in the east, either consolidating partner-ship with indigenous groups or establishing organizational networks of their own, as the tempo of organization-building was stepped up in a headlong dash to keep pace with integration in the wider economic and social order. Thus the emergent associational order was decisively marked by the logic of unification, as the institutional blueprint of the Federal Republic was superimposed upon indigenous initiatives. Only in rare cases did indigenous organizations succeed in finding a niche in the liberal democratic arena by establishing themselves as a reference point for those interests that were marginalized by socio-economic change in the transformation process.

Business organizations

Business organizations reflected the disjuncture between the old social order and the new, represented by the GDR managerial elite on the one hand, and the slowly emergent entrepreneurial middle class on the other. Pending privatization, economic life remained in the hands of planning bureaucrats and the managers of state enterprises. Rooted in the econ-omic structures of the planned economy, the managerial elite was ill adapted for the task of shaping the new associational order. Despite access to the networks of the planning bureaucracy, the initiatives on which they embarked in November 1989 were slow to take shape, and it was not until March the following year that a committee was formed in Leipzig to plan the establishment of an employers' association in the metal and electrical sectors (Gesamtmetall 1992: 4). From the outset, the initiative was oriented towards co-operation with employers' associations in the west, although the latter were initially apprehensive of contact with the managerial elite of the old regime (Ettl and Wiesenthal 1994: 7).

Organizational activity also emerged amongst those for whom the opening up of the private economic sphere signalled immediate oppor-tunities for entrepreneurship. This group constituted former owners of industrial and commercial property expropriated under the GDR regime and seeking restitution (reprivatizers), along with retailers and tradesmen for whom commercial independence beckoned. The interests of these prospective entrepreneurs conflicted with those of the old managerial elite, and their organizational initiative took an independent course, with the creation in November 1989 of the GDR Entrepreneur Association (Unternehmerverband, UV). The foundations of the new organization, however, reflected the weakness of the entrepreneurial middle class, and it led a tenuous existence, despite initial support from prominent Bonn patrons (interviews: UV Norddeutschland, Thüringen, Sachsen-Anhalt).

For the employers' associations in the Federal Republic, organization-building was a race for competitive advantage with the trade unions in the wage-bargaining arena. The primary purpose of organization was to provide a counterweight to the unions (interview: Nordmetall, Schwerin), and to buttress negotiating teams of inexperienced GDR managers in the wage round accompanying monetary and economic union. The West German employer and industry confederations BDA (Bundesvereinigung der Deutschen Arbeitgeberverbände, Confederation of German Employers' Associations) and BDI (Bundesverband der Deutschen Industrie, Confederation of German Industry) began to assert their presence in late February, establishing an information bureau in Berlin 'to mediate economic relations between east and west' (BDA/BDI 1990). The vanguard role, however, was played by the metals and electrical industry employers' association Gesamtverband der metallindustriellen Arbeitgeberverbände (Gesamtmetall) and its affiliated regional associations in the west. The latter had already established contact with GDR managers towards the end of 1989. As the unification process accelerated, Gesamtmetall took steps to consolidate the relationship. A month of talks culminated at the end of March in a co-operation agreement, establishing partnerships between the embryonic regional organizations in the east and their western counterparts, as a precursor to membership in Gesamtmetall. The key provision, and one that explains the haste with which the agreement was concluded, was a binding undertaking to 'work together in a strictly co-ordinated way' in wage-bargaining (Gesamt-metall 1992: 4–5).

The co-operation agreement formalized the assimilation of GDR managers into Gesamtmetall, signalling a rapid acceleration of organization-building and the intensification of activity on the part of the westerners. Gesamtmetall staff were despatched to the east to provide logistical and technical assistance in the formation of partner associations. By early May a branch of the Association of the Metal and Electrical Industry (Verband der Metall- und Elektroindustrie, VME) was established in all five of the new *Länder*, and were incorporated as full members of Gesamtmetall by the end of September. During this period, employers' associations were established across the spectrum of industrial and commercial branches, although none matched the organizational strength of the metal and electricals sector. Consequently the VME took the lead in building confederations of sectoral employers' associations on the foundation of its own apparatus in each of the new *Länder*. With these in place by October 1990, the formal infrastructure of employer organization was complete.

Industry associations lagged behind the employers in extending their organizational networks eastward. Their primary function of political representation was less pressing than the wage-bargaining functions of employers' associations, and there were no indigenous initiatives in this arena. The principal mover was the Association of German Machinery and Plant Manufacturers, Verband Deutscher Maschinen- and Anlagenbau (VDMA). which established an organizational presence in Sachsen in June 1990. Four months later, the VDMA sponsored the formation of the Landersverband der Sächsischen Industrie (LSI), a confederation of sectoral industry associations which also served as the representative of the BDI in Sachsen. For the most part, however, the representation of industrial interests was mandated by the BDI to the BDA employers' confederations.

Thus, in the absence of an entrepreneurial middle class, employers' associations emerged out of an essentially artificial alliance between western associations and the GDR economic elite. With its strategic location in the GDR economy, and effectively playing the role of the employer, the managerial elite was an indispensable ally for employer counterpart associations in the west. As one Gesamtmetall leader put it, 'there are no experienced market economy people at our disposal; we can't rely on pastors and teachers, and we can't wait for the emergence of people who had nothing to do with the old system' (*Kölner Stadt-Anzeiger*, 23 April 1990).

Despite its artificiality, however, and despite the pragmatism which motivated both sides, the relationship was not lacking in cordiality. Despite their initial reservations, westerners now took a broad view of the political background of their eastern partners. In some cases, as between the respective leaders of Nordmetall in Hamburg and Mecklenburg-Vorpommern, professional partnerships developed into close personal friendships:

We had no reservations about contact. We welcomed the managers of the DDR state enterprises . . . they were often very able, and had done the best they could under the circumstances . . . some of them had been SED [Sozialistische Einheitspartei Deutschlands, Socialist Unity Party of Germany] members, but that was inevitable. (Interview: UVB)

The relationship developed on the basis of trust . . . we had a great deal of contact with each other . . . we'd discussed all the problems together, so we really didn't have any difficulty relating to each other . . . the people in the west who had responsibility were *fully accepted* by the people in the east . . . the relationship went beyond the official level – we had a close personal relationship . . . we went through it all together. There were no differences between us. We were going backwards and forwards between Hamburg and Schwerin and Rostock and Neu Brandenburg . . . there were no problems. (Interview: Nordmetall, Hamburg)

Reliance on the GDR managerial elite greatly accelerated the formation of employers' associations, but it meant that the new organizations were rooted in the old economic structures. This had two negative implications. First, the privatization and restructuring of state industry inevitably led to the fragmentation of the old managerial class, creating instability in employers' associations. Secondly, the dominance of large-scale enterprises made the new associations uncongenial to the entrepreneurial middle class as it emerged slowly and hesitantly from economic liberalization. The ensuing legacy of alienation restricted recruitment amongst these elements, where the employers' association faced competition from the independent east German entrepreneur associations, Unternehmer-verbände (UVs).

The chambers of industry and commerce

Alongside these *GDR-wide* initiatives, organizational activity also emerged at the level of the *local* economy, in the form of chambers of industry and commerce (Industrie und Handelskammern, IHKs) The pattern of organization-building was similar to that amongst the employers, with partnership arrangements established between spontaneous initiatives in the east and their western counterparts, leading to a system of chambers modelled on the Federal Republic. Indigenous activity began in November 1989, with initiatives aimed at the reform of the GDR chambers, which had been made up largely of small retailers (interview: IHK, Schwerin). The decisive moves, however, were generally undertaken by managers in the local state enterprises, especially those with experience in export (interview: DIHT Büro-Berlin). From the outset, the reconstituted chambers sought the co-operation of their counterparts in the west. The latter were intensively involved in organization-building, seconding key personnel to provide expertise.

As with the employers, the new chambers were built upon an alliance between GDR managers and west German interests. Indigenous initiatives were orchestrated by the German Council of Industry and Commerce (Deutscher Industrie- und Handelstag, DIHT), the umbrella association bringing together local chambers of commerce in the Federal

Republic. In view of the quasi-public function of the chambers in trade certification and vocational training, organization-building in the east was an urgent priority for both the DIHT and federal government. Mediation between the founders of the chambers in the regions, the DIHT and the governments in Berlin and Bonn was orchestrated by a state secretary in the GDR Economics Ministry. A former official in the state planning apparatus, he was personally acquainted with many of the leading figures in the new regional chambers. Together they drafted the ministerial order establishing the legal framework of the chambers, which was adopted on 1 March 1990. Identified as the key mover by the DIHT in Bonn, he was subsequently appointed to head their liaison office in Berlin, and was responsible for orchestrating the affiliation of the new chambers to the DIHT. The formation of an autonomous confederation of chambers in the new *Länder* was never seriously considered by the founders (interview: DIHT Büro-Berlin).

Between February and April 1990 the old chambers were wound up and new ones established, affiliating with the DIHT in October. Supported by state subsidies and with an income derived from compulsory membership subscriptions, the new chambers quickly developed an organizational life of their own, under the leadership of elected bodies and salaried staff recruited almost exclusively from the new *Länder*. As quasi-state bodies, however, and originating out of the alliance of the old managerial elite and economic interests in the west, their roots amongst entrepreneurs were insecure.

Trade unions

Relative freedom from the burden of political association with the old regime enabled the managerial elite to adapt to economic change quite quickly, although their longer-term future was uncertain. For the trade unions, adaptation was much more problematical, due to their inseparability from the apparatus of the party-state. The central trade union organ, the FDGB (Freier Deutscher Gewerkschaftsbund, Confederation of Free German Trade Unions, GDR), was part of the state apparatus, its leadership intransigent in its refusal to recognize the consequences of democratization. Impervious to the opposition of autumn 1989, it was only after the collapse of the state that reform got underway, with a special congress of the FDGB at the end of January 1990 to introduce democratic statutes and a new leadership. Little more than an attempt to retain its organizational integrity in the face of political change, the reforms failed to establish any semblance of popular legitimacy.

In an attempt to free themselves from the dead hand of the FDGB, industry unions were established in the spring of 1990, orienting themselves towards reform based on co-operation with their western counterparts (Bialas 1994: 6–9). Totally ill adjusted to the representation of employee interests, however, their workplace structures were incapable of adaptation to new socio-economic circumstances. Without workplace representation, and lacking any confidence in the centralized union apparatus, the membership turned increasingly to trade unions in the Federal Republic. Union structures thus collapsed from below as much as from the failure of reform from above (Kirschner and Sommerfeld 1991).

Initially, the position of most trade unions in the Federal Republic was one of support for reform initiatives in the east. From November 1989, the engineering and electricals union IG Metall dispatched advisory personnel to assist its eastern counterpart in building a democratic organization. This was followed between December and February by measures geared to establishing an institutional framework for co-operation and, in the medium term, confederation. This strategic conception was built on the assumption that the unification of the two German states would take the form of a progressive confederation, allowing time for the reform and consolidation of union organization in the east as a precursor to its assimilation into all-German structures (Schmid and Tiemann 1992; Tiemann, Schmid and Lober 1993). With the acceleration of unification, however, the foundations of this strategy were fatally undermined. Bolstered by polls indicating a huge store of public confidence invested in the DGB (Deutscher Gewerkschaftsbund, Confederation of German Trade Unions) unions (Fichter and Kubjuhn 1992: 162), IG Metall undertook a strategic reorientation, abandoning the reform of existing structures in favour of institutional transfer from the Federal Republic (Bialas 1994: 12). The new course meant a complete legal break with the past, winding up the GDR union on 31 December 1990, and requiring members to rejoin IG Metall from 1 January 1991. A further implication of this course was the termination of contractual commitments to the staff of the GDR union.

IG Metall was unique in that it shifted abruptly from very close co-operation with reform initiatives in the east to root-and-branch organizational transfer. The other west German trade unions pursued one of three strategic models (Fichter 1993: 29–31). First, a number of unions took the road of *reform and incorporation*, steering reform initiatives, shaping new structures in their own image and subsequently assimilating them into their own organization. A second strategy can be described as *co-operative organizational transfer*: abandoning reform initiatives, western unions extended their own organizational structures eastward, but continued to co-operate with their GDR counterparts, without the strict

severance of legal succession in membership and employment characteristic of IG Metall. The third strategic option prevailed in those sectors
where GDR unions were irredeemably entwined with the state apparatus;
the police, education and science, and public administration. Here a
strategy of *non-cooperation* entailed institution-building initiatives based
in the west, with a minimum of contact with predecessor organizations in
the GDR.

The motives behind the strategic decisions of trade unions in the
Federal Republic were varied and often conflicting. On the one hand,
initially at least, organizational transformation through internal reform
appeared to offer the most rapid and cost-effective way of establishing
democratic trade union activity in the east. It might also have endowed
the emergent structures with social roots. On the other hand, such a
course risked the taint of political association with the past, and raised
unpredictable issues of inherited legal responsibilities. Amongst the
smaller unions with limited resources, financial considerations were predominant. For most other unions, it quickly became apparent that the
burden of organizational decrepitude, legitimacy deficit and legal uncertainty outweighed the advantages of the reform and incorporation of the
GDR unions.

For IG Metall, all these considerations entered the equation. In view of
its status as the locomotive of trade union wage-bargaining, however, the
decisive consideration was how best to secure a position in the emergent
structures of industrial relations in the east. As in the case of the employers' confederations, once the trajectory of the unification process
became clear, a strong presence in the collective-bargaining arena became an urgent priority:

We had to be in a position to support . . . workplace initiatives and to co-ordinate
these at regional level. For this purpose the established structures in the west were
of great importance . . . we had to be in a position to lead wage negotiations.
(Interview: IG Metall, Verwaltungsstelle Erfurt)

Under these circumstances, established organizational structures in the
west provided a firmer bridgehead than reform initiatives in the new
Länder. In the interim, however, the close co-operative relationship which
the union had established with its eastern counterpart proved useful,
enabling IG Metall to shape wage-bargaining from an early stage. In the
pay round of spring 1990 which established a provisional wage structure
in readiness for economic and monetary union, it was able to exert a
backstage influence, steering the official GDR negotiating team.

Whilst the employers' associations and chambers were built on the
basis of co-operation with the GDR managerial elite, the trade unions for

the most part avoided reliance on the structures and personnel of their eastern counterparts. Having abandoned its initial strategy of reform in favour of organizational transfer, IG Metall proceeded with the installation of its apparatus and staff. With one exception (Sachsen), the new *Länder* were merged with existing *Bezirke* (regions) in the west (see chapter 2). A network of local offices was established, based on the liaison bureaux set up in the early stages of democratization. From these offices a massive campaign of recruitment and shopfloor activity was launched, culminating in membership registration in January 1991 and the election of local management committees three months later (interviews: IG Metall, Verwaltungsstellen Erfurt, Dresden, Magdeburg, Schwerin; IG Metall, Bezirksleitung Berlin-Brandenburg, Dresden). Thus, despite its origins in institutional transfer from the west, the organizational network of IG Metall at the local level now provided a framework for indigenous union activity.

The Federation of German Trade Unions (DGB) was obliged to delay its formal establishment until the apparatus of its constituent industry unions was in place. Informally the DGB had been laying organizational foundations since early 1990, often in conjunction with those of its member unions – ÖTV in the public sector (Gewerkschaft Öffentlichen Dienste, Transport und Verkehr, Union of Workers in the Public Sector) and GEW (Gewerkschaft Erziehung und Wißenschaft, Union of Teaching and Scientific Workers) in education and science – which shared its aversion to contact with the GDR unions. By the middle of the year a network of regional offices had been established, offering assistance in organization-building and legal advice. Formal organizational structures were established at *Land* level in December 1990, but structures were not in place until the end of the following year, and did not begin functioning normally until early 1992. The relatively slow pace of organization-building gave the DGB time to recruit quite a high proportion of its officials from the east. Attempting to avoid hiring FDGB officials, it sought those with organizational experience elsewhere (often in New Forum, the citizens' movements in Alliance '90 or the SPD).

Professional organizations

Organizational activity in the professions exhibited a variety of patterns, corresponding to variations in the impact of socio-economic transformation from one group to another. Ultimately the decisive factors were the marketability of professional skills, issues of professional status and the recognition of qualifications. The medical profession and engineering represent two contrasting patterns of organizational development. Medical qualifications were unreservedly recognized, and the profession was integrated relatively easily into the structures of health care in the Federal Republic. Robbed of their raison d'être, the tentative organizational initiatives of GDR doctors either collapsed or were assimilated rapidly into professional associations in the west. For engineers, on the other hand, the recognition of qualifications was problematical. Their alienation from professional bodies in the west enabled the pre-existing GDR engineers' organization to establish a role in the new associational order.

Amongst doctors, the initial response to the opening up of the GDR was one of spontaneous solidarity within the profession. Organizational activity remained, however, at the level of informal social networks, 'mutual support groups' and discussion circles (Erdmann 1992: 327). The most important centre of activity was the Charité hospital in Berlin, which had been the flagship of medical science in the GDR, and was consequently in the forefront of the struggle between medical ethics and the political and ideological goals of the state (Stein 1992). The Charité thus had a strong professional and institutional ethos which served in some measure as a foundation for organizational activity. It was here that initiatives began on 8 November 1989 with a meeting of twenty doctors which concluded with a call to form a professional interest association (interview: NAV-VB, Berlin). Conceived in terms of the reform of GDR medicine, the group's main purpose was 'to exert influence for the improvement of doctors' working conditions in the interests of better health care' (Gebuhr 1993: 10). Similar developments occurred elsewhere, especially in cities like Leipzig and Dresden with large medical establishments. By the end of 1989 around 8,000 doctors had signalled their readiness for association membership (interview: NAV-VB, Berlin).

As in other spheres, organizational activity in the medical profession was transformed by the logic of unification. Professional associations in the Federal Republic now began mobilizing for recruitment in the east. Faced with this threat, indigenous initiatives sought to establish a firmer organizational base. Once again, the first steps were taken by the Charité group, culminating on 3 February with the formation of the VB, the Rudolf-Virchow-Bund (interview: NAV-VB, Berlin). The founders' aspiration that it would form the basis of a GDR-wide association was quickly dispelled. Whilst similar initiatives in Brandenburg and Mecklenburg-Vorpommern affiliated to the VB, Sachsen doctors preferred a looser form of co-operation. Elsewhere, the attraction of the west German associations overpowered autonomous initiative (Gebuhr 1993: 13–14).

The failure of the VB's aspirations was symptomatic of deep differences which emerged amongst doctors as unification became an immediate reality. For hospital doctors, integration into western structures of health care was relatively unproblematic. This part of the profession quickly gravitated towards the Marburgerbund, the salaried doctors' association in the Federal Republic, which conducted a recruitment campaign calculated to divide associational life in the medical profession between hospital and private practice doctors (interviews: NAV-VB, Sachsen; Marburgerbund, Landesverband Sachsen). The latter were themselves divided between those who wanted to retain the GDR system of *Polikliniken* (district health centres containing a wide range of medical specialists), and those who advocated the wholesale adoption of west German structures of outpatient care, based on private practice. Initially, there was considerable support for a separate system of outpatient care based on the *Polikliniken*. Only around one-quarter of outpatient doctors were attracted to private practice (Erdmann 1992: 329). With unification, however, this kind of 'third-way' option appeared increasingly incongruous. Moreover, in the face of a 'massive campaign' on the part of the western health care establishment (interviews: NAV-VB, Berlin-Brandenburg, Sachsen; Marburgerbund, Landesverband Sachsen), the balance shifted in favour of private practice. Adopting western structures was increasingly attractive as a rapid route to effective health care delivery and the improvement of the material conditions and status of doctors.

The disintegration of organizational initiatives in the medical profession reflected the inability of doctors to define their interests collectively. Without an independent professional reference system of their own, doctors gravitated towards that provided by professional associations in the west. This tendency was accentuated by the progressive assimilation of the medical profession into the structures of health care in the Federal Republic. As they were marginalized by the increasing support of doctors for the western model, it was difficult for indigenous initiatives to adapt programmatically to this shift in opinion since their western competitors already occupied this ground. Overtaken by events, they either collapsed or took a pragmatic decision to merge with one of their western counterparts.

The VB adopted the latter course, opting in September for a merger with the Association of Private Practice Doctors (Verband der Niedergelassenen Ärzte, NAV), although it retained some of its organizational identity (NAV-VB 1992: 4–10), keeping its title and maintaining a business office in Berlin. With the integration of doctors into the health care system of the Federal Republic, professional associations in the west, principally the Hartmannbund and the Marburgerbund, established a presence, forming *Land*-level associations in summer 1990.

Whilst the medical profession had lacked an independent professional body in the GDR, engineers had been organized in the Chamber of Technology (Kammer der Technik, KdT). A strong organizational base and relative freedom from politicization in the old regime enabled the KdT to survive democratization. Democratic procedures were introduced early in 1990, under which a new leadership was elected. Although membership fell steeply from the previous level of over 250,000, the KdT remained a mass organization (interviews: Verein Ingenieure und Wirtschaftler Mecklenburg-Vorpommern; Ingenieurtechnischen Verband Thüringen). Spanning the technical intelligentsia, however, from academically trained engineers to qualified skilled workers, the membership of the KdT was too diverse for it to act as professional association in the accepted western sense.

Above all, however, it was the issues of professional recognition which enabled the KdT to survive. Different professional structures in the GDR and the Federal Republic made integration acutely problematical, with a broadly inclusive professional community in the new *Länder* contrasting sharply with the hierarchical structure in the west. Encompassing a broad 'technical intelligentsia' of engineers, scientists, qualified skilled workers and economists, the KdT made no distinction between the academically qualified and those with vocational training (Eichener and Voelzkow 1992: 252–3). Only around one-quarter of engineers in the KdT possessed the Diplom-Ingenieur qualification, which served as the yardstick of the profession in the west. For the remainder, establishing equivalence between engineering qualifications was highly contentious, with acrimonious conflict between the KdT and the Association of German Engineers in the Federal Republic (Verein Deutscher Ingenieure, VDI). The elite-oriented VDI advocated highly restrictive criteria for the recognition of qualifications, effectively excluding the majority of engineers in the east from the profession. Its position was flanked by attacks on the KdT, focusing on its past, casting doubt on its new democratic credentials and questioning the quality of the profession in the east (interviews: Verein Ingenieure und Wirtschaftler, Mecklenburg-Vorpommern; Ingenieurtechnischen Verband Thüringen). Misfiring badly, VDI attacks on the KdT merely served counterproductively to strengthen solidarity amongst east German engineers. Geared to a differently constituted professional group, the VDI failed in its bid to structure engineering according to their elitist and western-oriented blueprint. Ill adapted to providing a frame of reference for the profession in the manner of west German doctors' associations, VDI recruitment in the east met with very limited success.

The capacity of the KdT to resist competition from the west stemmed principally from it demonstrable success in defending the interests of

GDR engineers. After the settlement of the qualifications issue, it retained a functional role as the engineers' advocate in the bureaucratic recognition procedures which ensued. This was a major undertaking: in Thüringen alone there were 60,000 applicants for recognition, one-third of which were still outstanding in 1994 (interview: Ingenieurtechnischen Verband Thüringen, Erfurt). Underlying its capacity for survival was the ability to provide a familiar reference point for a profession undermined by socio-economic upheaval. Essentially backward-looking, however, it resembled other organizations carried over from the previous regime in appealing largely to 'GDR traditionalists', predominantly in the older age range (Wiesenthal, Ettl and Bialas 1992: 14).

For the professions as whole, however, the assimilation model exemplified by the medical profession is more typical. Around 80 per cent of the GDR's medical school qualifications were recognized in the Federal Republic and the establishment of private practice in the professions was supported by large-scale programmes of financial assistance. Three years after unification, the majority of private practitioners, with the exception of the cultural and literary professions, reported an improvement in their professional situation. The integration of professional life led to concomitant assimilation of organizational activity within west German structures (BfB 1994: 30–45). Engineers represent an unusual case of socio-economic exclusion and independent organizational activity in the new *Länder*.

Conclusion

The expectation that democratic revolutions in the countries of east/central Europe would be accompanied by the rise of a pluralist civil society arose, first, out of an exaggerated perception of the scope for autonomous associational activity under communism. Even in those countries like Hungary where liberalization allowed some room for private economic activity, the interests it generated remained dependent upon the state. A second source of the 'civil society illusion' was a misreading of the significance of anti-communist opposition movements and their potential for reconstituting themselves as the foundation of the new order. Amorphous in composition, and transcending sectional interests, the movements which accompanied the breakup of communist regimes were unsustainable once their reforming mission was complete. Thereafter, associational activity was subordinated to party formation and parliamentarism, with interest representation confined largely to economic and intellectual elites, and conforming closely to the 'entrepreneurial' model of organization.

Associational activity was retarded by a syndrome that is endemic to post-communist society. Poised between state socialism and the market, economic relations were insufficiently developed to generate the complex patterns of social differentiation and interdependence that lie at the heart of civil society in sociological discourse. The slow development of market-based social structures in the countries of east/central Europe meant that associational activity continued to reflect the legacy of the past, with a 'nomenklatura bourgeoisie' engaged in customary forms of personal networking and clientelism, and labour movements dominated by trade unions retaining the apparatus inherited from the old regime.

The weakness of the state in east/central Europe may also inhibit civil society formation. The antithesis between state and civil society in democratic theory may obscure the role of the state in promoting associational activity. A number of observers have pointed to the role of the state as the 'patron' of interest group mobilization (Walker 1983), 'creating, maintaining and empowering organized interests', allocating roles and inducing interest groups to comply (Grant 1993: 90). From this perspective, far from opening up the field for autonomous associational activity, the weakness of the post-communist state deprives civil society of its essential institutional foundations (Ekiert 1991: 210). The German experience underlines the role of the state in promoting group mobilization. As 'para-public institutions' ascribed a clearly defined role in public policy, organized interests quickly established themselves in the new socio-economic order. Nowhere was this more apparent than in industrial relations, where a prescribed role in wage-bargaining provided a powerful incentive for employer and trade union mobilization. It was characteristic also of the medical profession, in which indigenous initiatives were rapidly eclipsed by doctors' associations entrenched in the west German system of health care.

Indigenous initiatives in organization-building were, for the most part, little more than an interlude between the disintegration of the GDR and the acceleration of the unification process. Characterized by hesitancy and disorientation, they remained at the informal level, few showing any potential for stable organizational activity. With unification, a new logic of collective action took over, west German organizations offering interest representation without the 'transaction costs' involved in self-organization. Access to a 'ready-made' institutional apparatus promoted organizational activity and brought about a sharp break with the past. Without a supportive social infrastructure, however, the new order was peculiarly inorganic, an *Apparat ohne Unterbau* (apparatus without foundations) which bore little resemblance to the conception of association outlined in the introduction.

2   Socio-economic foundations

In the introduction I located the source of associational activity in the issues and cleavages arising out of economic relations. Interest group configurations reflect patterns of social differentiation embedded in the underlying structure of capital ownership, and the ordering of employment relations and labour markets. For both employer and employee, the employment relationship is the source of the 'categoric cleavage' around which common interests form, and group formation is decisively shaped by the character of the relationship. Institutionalized employment relations and homogenous labour markets, it was argued, are the key to solidaristic forms of trade union mobilization. Employers also share common interests in labour market relations, but their interests are defined also in relation to their status as owners of capital. Business interests are thus shaped by the degree of capital concentration, the mix between national and international capital, and relations between large and small firms.

From this perspective, the attempt to identify emergent patterns of interest group activity in post-communist society should begin by examining the structures of capital ownership and employment accompanying market transition. In the early stages of transition, it has been argued, economic relations are insufficiently developed to generate the stable and clearly defined group interests and identities on which the associational order is based in group theory. 'In a society in which the labour market is unknown . . . the social structure lacks the requisite degree of differentiation . . . of status, interest and cultural identity that only a developed market society will generate' (Offe 1991: 876–7). The legacy of repressed social difference under communism may mean that post-communist society is too amorphous and atomized to generate the prerequisite social differentiation for the spontaneous emergence of organized interests.

Whilst the communist legacy of social homogeneity can be expected to recede in the face of an emergent market economy, the resultant social structures are likely to remain inchoate and unstable. Societies in transition from communism to capitalism are characterized by fragmentation, individualization and the absence of the broadly based social formations that underpin the classical model of interest mediation. Social fragmentation generates a broader and more diverse spectrum of interests than is usual in a mature capitalist economy. Business interests are highly diverse, with cross-cutting cleavages based on company size, ownership and commercial performance. A correspondingly fragmented labour market means that trade union interests exhibit a similar diversity. Professional groups are divided by the commercial pressures of establishment and survival in private practice. Thus the dynamics of post-communist transformation accentuate the conflicts arising from the logic of membership in groups of diverse socio-economic composition.

Economic relations and market transitions

The experience of eastern and central Europe supports Offe's view that post-communist society in the early stages of transformation lacks the social prerequisites for vigorous associational activity. Despite widespread privatization and the emergence of a market economy, tendencies towards 'post-socialist differentiation' are only weakly developed (Hausner et al. 1995). The group attitudes and interests which form the basis of pluralist association have been slow to form, with even less evidence of those broadly based social formations on which the associational order rests in group theory. Interest formation is strongly marked by the predominance of collectivism over private economy relations, reflected in an interest alliance between managers and employees in a common front against the state:

the distinction between competing 'factors' or 'class' interests is outweighed by a broad spectrum of common interests vis à vis the state administration . . . the interests of capital and labor more often than not appear identical. (Wiesenthal 1995b: 10–12)

This coalition of interests reflects the legacy of state socialism, which stifled managerial autonomy and trade union independence alike. Freed from the constraints of the command economy, both management and labour have been slow to divest themselves of the behavioural habits of repressive paternalism which characterized employment relations under communism. The emergence of clearly defined group interests is retarded by the weakness of ownership relations, reflecting the structure of capital and prevailing modes of privatization.

The pace and extent of privatization, of course, are subject to cross-national variation, reflecting the different strategies of market transition. Poland and the Czech Republic exemplify the most radical path, with 'shock therapy' strategies involving mass privatization. Whilst small business was rapidly divested into the private sector, however, the paucity of indigenous capital accumulation meant that large-scale privatization lagged behind. In Poland, shares in selected companies were sold to the public, but many state enterprises remained intact under the National Investment Fund. The Czech Republic pursued an even more consistent 'big bang' approach, with small businesses privatized by restitution to former owners or public auction and some 3,000 large companies subject to privatization through voucher distribution. Hungary initially adopted a more gradualist path, building on a private economic sector that had begun to emerge in the last years of the communist regime. A subsequent attempt to accelerate privatization through voucher distribution was only partially successful, large parts of the public sector remaining under the ownership of state holding companies. At the other end of the spectrum, in the Balkan countries where reformed communist parties retained power, market transition has followed a slower path. Exemplified by Romania, the model is characterized by a mixed economy, with strategic economic sectors remaining under state ownership, and entrepreneurial activity elsewhere subject to strict regulation (Berend 1995: 136–7).

Despite these different strategic approaches to market transition, however, the resultant ownership relations exhibit some similarities. Shock therapy strategies have been retarded by shortages of indigenous capital, and by the political fallout of rapid economic transformation. Even in those countries pursuing the radical path, privatization has hardly begun to crystallize the sharply defined patterns of ownership and social stratification from which class formations emerge. The predominant mode of voucher privatization, it has been argued, leads to a dispersal of capital and a weak property structure which retards the formation of an entrepreneurial business class (Nove 1995: 238–9; Frydman and Rapaczynski 1994: 9–41). Moreover, it often allows companies to be captured by 'insiders' in the form of management–employee buyouts, retarding role differentiation in the workplace (Bamber and Peschanski 1996: 76; Clarke and Fairbrother 1994: 390–3; Egorov 1996: 90–2; Kiss 1994: 142; Rutland 1992: 76). Direct sales, on the other hand, are often subject to foreign acquisitions. In Hungary, foreign capital accounted for three-quarters of privatization revenues in 1991–2, whilst in Poland most large to medium-sized enterprises went to foreign buyers (Poznanski 1995: 214–15). The formation of a liberal bourgeoisie is also retarded by the reconstitution of the communist elite. By the end of 1990, it has been estimated, 20 per cent of all productive assets in Poland had been converted to the personal property of the 'nomenklatura bourgeoisie' (Crawford 1995b: 29).

Cleavages between the state and private sectors, indigenous and foreign capital, and liberal and 'nomenklatura bourgeoisie' are compounded by polarization between large and small firms. Newly established businesses are ascribed a key role in emergent market economies. Representing the grass-roots of entrepreneurial class formation, business start-ups have proliferated across the region. Undercapitalized and occupying a precarious position on the margins of economic survival, their interests are sharply divergent from those of the large company sector (Grant 1993: 95–7).

This hybrid structure of capital ownership is reflected in the fragmentation of associational activity, with a multiplicity of general associations ranged broadly along the lines of cleavage between state and private economy, between large and small business, and sometimes between domestic and international capital. Sectoral organization is weak or nonexistent. Beneath the general associations, fragmentation intensifies in an anarchic plurality of business circles and entrepreneur clubs. Hungary, the Czech Republic and Poland each have several hundred such groups, whilst Russia has around seventy groups active at national level, and many more in the regions (Cox and Vass 1994: 169–72; Héthy 1994: 317; Stykow 1996: 5–6). Lacking any semblance of co-ordination or articulation, the kaleidoscopic organization of business interests reflects the inchoate character of economic relations in post-communist society, and the absence of the social infrastructures that support collective action in the west.

Underdeveloped structures of capital ownership and the continued dominance of economic life by the state are reflected in employment and labour market relations. The cleavage between employer and employee is weak, and role differentiation is often unclear. Several business associations in Russia claim to represent the common interests of managers and employees, whilst some trade unions include the managers of state enterprises. Governments are the chief target of trade union demands, in which wage claims are often secondary to the wider issues of prices, job protection and company restructuring. Labour movements remain subject to the domination of trade unions with roots in the old regime, for which adversarial industrial relations are alien. Identifying strongly with the enterprise, the union leadership does little more than ratify pay scales determined by management. Post-communist unions are more adversarial in wage-bargaining, but they are restricted to skilled workers in strategically important sectors, and their impact is limited by organizational weakness, with local unions exercising virtual autonomy in company-level industrial relations (MacShane 1994: 364; Myant 1994: 74; Kloc 1994: 126–7; Clarke and Fairbrother 1994: 380).

Employment relations are subject to cross-national variation with the intensity of market economy development, but the dominant trend is towards decentralization and individualization. In Russia, 80 per cent of private sector enterprises report company wage-bargaining, with industry-wide agreements playing little role (Bamber and Peschanski 1996: 86). Only a very few firms, however, have adopted the 'capitalist' model of managerial authority, incentive structures and wage differentials (Clarke 1994: 143). In the Czech Republic, where privatization and the market economy have advanced furthest, decentralized pay-bargaining predominates, with strong tendencies towards individualized employment contracts, especially amongst small firms in which the union presence is tenuous (Pollert and Hradecka 1994). In larger companies, individual pay-bargaining is associated with a tendency towards managerial autonomy, with pay policy falling increasingly within the remit of line managers rather than company personnel departments (Hegewisch, Brewster and Koubek 1996: 60–1). These tendencies are far removed from the standardized and institutionalized structure of employment relations out of which the pluralist model of economic interest groups emerged. As was concluded from the foregoing analysis of the structure of capital, employment relations provide a weak infrastructure for solidaristic forms of collective action.

The structure of the advanced post-communist economy

Interest group politics, it was argued above, are embedded in political economy, reflecting ownership relations and the structure of capital and labour markets. In the previous section we saw that group formation is retarded by the weak ownership relations characteristic of post-communist societies in eastern Europe. In the early stages of economic transformation, eastern Germany conformed to this model with ownership vested in the Treuhand (state privatization agency); private capital did not yet play a significant role in economic life, and, in its absence, social and political roles were ill defined. Economic transformation generated its own distinctive pattern of interests, with management and workers drawn together by a preoccupation with survival in the face of the Treuhand's plans for restructuring. The private economy is accompanied by the emergence of market-based social structures – an entrepreneurial/ managerial middle class, and the variegated strata of salaried white-collar staff and manual wage-earners. The predominant characteristics of east German society, however, are social fragmentation, individualization and the absence of the broadly based social formations that underpin the associational order in mature industrial societies.

Capital–labour relations under the Treuhand

Whilst economic and monetary union transformed the legal and economic basis of corporate life in the new German *Länder*, enterprise management remained largely unchanged pending privatization. Ill equipped to deal with the commercial pressures of the market and facing an uncertain future, managers tended to see themselves as the victims of system change, identifying with their employees. The ambivalent status of Treuhand company managers 'between employers and employees' militated against 'a proper separation of interests' (interview: Nordmetall, Schwerin). Moreover, with wage costs and redundancy settlements underwritten by the Treuhand, managers were largely free from the 'hard budget constraints' of the private economy. Interest representation was thus characterized by 'mutual accommodation' (Czada 1996: 112), often taking the form of advocacy coalitions of employers and trade unions lobbying for state support.

Threatened by corporate restructuring and redundancy, employee interests were tightly bound to the survival of the company. *Betriebsegoismus* (identification with company interests) was part of the culture of industrial relations under state socialism, the planned economy engendering an alliance of workers and management against the system. With unification, company identification was reinforced by the institutionalization of management–employee consultation through the works council apparatus. Statutory rights of consultation on personnel issues meant that works councils were party to redundancy negotiations, frequently co-operating with management in a strategy of *Rettung durch Anpassung* (rescue through restructuring). The syndrome of 'co-management', rooted in perceptions of a 'community of fate in adversity', served to marginalize the trade unions, undermining their attempts to mobilize a broad front of 'class' protest against rationalization and redundancy (Bialas 1994: 18– 21; C. Lane 1994a: 192).

Mutual accommodation and co-management at enterprise level were reflected also in the sectoral interest cartels between employers and trade unions that emerged in some of the new *Länder*. Indeed, it was not uncommon to find the trade unions aligned with regional employers in a broad-fronted campaign demanding a more activist industrial policy on the part of *Land* or federal government (*Die Welt*, 30 September 1993). The most striking example of this tendency was the Interessenverband Chemnitzer Maschinenbau (Interest Association of Chemnitz Machine-

Builders, ICM), formed in April 1992 on the initiative of IG Metall. The culmination of increasingly close sectoral co-operation, the association served two main purposes (Bluhm 1995: 166–9). First, it brought together enterprise managers, works councils and trade unions in a lobby aimed at influencing Treuhand policy. Insecure managers facing the uncertainties of privatization were attracted by the organizational resources of IG Metall. Alliance with the union was doubly attractive in view of their own organizational weakness. The machine-building trade association (VDMA) had only a tenuous presence in the east, whilst the engineering employers' association (VME) was crippled by internal instability and conflict. Secondly, the association served as a support network for sectoral co-operation and co-ordination in marketing and research, functions previously carried out within the networks of the planning apparatus. Regional crisis coalitions, as we shall see in chapter 6, were not uncommon in the new *Länder*. The unusual feature of the ICM was that the coalition was formally constituted as an independent organization.

The ICM was a product of a constellation of interests specific to post-communist economic transformation, representing the shared interests of the participants in the survival of a sector in which privatization was particularly problematical. With the conclusion of the privatization process, lobby activity declined in strategic importance. Entrepreneurship was accompanied by the displacement of co-operation by a more competitive pattern of intercompany relations. At the same time, the intensification of conflict in wage-bargaining (excluded from the remit of the association) undermined the partnership between employers and IG Metall on which the ICM was built. Its decline was indicative of a new pattern of interests reflecting the emergence of private economy relations in the new *Länder*. The rapidity of privatization, relative to the slower pace of economic transformation in the countries of eastern Europe, meant a more clear-cut differentiation between the interests of capital and labour. Whilst privatization was accompanied by the emergence of a more sharply defined role differentiation, however, both employers' associations and trade unions continued to exhibit weaknesses that can be traced to the structure of capital and employment relations in the advanced post-communist economy.

Privatization and the structure of capital

The traditional German model of business organization is rooted in dense intercorporate networks amongst firms, with interlocking ownership relations and an extensive overlap in company control generating an 'insider system' of corporate governance in which competition is combined with interdependence (Schneider-Lenné 1992). Business associations are broadly encompassing, built on the bedrock of a large and cohesive *Mittelstand* which serves to mediate conflicts of interest between large and small firms. By contrast, the structure of east German economy is unconducive to this type of business organization, polarized as it is between the subsidiaries of large west German companies and a substratum of small firms.

The structure of capital reflects a privatization process that, uniquely amongst the post-communist countries, was accompanied by systematic restructuring under a central authority, the Treuhand. Thus, around 800 mega-enterprises were broken up into some 12,500 companies for disposal into the private sector. Most large firms were acquired by west German capital, which accounted for some 90 per cent of the total asset value. East German acquisitions were restricted, for the most part, to small privatizations. Reprivatization (the restitution to former owners of firms expropriated under the GDR) accounted for around 4,000 of these, whilst some 2,000 firms were subject to management buyouts (Flockton 1996: 227; Hall and Ludwig 1995: 499–500; Priewe 1993: 340). Restructuring, combined with subsequent rationalization, meant a radical process of downsizing, with a decline in the average company workforce from 293 to 117 between 1991 and 1993, as against 149 in western Germany (DGB Landesbezirk Berlin-Brandenburg 1993).

Augmented by a proliferation of new business start-ups, management buyouts and reprivatizations constitute the indigenous *Mittelstand* of predominantly small firms with fewer than twenty employees (only 10 per cent have a payroll of more than 200), confined largely to secondary activities such as food processing and the artisan trades (Hall and Ludwig 1995: 502). Undercapitalized, heavily reliant on credit finance and lacking entrepreneurial expertise, the circumstances of the indigenous *Mittelstand* generate interests which are hard to reconcile with those of large firms with an ownership base in the west.

Business interests are also differentiated by sector, reflecting differences in corporate structure, product markets and public policy preoccupations. In the east German economy, sectoral differences are sharpened by wide disparities in economic performance between relatively successful sectors, like construction and the service industries, and sectors like engineering and electricals experiencing severe decline. Extensive regimes of state support exacerbate these differences, generating tension between market-oriented sectors, and those in which many member firms remain heavily dependent on public subsidy: 'some of our member associations are vehemently opposed to the market' (interview: LVSA). Sectoral differences, like the cleavage between large and small firms, are endemic to business organization, but may be more virulent in the post-communist economy.

Reconciling the divergent interests of larger, profitable companies based in the west with a commercially weak indigenous *Mittelstand* remains the central problem of business interest representation in post-communist Germany (Berger 1994, 1995). Conflicts of interest between large and small firms are bound up with the dynamics of post-communist transformation, reflecting tension amongst competing priorities of economic renewal. Modern capitalist economies are based on mixed structures, with SMEs servicing and supplying the large company sector. Capital accumulation in large firms can thus be seen as a prerequisite of a healthy *Mittelstand* economy. However, this long-term strategy has little resonance amongst small and medium-sized entrepreneurs under acute and immediate financial pressures. The *Mittelstand* has therefore pressed for economic development instruments targeted towards its specific requirements.

The cleavage between large and small firms is very clearly reflected in business organization. The sectoral associations affiliated to the Confederation of German Employers Association (the BDA) have attempted to bridge the gulf with very limited success. Significantly, business is one of the very few areas of the associational order in which indigenous organization has survived colonization from the west. Targeting small, east German businesses, the entrepreneur associations (Unternehmerverbände, UVs) have had some local success in exploiting the weakness of the employers' associations in this sector as has the Bonn-based Bundesverband der Mittelständische Wirtschaft (Confederation of the *Mittelstand* Economy, BVMW) (interviews: UV Norddeutschland, Rostock, Umgebung, Sachsen-Anhalt; Verband der Mittelständische Wirtschaft, Rostock).

Competition from these quarters means that the employers' associations have to adjust to the interests of smaller firms, and all have taken steps in this direction. The Thüringen employers, for instance, lobby hard for the interests of reprivatized companies, whilst in Sachsen the employer confederation appointed a chief executive with a *Mittelstand* background in an attempt to attract this clientele (interview: VAS). Advocacy of the *Mittelstand*, however, is tempered by warnings against exaggerating its claims at the expense of large-scale industry. 'The experience of Opel in Eisenach shows that large-scale investment is an indispensable condition for the success of the *Mittelstand* economy' (spokesman, VWT, *Handelsblatt*, 22 January 1991). Constrained by their strong connections with the large company sector, the response of the employers' associations to the concerns of the indigenous *Mittelstand* often appears ambivalent. Virtually all business groups claim to be *Mittelstand* associations first and foremost, although it should be noted that the *Mittelstand* preoccupation in German economic culture often makes it politically prudent for large firms to present their interests as those of an industry dominated by small business. Outside the employers' associations, however, this claim is dismissed as rhetoric: '*Mittelstand* industry feels very badly represented by the employers' associations' (interview: LSI).

Mittelstand interests are much more central to the UVs which challenge the dominance of the employers' associations in some of the new *Länder*. Based exclusively in the east, they are able to focus on the interests of indigenous business: 'we're closer to business . . . more attuned to popular needs, so we're more effective at political representation' (interview: UV Sachsen-Anhalt). As cross-sectoral organizations spanning the whole range of industrial and commercial activity, their membership is highly diverse, but sectoral differences are counterbalanced by the common interests of SMEs. The German experience thus underlines that of its eastern neighbours, pointing to the difficulty of encompassing the interests of large and small firms in unitary business associations.

Employment relations

Introduced by institutional transfer from the Federal Republic, the formal structures of employment relations are those of the German model. Multi-employer bargaining generates broadly encompassing wage agreements exerting legally binding force across industrial sectors, with labour relations institutionalized in a dense network of legal regulation. It is a model of stability and predictability which has often been seen as a cornerstone of the Federal Republic's economic success. In the 1990s, however, attention has turned to the institutional rigidities of the model which are now seen as retarding the German response to economic globalization and jeopardizing national economic performance. Tendencies towards decentralized wage-bargaining, seen for a decade in the west, are greatly intensified in the post-communist economy. The rapidity of structural economic change places a premium on flexible strategies of capital accumulation and there has been a massive shift towards works council bargaining as informal deals at the level of the firm.

The German model of industrial relations mirrors trade union and employer organization, based on sectoral principle. Unlike the Scandinavian model, in which strong peak organizations assume major bargaining responsibilities, the BDA and DGB have no more than a co-ordinating role, with industrial unions and sector employers' associations exercising autonomy in their respective domains. Collective bargaining is supported by a legal requirement that member firms must abide by the terms of agreements concluded by their employers' association. The wage-bargaining arena is thus dominated by collective, multi-employer agreements enforceable across the sector (*Flächentarifverträge*). Sectoral agreements accounted for over 70 per cent of wage contracts in force in 1990. Company agreements are generally restricted to SMEs, outside the associations, and even here there is a strong tendency to conform to sectoral pay levels. The result is a high degree of wage standardization, with relatively little variation within sectors (Jakobi et al. 1992: 230–48, 249–51).

Whilst wage-bargaining is the province of trade union and employers' associations, shop floor and personnel issues are dealt with by the works council (*Betriebsrat*), in a system of institutionalized co-operation between workers and management. Elected by the workforce, the works council has extensive statutory rights of consultation and negotiation, set alongside a legal obligation to work with management in a spirit of mutual trust, and in the common interests of employees and the firm. Its remit is broad, encompassing recruitment and dismissal, working-time schedules, and remuneration issues like bonuses, performance-related pay, and fringe benefits. It is increasingly common for sectoral pay agreements to be supplemented by deals negotiated between management and works councils, company bargaining on these lines offsetting the rigidities of collective agreements. The works council system can thus be seen as a legally ordained form of company-level industrial relations.

In practice the separation between sectoral wage-bargaining and the penumbra of issues subject to works council agreements is rather fluid, facilitating adaptation to globalization and technological change through a shift towards company-level bargaining between management and works councils (Crouch 1993: 262; Koch 1995: 151–2). Whilst wage-bargaining remains centralized, *qualitative* issues related to working hours, the introduction of new technology and human resource management practices have progressively shifted to company level. The post-Fordist revolution in industrial relations has thus been mediated by the works council system, without any large-scale upheaval in the system. Employers have gained in influence without pushing their advantage to its limits, whilst the unions have acquiesced in the shift towards company-level bargaining (C. Lane 1994b: 182–5), seeking to reconcile their interest in reduced working hours and the 'humanization of the working environment' with the new industrial relations agenda.

Transnational tendencies towards flexibility and company autonomy have been partly absorbed and partly resisted by the German model, the rigidities of which are offset by its capacity for incremental consensual change through works council bargaining. Critics point to the insensitivity of the *Flächentarifvertrag* principle to variations in economic performance amongst firms, seeing institutionalized industrial relations as a constraint on innovation and a burden on economic competitiveness (Flockton 1996: 212). Nevertheless, whilst demanding more latitude for productivity-related wage differentiation, employers in western Germany continue to invest in the system as a source of order and predictability. In the new *Länder*, however, the circumstances of economic transformation exacerbated the strains on the German model, opening up fissures in the institutional order of industrial relations.

The challenge for the employers' associations is to adapt the architecture of collective bargaining to the demand for flexibility, without relinquishing the underlying principle of sectoral centralization. The employers' response is the concept of the 'wage corridor', with a broad agreement at sectoral level allowing scope for some in-house variation at the level of the firm. Instrumentalizing the sense of crisis in German industrial relations, Gesamtmetall has attempted to weaken the resistance of the trade unions to the principle of flexibility. 'Wage-bargaining structures are jeopardized', they argue, 'when firms in the east are exposed to unsustainable wage settlements' (*Handelsblatt*, 10 June 1991). Employer attempts to open up a 'second front' of wage-bargaining at company level are characterized by the trade unions as an attack on the foundations of institutionalized industrial relations (*Handelsblatt*, 5 April 1993).

For the employers, company-level bargaining is an escape from the institutional rigidities of industry-wide agreements, and allows them greater scope to exploit favourable labour market conditions with reduced wage settlements. The organizational weakness of the employers' associations in the new *Länder*, and the resultant asymmetry of institutionalized collective bargaining makes in-house settlements doubly attractive. To be sure, the rediscovery of the firm threatens to marginalize employers' associations from their traditional role in the bargaining arena, but for many companies this is a price worth paying for a system of wage-bargaining with greater sensitivity to the realities of the post-communist economy.

Decentralized bargaining is more of a threat to the trade unions. In western Germany, the unions have an ambivalent attitude towards works council bargaining. Notwithstanding the pervasive company egotism (*Betriebsegoismus*) of which they often complain, works councils are largely under union control. Union success in elections means that between two-thirds and three-quarters of works councillors are trade union members, with a 'stable coalition of interests' in which the councils serve almost as an extension of the union apparatus (Jakobi et al. 1992: 244; C. Lane 1994b: 182–5). In the new *Länder*, however, the relationship is more complex, with sharper lines of demarcation between works councils and trade union organization. Although union penetration is as extensive as in the west, works councillors tend to be more rigorous in asserting their formal independence, identifying more closely with the company than the union apparatus, strengthening company loyalties at the expense of trade union solidarity (interviews: IG Metall, Bezirksleitung Berlin-Brandenburg; IG Metall, Verwaltungsstelle Erfurt).

The more company-focused orientation of the works council in the new *Länder* represents a challenge to trade unions, which are dependent on this forum for the representation of their interests and objectives in the company (C. Lane 1994a: 194). Lacking experience and political sophistication, works councillors were initially unprepared for handling the claims and obligations arising in the dual system of interest representation (Mahnkopf 1991: 279). Moreover, the relative weakness of trade unions in works councils is compounded by their tenuous presence on the shop floor. In the west, the unions are able to deploy their shop steward (*Vertauensleute*) apparatus. In the new *Länder*, IG Metall has difficulty in recruiting *Vertauensleute*, reducing the union's influence in works councils. There are some indications that, with the further development of private economy relations, and with the sharpening of wage conflict, works councils are beginning to assimilate west German practices (Kädtler and Kottwitz 1994). The tenuous presence of the trade unions on the shop floor, however, means that works councils are more susceptible to company identification than in the west. The shift to company-level bargaining and the expanding role of the works councils thus means relinquishing central union control over the bargaining arena to local actors. At local level, where the pressures of company survival are most intense, there is often a strong tendency towards 'concession bargaining', sacrificing wages and working conditions for security of employment. Moreover, the legal prescription against works council engagement in industrial action makes the entry of the councils into the wage-bargaining arena deeply unattractive for the trade unions.

Trade union strategy to counter the pull of company interests has centred on the attempt to mobilize broadly based campaigns against company closure. In Thüringen, for instance, the DGB initiated an *Aktionsbundnis* (alliance for action) between otherwise isolated works councils, co-ordinating token work stoppages and orchestrating mass protest (DGB Landesbezirk Thüringen 1994: 17–18). Here and elsewhere, the DGB has convened regional conferences of works councils in the attempt to co-ordinate plant-level action (interview: DGB, Landes-bezirk Sachsen-Anhalt). Bids to broaden the front of protest against redundancy, however, have run up against the narrow preoccupation of workers with the conditions and prospects of their own company, reflec-ted in the *Betriebsegoismus* of the works councils.

Fragmented labour markets

Trade union solidarity, it was argued in the introduction, is engendered by homogenous labour markets which serve to counteract those interests which workers share with their firms. Uneven patterns of productivity and profitability in the post-communist economy are reflected in sharp labour market variations, with income differentials correspondingly wider than in the west (Bialas and Ettl 1992: 31–4). A number of cleavages can be identified. The first arises from 'two-speed labour mar-ket', divided between skilled workers in technologically advanced, high-productivity companies, and semi-skilled and unskilled labour employed in the low-productivity rump of the GDR economy (Bastian 1997: 18; Wenger 1995). Labour market segmentation is compounded by the gulf between investment-rich companies with an ownership base in the west, and the undercapitalized indigenous *Mittelstand* sector (Bialas 1994: 49–50). The resultant fragmentation of the workforce generates conflicts of individual and collective interest which are difficult to reconcile within customary forms of trade union representation.

Income differentials are wider than in western Germany, both between and within sectors. The average manual worker's wage in the construc-tion industry is more than double (204 per cent) that in the textiles sector, against a differential of around 150 per cent in western Germany. A similarly broad income range is evident within sectors. Amongst manual workers in the retailing sector, the highest incomes are almost double (196 per cent) those of the low-paid. In the majority of sectors, income differentials are wider than in the west, reflecting the diversity of the economic landscape in the post-communist economy (Bispinck 1993: 320–3; Bosch and Knuth 1993).

Alongside the fragmentation of employee interests is a syndrome of interest conflict between the employed and the unemployed. The conflict is characteristic of all western European economies in the 1990s as rising levels of unemployment force trade unions to shift their priorities from wage maximization to job protection. In the post-communist economy, however, the dilemma is sharpened by the scale of de-industrialization and mass unemployment. Between 1990 and 1992 the number of regular jobs in the primary labour market declined from 9.8 million to around 5.7

million. Some 2.2 million workers were absorbed into the secondary market or early retirement, short-time working or job creation and re-training programmes. Initially seen as a temporary expedient for cushioning the effects of economic transformation, the secondary labour market has become an institutionalized feature of the east German economy. Despite these measures, however, and an annual GDP growth rate approaching 10 per cent from 1992 onwards, unemployment remained steady at around 14–15 per cent, rising to 17 per cent as growth was stifled by recession in the west German economy. Around 80 per cent of the labour force has experienced job change or unemployment since unification.

The conflict of interest between the employed and the unemployed can be seen in terms of the 'wages–employment dilemma', one of the central problems of economic reconstruction in the new *Länder*, in which public policy and the private economy are entwined in a problem complex that defies resolution through the normal channels of interest representation. Against the background of the intense political pressures generated by economic transformation, public policy has been geared to sustaining a higher level of employment and wages than could be supported by the productive economy. The gulf between employment and wages on the one hand and productivity on the other has been met through public support of the labour market, and by a squeeze on private-sector profitability. Thus the social and political costs of transformation have been reduced in the short term, but at the expense of the long-term objectives of economic reconstruction. Uneconomic wage levels and subsidized employment inhibit recovery, with the prospect of 'high rates of employment lasting for decades' (Hughes-Hallett, Ma and Mélitz 1996: 538).

The trade union response to the wages–employment dilemma has been to reject the linkage between increasing wages and rising unemployment, arguing that job losses are an inevitable consequence of the exposure of a backward economy to the rigours of the market (IG Metall 1995: 4). Union strategy has been to combine strong wage pressure with demands for industry and labour market support on the part of the state (Flockton and Esser 1992: 295–300). With state subsidies cushioning the employment effects of rising wage costs, wage-bargaining ceases to be a zero-sum conflict between wage-earners and the employed. Indeed, with unemployment support linked to wages under the Labour Promotion Act (Arbeitsforderungsgesetz), a high-wage policy has a positive spinoff for the unemployed, at least for the duration of their benefit entitlement. Trade unions are thus able to transfer the costs of high-wage policies to state, *externalizing* the negative consequences of their actions, and releasing them from the wages–employment dilemma (Bialas 1994: 51).

This strategy rested on the assumption that the political economy of the new *Länder* would be progressively assimilated with the German model of a high-performance, high-wage economy coupled with a socially responsible state, *Sozialstaat*, based on the principle of social solidarity. Increasingly difficult to reconcile with the dynamics of economic globalization and recession, however, the German model itself is subject to a fundamental reappraisal, creating a Gordian knot of economic problems and organized interests. As we shall see in chapter 6, the trade union response to the intensification of the wages–employment dilemma is to fall back on the customary routines of bargained adjustment, seeking a consensual formula for wage flexibility in the interests of job protection and creation. The quest for this elusive objective has exposed sharp political differences between the industrial unions, and the inability of the DGB to reconcile the ensuing conflicts has underlined the limits on its unifying role. In the new *Länder*, the scope for compromise is restricted still further by a logic of trade union membership which depends upon the capacity of the unions to realize their members' aspirations towards wage parity with the west.

Thus the package of measures in IG Metall's 1996 Bündnis für Arbeit (alliance for jobs) in the east was more restrictive than that offered in the west. Its proposed reduction in working hours was only partially reflected in reduced wages, whilst the commitment to wage parity remained non-negotiable. Rejected by employers who see labour market crisis as an opportunity to open up collective bargaining, IG Metall's initiative collapsed. In the absence of a political solution to the wages–employment dilemma, centralized wage-bargaining is under increasing pressure from plant-level agreements, leading to progressive reduction of union control over this central arena of interest representation.

Professional interests

Interest representation in the profession is inherently fragmented, with professional groups divided along the lines of disciplinary specialisms, and by differences in the commercial basis of professional practice. There are, for example, over 100 engineers' organizations in Germany. In medicine, broadly based associations like the Hartmannbund, the NAV and the Marburgerbund coexist with a large number of more specialist groups. Divisions along the lines of disciplinary specialism are compounded by divisions between salaried employees and private practitioners. Amongst the latter, professional solidarity is often undermined by commercial competition and rivalry. The competitive ethos is often exacerbated by the upheaval of professional life accompanying post-communist social transformation, with the struggle for survival in private practice generating a competitive individualism that undermines the sense of vocational ethos in which professional interest associations are rooted.

The main division in the medical profession runs between the hospital sector and ambulent (outpatient) health care. The ambulent sector was subject to a massive transformation with unification: 'in no other sector of health care was the difference between the GDR system and that of the Federal Republic as great as in ambulent care' (Ministerium für Arbeit, Brandenburg 1994: 88). With the breakup of the GDR's polyclinic health centres, ambulent care was established on a private practice basis. Privatization coincided with a tightening-up of health system finance in the Federal Republic. Doctors already hard pressed to meet the costs of establishing themselves in private practice were immediately faced with a squeeze on payments for treatment under the health insurance funds. The professional associations of ambulent doctors (the NAV and the Hartmannbund) are heavily preoccupied with the commercial basis of private practice. Representing hospital doctors, the Marburgerbund is more in the nature of a trade union, with a primary function of conducting salary negotiations. Divisions between the ambulent sector and hospital doctors reflect the structure of health care in the Federal Republic and are not unique to eastern Germany. In the east, however, the financial pressures on private practitioners sharpen these divisions in the profession.

The medical profession is also differentiated on political lines. In the Federal Republic, the Hartmannbund represents the conservative, elitist face of the profession. By contrast the NAV is more 'progressive' and democratic, and is less inclined towards the centre-right parties. In the new *Länder*, these differences of political accent are sharpened by the legacy of socio-economic transformation. In the debate over the restructuring of GDR health care in 1990, all the west German doctors' associations advocated private practice, but the Hartmannbund was particularly strident in denouncing the polyclinics, whilst the NAV was more moderate. With unification, the Hartmannbund simply extended its organization eastwards, whereas the NAV incorporated the GDR profession through partnership with the newly formed Rudolf-Virchow-Bund (VB). Subsequently, the NAV has been more ready to embrace eastern interests: 'it has really become much more progressive in the last few years' (interview: NAV, Sachsen). The NAV is more receptive than the Hartmannbund to the financial difficulties of private practitioners in the east, and east–west differences have dissolved in a common front against Health Ministry reforms to health care finance. Moreover, NAV support for *Arztehause* (health centres based on partnership practices that are beginning to appear in both parts of Germany) endears it to doctors in the east who retain an attachment to the principle of collective practice.

Relations between the respective associations are characterized by 'competitive co-operation'. Co-operation is based on a pragmatic recognition that, for all its internal differences, the medical profession shares common interests. Professional unity, however, is undermined by commercial pressures:

We don't love each other, and we don't have any more contact than is absolutely necessary, but we do sometimes co-operate. (Interview: Marburgerbund, Landesverband Sachsen)

We have little reason to regard each other as competitors . . . and we don't poach each other's members . . . on the other hand there is little solidarity amongst doctors due to the intensity of the economic problems and the struggle for survival. (Interview: Hartmannbund, Landesverband Mecklenburg-Vorpommern)

The weakness of professional solidarity also undermines the representation of a common front in relation to the 'specific constellation of problems' in the new *Länder*. Attempts to speak with one voice have proved abortive: 'some organizations were not prepared to co-operate' (interview: NAV-VB, Sachsen). The fragmentation of associational activity reflects the competitive individualism of a profession newly exposed to commercial pressures.

As we have seen, engineering provides one of the few examples of the survival of a GDR interest organization, albeit for only four years beyond unification. Encompassing the whole range of science and technology from academically trained scientists to skilled workers (*Facharbeiter*), the rationale of the KdT was rooted in the interest spectrum of communist society (Eichener and Voelzkow 1992). Its role was twofold. First, it served as the state's instrument for the promotion (but also control) of international exchange between the GDR intelligentsia and science in the capitalist world. Secondly, it provided a home for the technical intelligentsia. Worse paid and more heavily taxed than the average manual worker, and with its members' children receiving low priority in access to higher education, this group regarded itself as a disadvantaged class. From the late 1980s, the technical intelligentsia used the KdT as a forum for its interests, and as a safe haven from which to criticise the regime.

The survival of the KdT after unification was due to its ability to find a new role: representing engineers with non-academic qualifications in their struggle for professional recognition. It was well equipped for this campaign, with a number of high-profile representatives in the

Bundestag, mobilized through a parliamentary committee. With the successful resolution of the qualification issue, it continued to serve its members through the provision of advice and advocacy in the official procedures that were subsequently established for the recognition of GDR-qualified engineers. A classic example of Olson's 'selective membership incentives', this role underpinned the existence of the KdT in the early years after unification. Ultimately, though, it remained rooted in the GDR, and was ill equipped for the representation of professional interest in the more differentiated occupational structures of liberal market society.

In engineering as in other professions, interest representation is combined with information networks, technical services and career opportunities (interview: Verein der Ingenieure und Techniker, Thüringen). With the construction industry dominated by large west German companies, and with private practice run on western lines, the professional elite of university qualified engineers look towards the specialist services provided by the VDI, or to the multiplicity of specialist professional associations in the Federal Republic. For skilled employees in the engineering sector, the trade unions offer a more appropriate form of representation. It is the *Mittelstand* sector of self-employed entrepreneur-engineers (often without academic qualifications) that remain outside the professional associations. For them, commercial survival is more pressing than professional concerns. and it is to this group that KdT successor organizations have looked in their bid to find a niche in the new structure of interest representation (interview: Verein der Ingenieure und Wirtschaftler, Mecklenburg-Vorpommern).

Conclusion

The experience of east/central Europe suggests that post-communist society is insufficiently differentiated for the spontaneous generation of pluralist interest representation. An underdeveloped private economy retards the emergence of those socio-economic distinctions around which group interests form. Prevailing modes of privatization in the countries of eastern and central Europe have failed to crystallize economic relations. The structure of capital ownership remains diffuse, and with distinctions between managerial and employee interests ill defined, there is little foundation for the emergence of a differentiated interest landscape. The common interest of managers and employees in company survival results in a syndrome of co-management in which the company serves a the focal point of collective interest, marginalizing associational activity on the broader front. The German case is distinguished, of course, by the institutional transfer of a 'ready-made' apparatus of interest representation. In the early stages of economic transformation, however, it was 'subverted' by the inchoate character of capital ownership and a pattern of employment relations marked by the same syndrome of co-management observed elsewhere in east/central Europe.

Rapid and thoroughgoing privatization transformed ownership and employment relations, sharpening the profile of socio-economic interests, but the evidence suggests that the configuration of interests is more fragmented than in the west. The advanced post-communist economy is characterized by a distinctive pattern of capital accumulation, concentrated around a relatively small number of large companies with an ownership base in the west, alongside an undercapitalized substratum of SMEs in the indigenous *Mittelstand*. The structure of corporate ownership thus conforms to the polarized model outlined in the introduction, generating divergent definitions of collective identity and interest that are difficult to contain within a system of business organization based on the sectoral principle. Interest conflicts reflecting a polarized structure of corporate ownership are compounded by those arising in cross-sectoral differences in economic performance. Some sectors adapt more readily to market transition than others. The market orientation of the leading sectors conflicts sharply with the state dependency of the laggards, creating conflicts of interest which undermine the cohesion of cross-sectoral business confederations. Variations in the structure of corporate ownership, company size and profitability are reflected in a mêlée of conflicting interests and public policy preferences in which the tension between large and small firms, endemic to organized business, is particularly acute.

Employment relations in the advanced post-communist economy provide a similarly unstable foundation for associational activity. With market transition, tendencies towards co-management give way to more adversarial relationships, but there is little to suggest that employment relations will gravitate towards the institutionalized model outlined in the introduction. Indeed, the German case shows the limitations of institutionalized collective bargaining in the context of the post-communist economy. A more pronounced pattern of productivity-related wage differentiation is difficult to reconcile with uniform sectoral wage agreements. The rapidity of structural change places a premium on flexible strategies of capital accumulation, especially for 'home-grown' entrepreneurs facing problems of undercapitalization, for whom the attractions of flexibility are disproportionately strong relative to the benefits of stability inherent in institutionalized collective bargaining. Labour market fragmentation, on the other hand, generates a divergent pattern of wage-earner interests that is difficult to accommodate within the structures of a unitary labour movement. Similarly, in the professions, fragmentation by disciplinary specialism is compounded by the competitive individualism generated by the commercial pressures of newly established private practice. A diverse and fragmented spectrum of interests in the advanced post-communist economy militates against the solidaristic values and communitarian identities on which the associational order rests, undermining, as we shall see in chapter 4, the organizational resources and incentive structures of collective action.

3 Organization

Interest organization exhibits a striking diversity of structural forms in different national contexts. The range of variation can be expressed in terms of a spectrum from the loose-jointed 'pluralistic' interest group system in the United States – 'untidy, competitive . . . and very varied' (Wilson 1993: 139), to the more formally structured, tightly integrated corporatist systems in some of the northern European countries. Cross-national heterogeneity can be explained by different patterns of economic development and corresponding differences in the class configurations from which organized interests emerge. It may also reflect differences in the institutional environment, which shapes the institutional design of the organizational landscape. The fragmentation of the American system, for instance, has been explained by the dispersal of power within the apparatus of the state (Salisbury 1979: 218–20). In short, 'the characteristics of associational systems . . . are deeply influenced and determined by the socio-economic and political history of each single country' (Lanzalaco 1992: 199–200).

The centralized, hierarchical design characteristic, as we have seen, of corporatist systems is unlikely to emerge spontaneously in the early stages of democratic transformations. Corporatist design is associated with sharply defined and cohesive class formations. With its social structures as yet ill defined, post-communist society is likely to generate a more fragmented spectrum of interests, reflected in interest group systems which approximate more closely the more untidy and varied pattern of the pluralist design.

Interest organization in post-communist society

The organizational landscape in the countries of east/central Europe is the antithesis of the corporatist model, displaying neither the disciplined hierarchy of centralized systems nor the structured interdependence of the articulated variant. Fragmentation is its hallmark, with a multiplicity of competing trade unions and business associations reflecting the social and political instability of societies in transition. Trade union structures are characterized by bifurcation between unions inheriting the apparatus of their communist predecessors and newly formed unions, often born out of the democratic revolution. Bifurcation between old and new unions is compounded by political and occupational differences to produce a multiplicity of competing confederations. The autonomy of company-level unionism leads to the disempowerment of the confederations in a decentralized structure in which articulation between confederal leaders and the organizational base is almost entirely absent. Membership levels are subject to acute cross-national variation, and are highest where the labour movement is dominated by unions with their organizational foundations in the old regime. Membership is at its highest in large firms remaining under state ownership, the heartland of the old unions.

Business organization is kaleidoscopic in character. Beneath the semblance of order imparted by a few large general associations lies a chaotic multiplicity of sectoral, regional and club-type entrepreneur groups, with little articulation between the two organizational levels. Where the associational order exhibits any indication of consolidation and stability, it is along lines which reflect the heterogeneity of interests in the post-communist economy. There is little reliable data on business group membership, but the indications are that membership is low, especially amongst private sector entrepreneurs.

Organizational design

In the labour movements of east/central Europe three organizational types can be observed: centralized systems with a unitary trade union confederation; polarized systems with a communist successor confederation competing with an anti-communist rival; and fragmented systems containing a multiplicity of confederal organizations. The Czech Republic is the only example of the unitary model. Here the old unions retained both a measure of organizational integrity and a monopoly over the labour movement (Myant 1994: 61–4). Communists and anti-communist elements co-operated in the reform of the old structures, with the latter quickly acquiring a majority in the Czech and Slovak Confederation of Trade Unions, CSKOS (CMKOS after the partition of the Czech Republic from Slovakia). Poland provides the classic case of polarization, with bifurcation between the old official All-Poland Alliance of Trade Unions (OPZZ) and Solidarity, mirrored in Bulgaria by division between the reconstituted official union CITUB and the anti-communist Podkrepa.

A more pluralist structure is to be found in Hungary, where the communist successor National Association of Hungarian Trade Unions, MSZOSZ, coexists with a number of breakaway confederations, as well as the newly formed Democratic League of Independent Trade Unions and the National Alliance of Workers' Councils. In all, there are seven confederations in the Hungarian labour movement, although pluralism is offset to some extent by the dominance of the MSZOSZ, and by the occupational specialization of some of its rivals (Tóth 1994: 86). Trade union structures in Russia are both fragmented and subject to the fissiparous tendencies characteristic of national political life. The Federation of Independent Trade Unions of Russia, FNPR, was created in an attempt to reconstitute an official trade union apparatus which had collapsed with the disintegration of the Soviet Union. Little more than a loose confederacy of industrial unions and regional committees, the FNPR is just one of a number of competing union confederations in a highly pluralist structure (Clarke 1994).

Fragmentation amongst rival confederations is compounded by internal fragmentation. A proliferation of unions based on craft and occupation has led to a progressive decentralization of trade union organization, with increasing autonomy at enterprise level and the 'disempowerment' of peak organizations (Reutter 1996; Stykow 1996: 7). With the disintegration of the hierarchical relationships of the old regime, central and regional bodies have lost their authority over the lower levels of organization (Clarke 1994: 149) with a wide gulf between the particularism of enterprise-level activity, and a national leadership engaged primarily in political manoeuvre. Relations between the different levels of trade union activity are ill co-ordinated, with an organizational vacuum at the sectoral level.

Unions emerging from anti-communist opposition movements like Solidarity and Podkrepa resemble general unions rather than organizations at the apex of a tightly structured confederal hierarchy. Sectoral organization is discouraged as a breeding ground for personal rivalries and 'branch egoism'. A key characteristic of the general union is direct membership rather than a membership mediated through constituent affiliates. Sector or industry organization is stronger in the communist successor unions, but even here the autonomy of industrial unions is often more symbolic than real, and enterprise unions remain the dominant form of organization (MacShane 1994: 347). Seen against the backdrop of corporatist analysis, then, trade unions in east/central Europe have neither the hierarchical discipline of the centralized model nor the interdependence between leadership and grass-roots characteristic of the articulated variant.

Entrepreneurial organization is even weaker and more fragmented than the trade unions with a bewilderingly complex mosaic of business associations to which the principle of hierarchical centralization is entirely alien. Only the Czech Republic and Slovakia have anything approaching overarching confederations. An artificial product of state-sponsored tripartism, the Co-ordination Council of Entrepreneur Unions and Associations in these countries is no more than a loosely confederal umbrella organization, interlocuting sporadically and ineffectually between government and a multiplicity of independent business groups (Desai and Orenstein 1996). Most post-communist countries lack even this gesture towards centralization. The model of specialist sector groups exercising a monopoly over their respective domains and affiliated to a central confederation is unknown.

The prevailing pattern is of several competing *general* business associations ranged broadly along lines of cleavage between state sector and private economy, between large and small business, and sometimes between domestic and international capital. In Hungary, for instance, the National Association of Entrepreneurs (VOSZ) represents private firms in the SME sector, whilst the National Confederation of Hungarian Employers (MAOSZ) is the organization for large-scale business (across the state/private sector divide). The latter competes in the big business sector with the Hungarian Association for International Companies. Hungary exhibits the most consolidated organization, but even here there are six business confederations, excluding agriculture (Cox and Vass 1994: 170). Although there are some indications of rationalization, no single organization is able to establish a monopoly over its domain (Héthy 1994: 317–18). Moreover, general business associations are not confederations in the accepted sense, since they enlist member companies directly, alongside their affiliated sector and regional organizations.

As might be expected, economic backwardness and organizational underdevelopment go hand in hand, with Russia providing the paradigm case. Here the slow and halting pace of privatization means that business is still dominated by the state sector. The high-profile Russian Union of Industrialists and Entrepreneurs (RUIE) represents backwoodsmen in state enterprises, and has close ties with the leadership of the FNPR trade unions (Clarke 1994: 151). Aspiring to dominance over private economy interests is the Leaseholders and Entrepreneur's Union, representing some 10,000 small enterprises privatized through leasing arrangements. Beneath the big general associations, fragmentation intensifies still further with an anarchic plurality of business circles and entrepreneur clubs: 'organizations come and go with bewildering speed', with constant shifts in title, leadership and location (Rutland 1992: 17–20).

Hungary, the Czech Republic and Poland each have several hundred groups based on sector, region or personal faction, in an organizational mêlée characterized by the absence of co-ordination or articulation (Stykow 1996: 5–6). Russia has around seventy groups active at national level and many more in the regions, where formal organization is enmeshed with semi-organized networks embedded in a clandestine substratum of informal clan relations, corruption and criminality (Stykow 1994: 15).

A further complicating factor in some countries is the coexistence of voluntary business associations with quasi-official chambers of commerce. The status of the chambers and their relations with voluntary associations vary from one country to another. The Hungarian chambers have acquired public law status and compulsory membership on the German model. Combining their official functions with the articulation of private economy interests, they coexist uneasily with the voluntary associations in the representational domain (Brusis 1994: 8). In most other countries, however, the chambers have relinquished their public law status, distancing themselves from the state and assuming a new identity as the independent voice of private business. In Slovenia and Croatia, the weak development of voluntary organization means that the chambers occupy centre stage in the associational order (Grant 1993: 93).

Membership

Across east/central Europe, organized labour is dominated to a greater or lesser extent by trade unions with their origins in the old regime, their organizational strength rooted in a membership inherited from their predecessors. In Poland, Solidarity members are outnumbered by a factor of two to one by members of the old official trade union OPZZ. Similarly, the opposition union Podkrepa in Bulgaria is less than half the size of the official CITUB. With its communist origins, the MSZOSZ in Hungary more than doubles the combined membership of all eight of its rival confederations (Waller 1994: 26–7). Newly formed, independent trade unions like Sotsprof in Russia have failed to make an impact, and are restricted largely to white-collar employees and strategically placed groups of skilled workers (MacShane 1994: 349–50; Cox and Vass 1994: 169). Organizational density is difficult to assess with confidence. In larger enterprises remaining under state control, membership density can often be as high as 75 per cent (Bamber and Peschanski 1996: 80; Myant 1994: 63). Organization is weakest in the emergent private sector, where SMEs predominate. Here 'trade unions . . . have major problems in maintaining membership and a role for themselves' (Hegewisch,

Table 3.1. *Trade union membership: Germany and east/central Europe*

	% labour force	% manual workers	% non-manual workers	% age 15–39	% age 40+
Albania	61	47	66	66	61
Armenia	34	33	47	33	51
Belarus	93	90	95	90	95
Bulgaria	48	42	54	41	55
East Germany	39	40	32	35	44
Estonia	44	42	44	36	53
European Russia	80	80	80	75	86
Georgia	46	44	54	42	57
Hungary	39	33	40	34	44
Latvia	58	55	60	50	66
Lithuania	14	13	16	12	17
Macedonia	41	29	56	39	43
Moldova	78	75	83	74	82
Poland	23	13	24	20	28
Romania	46	41	39	46	46
Slovenia	55	–	–	53	60
Ukraine	82	80	85	78	88

Source: Budge, Newton et al. 1997: 170–2.

Brewster and Koubek 1996: 62). A low level of organization in the private sector suggests that, as economic transformation runs its course, trade union membership can be expected to decline steeply.

A striking feature of the trade union membership data shown in table 3.1 is the very wide cross-national variation. It is difficult to establish clear patterns of variation, except perhaps that the highest membership levels are to be found in those countries where there has been most resistance to market transition (Budge, Newton et al. 1997: 169). High membership levels may also be linked with the predominance of ex-communist trade unions, which often form bastions of resistance against market reform. Union membership may thus be seen as a defensive response to the threat of the market on the part of vulnerable workers, an interpretation which will be pursued further in chapter 4.

Business organization is retarded by the continuing dominance of economic life by the state. Despite a proliferation of capital clubs, business round-tables and industry associations, membership remains low: 'most employers feel no special need to combine' (Bamber and Peschanski 1996: 76–7). Organization is strongest amongst large firms, but even here the private sector has been hesitant in emancipating itself from the state. The Association of Hungarian Manufacturing Industry

(MGYOSZ), for instance, embraces the managers of state enterprises amongst its membership. Amongst SMEs, membership levels are extremely low (Brusis 1994; Wiesenthal 1995b: 5–7).

There is little to suggest the emergence of strong patterns of association in post-communist society. The dynamics of collective action here exhibit a marked continuity with the past, focused on the state rather than on market relations. It is the emerging private economy that could be expected to generate the strongest impetus for collective action, but it is here that trade unions and business associations are at their weakest. Dominated by SMEs in construction, retail and service sectors, the private economy appears to be infertile ground for collective action. This conclusion is strengthened by the analysis of membership *motivations* contained in the next chapter.

The German model: institutional design

Introduced by institutional transfer from the west, the associational order in the new *Länder* inevitably reflects the German model. In sharp contrast to the countries of east/central Europe, the model is characterized by very intensive organization within an institutional design based on hierarchy and order. Its main strength lies at sectoral level, with business associations and trade unions based on the unitary principle exercising a monopoly over their representational domain. Maintaining regional and often local networks, sector organizations serve to mediate between membership and confederal leadership. At peak level, business and the trade unions are organized under unitary confederations, although the latter are somewhat loose-jointed with only limited authority over their members. The associational order thus conforms more to the concentrated, articulated model of corporatism than to the centralized variant.

Whilst the new *Länder* are assimilated to the German model, there are some distinctive features which reflect the circumstances of post-communist transformation. First, whilst support from the west means that organizational intensity is far greater than in the countries of east/central Europe, resource constraints mean that organization is *leaner* than in western Germany, particularly in weaker economic sectors and the professions, where organization is tenuous. Secondly, the associational order is more *competitive* than in the west, with competition amongst business groups in the small firm sector, and sharp jurisdictional disputes amongst the trade unions. Thirdly, economic and social divisions between east and west Germany accentuate the *territorial* dimension in an associational order endowed by the federal system with a strong regional character (Mayntz 1990).

Business organization

German business is exceptionally highly organized, in a tripartite structure in which employer interests, industry and commerce are represented separately. The overall appearance is one of order and hierarchy; in each of the three spheres, associational activity culminates in a single unitary confederation, although centralization is offset by the autonomy exercised by sectoral or regional affiliates. Employer organization resembles a pyramid; at its apex is the BDA, a 'peak' confederation of forty-six sectoral associations. The largest and most powerful of the latter is the sectoral association of the motors, machine tools and electricals sectors, Gesamtmetall, encompassing some 8,300 firms. In common with its counterparts in other industries, Gesamtmetall exercises a monopoly over the sector. The main function of the sector associations is collective wage-bargaining in which the BDA plays only a secondary role, its remit restricted to co-ordination. The main function of the BDA is the representation of employer interests in the public policy arena. Multiple linkages between confederal, sectoral and regional level mean that, whilst employer organization is less centralized than the appearance of hierarchy suggests, it is nevertheless characterized by a high degree of internal articulation.

Formally, employer organization in the new *Länder* replicates the western model, although in practice resource constraints mean that there are some significant differences. With the exception of Brandenburg, which is merged with Berlin, each *Land* has its own regional confederation, affiliated to the BDA headquarters in Cologne. The relatively loose structure of the latter endows the *Land* confederations with a considerable degree of autonomy, enabling them to serve as the focus of a regional coalition of employer interests, and the representation of those interests with the *Land* government. At sectoral level, however, organization is much sparser than in the west, with only Gesamtmetall maintaining a full-scale infrastructure.

Gesamtmetall is organized on regional lines with fifteen regional associations across the Federal Republic. The new *Länder* are represented in this structure, with an Association of the Metals and Electricals Industry (Verband der Metall- und Elektroindustrie, VME) in Sachsen, Sachsen-Anhalt and Thüringen. Each maintains an independent organization with its own elected leadership and administrative apparatus, supported by membership subscriptions paid direct to the *Land* association rather than to Gesamtmetall. In the remaining *Länder*, the VME is merged in regional organizations cutting across east–west lines. Subject to the gravitational pull of Berlin and with no competing industrial centre, Brandenburg was incorporated from an early stage in the VME, Berlin-Brandenburg. Mecklenburg-Vorpommern exhibits structural similarities with its coastal neighbours in the western part of Germany, and the merger of the metal and electrical employers with the Hamburg-based Nordmetall thus followed economic logic. However, it also means that there is less scope for the representation of a distinctive east German identity. In addition to its bureaux in the *Land* capitals, the VME maintains quite an extensive 'on-the-ground' organization with eleven regional offices in the east. Of the other industrial sectors, none comes close to matching the intensity of its organization. Resource constraints mean that the smaller employers' associations have a sparser territorial basis, with organizational infrastructures encompassing a number of *Länder*, and with some operating from a base in the west.

As in the west, the BDA-affiliated *Land* confederations are very heavily dependent on the organizational apparatus and resources of the VME. It is standard practice in the west for the VME to play host to the BDA-affiliated *Land* confederations. In the east, however, the tenuous presence of the other sectors increases the reliance of the confederations on the VME, which provides two-thirds of the financial backing, as well as the office premises and staff. Thus the regional employer confederations are served by VME staff, although the elected leadership of the respective organizations remain separate. VME officials maintain that anchorage in a strong sector provides the confederations with organizational stability. On the other hand, it has been argued that the dominance of the VME imparts representational bias to the confederations (Boll 1994: 117).

The organization of German industry replicates that of the employers, with a pyramidical structure culminating in a single peak confederation, the Confederation of Germany Industry (Bundesverband der Deutschen Industrie, BDI). Composed of thirty-four affiliated sectoral associations, the BDI brings together over 500 trade and regional groups encompassing some 80,000 firms before unification. The BDI has a high profile in the public policy arena; whilst the BDA restricts itself largely to labour market and social issues, its brief extends to the whole range of economic and industry policy. Focused primarily on federal government, however, BDI organization is heavily centralized. Organizational weakness at regional level means that it usually delegates its representational mandate to the BDA-affiliated *Land* confederations. Industry organization is most intensive at sector level with 'an exhaustive exchange of information, ideas and experience' between the associations and their member firms (VDMA 1993: 13–14). In the larger sector associations like machine-building or chemicals, there are specialist subgroups for particular products. In the chemicals sector, the Verband der Chemischen Industrie maintains thirty-three specialist groups, in a model designed to accommodate sectoral diversity, counteracting tendencies to subsector fragmentation, and enabling sector associations to maintain a monopoly over their interest domain (Grant, Paterson and Whitston 1987).

Sectoral centralization at the expense of regional organization means that the BDI and its affiliates are largely absent from the new *Länder*. Only the larger sector associations have a presence on the ground, and even here it is restricted to skeletal proportions. In machine-building, the VDMA has only two regional groups in the east, and one of these is run from its west Berlin office. The extent of its apparatus in the east is one small bureau in Dresden, which also serves as the headquarters of the regional Confederation of Sachsen Industry (Landesverband der Sächsischen Industrie, LSI), the sole outpost of the BDI in the east. Elsewhere its representational mandate is given to the employers' confederation. The BDI presence in Sachsen is explained by the symbolic importance of visibility in the heartland of east German industry. The weakness of the BDA-affiliated employers' confederation in Sachsen means that the LSI acts as the principal interlocutor between business and the *Land* government (interview: LSI).

The third pillar of business organization consists of the chambers of industry and commerce (Industrie- und Handelskammern, IHKs). Their structure reflects their principal function of ordering the regional economy, with independent chambers in all the major urban centres. With their legally assigned responsibilities for vocational education and training and the certification of trade, the chambers are quasi-state bodies, incorporated in public law. Membership is compulsory across the whole range of commercial and business activity. Thus the chambers do not conform to the usual definition of organized interests in democratic societies, where membership is normally voluntary. Alongside the responsibilities ascribed by the state, however, the chambers perform a range of functions emerging out of the interests of their members. As representatives of business interests in the regional policy arena, the chambers form a part of the associational order, participating in interest representation at the federal level through their peak organization, the German Council of Industry and Commerce (Deutscher Industrie- und Handelstag, DIHT). In contrast to the BDA and BDI, where the interests of large-scale industry tend to predominate, the DIHT represents the perspective of small and medium-sized business.

With unification, chambers proliferated in almost every large town and city, often based on the structures and personnel of their GDR predecessors. Rationalization, orchestrated by the DIHT in order to secure their financial base, has left the chambers more sparsely distributed than in the west, reflecting the weakness of economic activity. There are fourteen chambers in the main cities, the larger of which maintain two or three branch offices to service neighbouring centres too small to sustain independent organizational activity. Under the chamber law (*Kammergesetz*), regional chambers have complete territorial sovereignty and financial autonomy, limiting the functions of the DIHT in Bonn to co-ordination and political representation with federal government.

Competing with business organization originating in institutional transfer from the west are the independent east German entrepreneur associations, UVs. Initially formed on the territorial basis of the whole of the GDR, this indigenous initiative of (for the most part) small business subsequently reconstituted itself along the lines of the federal system (Ettl 1995: 46–52). UVs are present in all the new *Länder*, but are strongest in Brandenburg and Sachsen, and in Mecklenburg-Vorpommern, where there are four independent associations, reflecting economic rivalries between the regions. To the employer confederations, the UVs are unwelcome intruders in the associational order. The employers reject any form of co-operation, regarding the UVs as a temporary product of economic transformation and attempting to drive them into extinction through competitive recruitment. The exception to this pattern of interorganizational competition is Mecklenburg-Vorpommern, where co-operative relations were established at an early stage and the UV is an affiliated member of the employers' confederation. In the other *Länder*, however, the employers have established a new form of general business association, Allgemeiner Arbeitgeberverbände, offering direct membership to firms which prefer to remain outside the sector associations. This initiative is designed to attract precisely those small and medium-sized firms which form the clientele of the UVs. One of very few specifically east German organizations to survive unification, the UV network continues to exploit the weakness of sectoral associations amongst smaller firms.

Trade unions

The structure of the German trade unions reflects the organizational principles of the unitary union (*Einheitsgewerkschaft*) and the industry union (*Industriegewerkschaft*). A single union exercises a monopoly over its industrial sector, transcending political divisions and distinctions of skill and status. Organization is characterized by a high degree of concentration, with thirteen internally centralized and largely autonomous industrial unions dominating the landscape. The industrial unions vary widely in size, with the largest, IG Metall, around ten times the size of the smallest. With virtually all facing membership decline and financial crisis, moves towards merger are underway, held back only by political differences and interorganizational turf struggles (Silvia and Markovits 1995). Already, super-unions are beginning to emerge, with IG Bergbau, Chemie, Energie formed in 1996 from a merger of two previously separate unions in the mining, energy and chemicals sectors, and the amalgamation of the constructive, agricultural and horticultural workers unions in IG Bauen-Agrar-Umwelt in 1995.

Collectively the industrial unions constitute the Confederation of German Trade Unions (Deutscher Gewerkschaftsbund, DGB), a relatively loosely confederated peak organization, within which individual unions retain a large measure of autonomy. With no role in wage-bargaining and little authority over its members, the DGB's function is limited to political representation. Even here, the capacity of the DGB for co-ordination is undermined by political differences between the constituent unions. Combining tight *sectoral* discipline with loose-jointed confederation, the German model is thus one of concentration without overall centralization. Both characteristics are likely to be exacerbated by the impending organizational upheaval which will probably result in a handful of multi-branch super-unions exercising increasing autonomy from the DGB.

Between national headquarters and the shopfloor, the industrial unions maintain an intermediate tier of organization, corresponding broadly to the territorial structures within which wage-bargaining takes place. Regional organization serves to co-ordinate branch-level activity and to mediate relations between leaders and members. All the industrial unions have a regional apparatus in eastern Germany, although the scale and intensity vary widely with membership size, and to some extent also with strategic outlook. Even before its merger with IG Bergbau, for instance, IGCPK had a relatively centralized structure, amalgamating Berlin, Brandenburg and Sachsen in one *Bezirk* and Sachsen-Anhalt and Thüringen in another. For smaller unions facing resource constraints this model has the merit of economy. In IG Metall, on the other hand, regional organization bridges the east–west divide, with four west German regions extended to assimilate neighbouring eastern *Länder,* only Sachsen remaining independent (Bezirk Dresden). Mixed regions are seen as a way of avoiding the institutionalization of east–west divisions, and serve also to harness established strength in the west to the task of organization-building in the east. In most other unions, regional structures mirror the federal system.

The disparity in socio-economic circumstances between eastern and western Germany places a premium on a system of territorial representation attuned to the specific interests of the new *Länder*. IG Metall officials in the east recognize the significance of regional representation: 'a leadership in Frankfurt is not favourably positioned to speak for Thüringen' (interview: IG Metall, Verwaltungsstelle Erfurt). As we shall see in chapter 6, the autonomy of IG Metall's organization in Sachsen made the union highly effective as a local actor, contributing to the strength of regional corporatism.

The absence of regional organization in IG Metall is partially offset by an extensive local organization, with thirty-five district offices (*Verwaltungsstellen*) across the east. District offices have autonomous control over budgets (20 per cent of membership revenues accrue to them) and the appointment of officials, under the supervision of an assembly elected in the workplace branches. Their capacity to articulate the local voice is indicated by variations in political orientation from one district office to another: 'we're quite conflict-oriented here; in Eisenach or Jena they're much more moderate'. Similarly, political alignments between unions are subject to local variation: 'ÖTV in Thüringen is very progressive . . . we're much closer to them than in the west' (interview: IG Metall, Verwaltungsstelle Erfurt). District organization is sparser than in the west, IG Metall's organizational parsimony in 1990–1 anticipating subsequent membership decline. Nevertheless there is a district office servicing every major town and city in the new *Länder*. Only ÖTV are able to approach such intensity of organization. The smaller unions are often restricted to one small office in shared trade union premises in the *Land* capital.

The weakness of some of the smaller unions in the east is compensated to some extent by the presence of the DGB, which is a bigger player in regional trade union life than is common in the west. As a peak confederation, the DGB assumes responsibility for political representation and for conducting relations with the *Land* government. It has an organizational presence in each of the new *Länder* (Brandenburg is combined with Berlin). With the exception of Sachsen (where IG Metall's leadership assumed the role), the *Land* chairman of the DGB is the recognized spokesman for trade union interests in the public domain. The DGB also plays a co-ordinating role at local level, through its infrastructure of district (*Kreis*) offices. District bureaux also act as service provision centres, especially for legal advice. In common with IG Metall, the profile of the DGB's local organization is relatively 'lean', with 31 districts against 180 in the west.

The DGB also has a role in mediating jurisdictional disputes between the industrial unions, which occur more frequently than in the west. The giant conglomerates which formed the basis of the communist economy crossed sectoral boundaries, and their breakup often entailed the renegotiation of union jurisdiction for the component plants. The fiercest of these conflicts was between IGBE and ÖTV over the union affiliation of power station workers (Wilke and Müller 1991: 115). Jurisdictional conflict is sharpened in the east by financial pressures which intensify competitive recruitment.

Professional associations

Business associations and trade unions are the mainstay of the associational order in eastern Germany, with pervasive networks of regional and local organization encompassing all the main urban centres. In the professional associations the territorial dimension is less pronounced. Without either the mass membership of the trade unions or the financial muscle of organized business, professional groups lack the resources to support regional networks. Organizational activity is more centralized, orchestrated from headquarters in the west and relying heavily on voluntary effort to co-ordinate a widely dispersed membership. Virtually all the professions maintain a rudimentary infrastructure at *Land* level in eastern Germany, but few can aspire to regional or local organization.

In the medical profession, the Hartmannbund is the strongest group, with a functioning organization in all five new *Länder*. Organization-building at *Kreis* (district) level has been identified as a priority (Hartmannbund 1991: 43–51), but with membership in decline this remains no more than an aspiration. The NAV-VB cannot even aspire to organizational activity below *Land* level (interview: NAV-VB, Dresden). The main contact between the NAV-VB and its membership is through the provision of services (scientific seminars, financial and legal advice), mostly orchestrated from its single branch office in Berlin (*Der Niedergelassene Ärzt*, 10 November 1993: 39).

Amongst engineers, organization reflected the roots of the Chamber of Technology (Kammer der Technik, KdT) in the old regime. Leadership was centralized in an overstaffed and bureaucratic headquarters in Berlin, with fifteen regional organizations responsible for the educational, scientific and social functions of the chamber. The reform of the KdT under its new title of the Engineering-Technical Association (Ingenieurtechnische Verband) was not accompanied by decentralization, despite demands from the regional level for greater autonomy (*Ingenieur Nachrichten* 1994). The collapse of the KdT in bankruptcy in 1994 has been attributed to the failure to rationalize cumbersome and resource-intensive structures which became impossible to sustain in the face of membership decline (interview: Verein Ingenieure und Wirtschaftler, Mecklenburg-Vorpommern).

Reacting against the overcentralization of their predecessor, the regional engineers' organizations that emerged from the ruins in 1994 retained complete territorial autonomy with an Engineering-Technical Association in each of the new *Länder*. Financially crippled, their premises subject to KdT liquidation proceedings and their membership decimated, the new associations face a bleak future. With the collapse of the KdT, the Association of German Engineers (Verein Deutscher Ingenieure, VDI) consolidated its hitherto skeletal regional infrastructure, but, although it now has branch offices in each of the new *Länder*, the VDI remains an essentially western association.

The rise and decline of group membership

Across the associational order in eastern Germany, membership trends exhibit a clearly defined pattern. In the employers' associations and trade unions, organizational density was initially as high or higher than in the west, and, whilst membership in the professional associations never attained western levels, they nevertheless enjoyed buoyant recruitment. Initial recruitment success, however, was unsustainable, and from 1992 interest groups across the associational order experienced membership decline. The most dramatic decline is seen in trade union membership, reflecting the shrinkage of the labour market in the course of economic transformation. Although the rate of decline has slowed down, membership continues to fall, converging rapidly with west German levels that are themselves in decline. Market transition also accounts in large part for the exodus from the employers' associations, but the resistance of managers and entrepreneurs in the newly emerging private sector to subscribe to association membership may be indicative of the limited potential for business organization in post-communist society. Low levels of professional association membership suggest that these groups are particularly resistant to collective organization.

Trade unions

Initially, the DGB trade unions were extremely successful in recruitment. At the end of 1990 DGB membership in the east stood at 3.6 million, rising to almost 4.2 million by the end of the 1991. At its height, DGB membership in the new *Länder* stood at 36 per cent of the total for the Federal Republic as a whole (Fichter 1993: 35). As we saw in chapter 1, most unions inherited the membership of their GDR predecessor, although they tried to ensure that members made an individual application. IG Metall was one of a minority of unions which declared a complete legal break with the past, requiring members to rejoin. The recruitment of almost 1 million members out of the 1.6 million membership of its GDR

Table 3.2. *Trade union membership: eastern Germany 1991–7*

	1991	1992	1993	1994	1995	1996	1997	1997 as a percentage of 1991
IG BSE	330,011	248,885	221,826	212,724	205,590	–	–	⎫ 51
GGLF	92,522	78,602	62,944	51,220	45,153	232,920[a]	215,370	⎬
IGBE	193,442	154,463	117,220	113,390	116,567			
IGCPK	209,823	158,779	137,394	120,393	110,143	188,219[b]	174,261	⎫ 41.8
Gew. Leder	13,952	6,265	4,917	3,884	3,333	–	–	⎬
GdED	221,373	172,603	158,010	143,515	132,459	127,503	118,396	53.5
GEW	186,903	175,306	161,020	149,319	141,041	131,551	123,550	66.1
HBV	348,841	244,464	204,598	177,088	156,189	142,189	129,530	37.1
GHK	82,860	44,674	38,714	31,212	26,890	22,398	22,054	26.6
IG Medien	63,496	56,045	47,812	43,937	40,535	36,740	34,932	55.0
IG Metall	990,553	802,859	662,526	588,046	518,722	461,217	420,688	42.5
GNGG	162,256	126,606	94,992	84,020	76,567	70,146	63,250	39.0
ÖTV	950,364	866,943	776,235	682,224	606,968	563,348	518,787	54.6
GdP	55,218	49,002	49,905	48,199	51,540	52,178	51,765	93.7
DPG	151,375	146,710	125,113	103,578	98,311	94,066	85,567	56.5
GTB	104,837	59,181	43,426	36,049	31,171	22,535	20,752	19.8
DGB	4,157,826	3,391,387	2,906,652	2,589,250	2,361,179	2,145,010	1,987,902	47.8

Notes: With the exception of those trade unions that have been grouped together to indicate amalgamation, the ordering follows the German convention, based on alphabetical order but disregarding the Industriegewerkschaft or Gewerkschaft prefix.

[a] IG BSE and GGLF merged in 1996.

[b] IG BE, IGCPK and Gew. Leder merged in 1997.

Sources: DGB Mitgliederstatistik (unpublished).

predecessor indicated a strong orientation towards collective action in this sector.

The very steep downward trend in trade union membership from the end of 1991 can be related to labour market shrinkage consequent upon economic transformation. Decline coincided with a rapid escalation in unemployment from 11.9 per cent to 17.0 per cent in the last quarter of 1991 (DGB Landesbezirk Sachsen-Anhalt 1993: 18). As can be seen from table 3.2, DGB membership fell by 18 per cent during 1992, with a further decline of 14 per cent the following year. Although the *rate* of decline slowed down thereafter, *absolute* decline continued, with annual membership losses of 8.4 per cent over 1994–7 and no indication of stabilization. By the end of 1997, DGB membership stood at less than half (47.8 per cent) of its 1991 level; IG Metall was amongst the hardest-hit, its 1997 membership representing just 42.5 per cent of its peak in 1991, reflecting the collapse of employment in the metals and electricals sectors. Where employment was more stable, the rate of decline in union membership was lower. The public sector union ÖTV, for instance, has retained over half (54.6 per cent) of its 1991 membership. In construction, after a 22 per cent fall in 1992, membership was consolidated, with an annual decline confined to around 3 per cent after 1994 as the sector experienced some growth.

The effect of mass unemployment on union membership is moderated by the tendency of the unemployed to retain their union membership for some time after job loss (benefiting from a much reduced subscription rate). With a proportion of unemployed members approaching 50 per cent (Bialas 1994: 15), IG Metall pays particular attention to servicing this constituency, supplementing traditional forms of workplace organization by local offices providing legal advice and unemployment counselling. Nevertheless, union officials report that organization is hard to establish amongst the unemployed (interview: IG Metall, Verwaltungsstelle Magdeburg). Union ties are weak and membership is often allowed to lapse after around twelve to eighteen months of unemployment (interview: IG Metall, Bezirksleitung Dresden). For those excluded from the labour market, trade union membership confers diminishing returns as expectations of re-employment recede. Nevertheless, the tendency of the jobless to remain in the union is indicative of the effectiveness of service provision as a membership incentive.

Whilst membership decline was primarily a consequence of rising unemployment, further explanations are to be found in the structural dynamics of the post-communist economy. The predominance of SMEs in the post-communist economy is also prejudicial to trade union membership. The correlation between membership density and company size is well established, with data from western Germany suggesting variations in union membership from 4 per cent in firms with fewer than nine employees to 58 per cent in those with a labour force of over 2,000 (Visser 1994: 91–2).

IG Metall officials report that, immediately after unification, membership levels in very large, formerly state-owned enterprises were exceptionally high, and, in the few that survive, the rate of organization approaches 80 per cent. In the large privatized companies where IG Metall has a well-established organizational presence, membership is generally around 60–70 per cent of the workforce. Outside these 'core' plants, membership is considerably lower, especially amongst SMEs (interview: IG Metall, Verwaltungsstelle Erfurt). The decline of trade union membership can thus be related to the corporate downsizing that accompanied the breakup of giant state-owned enterprises and the growth of a private sector in which small and medium-sized companies predominate.

Despite membership decline, organizational density (membership as a percentage of the total labour force) is significantly higher than in western Germany. DGB membership at the end of 1991 represented 52 per cent of the labour force, as against 27 per cent in the west, whilst IG Metall claimed a membership density of 60 per cent compared to a western level of 46 per cent. Declining to 38 per cent by the end of 1997, the rate of organization in the DGB nevertheless remained higher than western membership levels which had by now fallen to 25.5 per cent. The narrowing gap between east and west has led some to predict a progressive convergence at a level slightly below current western levels (Fichter and Reister 1996: 19–20). This analysis assumes, however, that the labour market in the east will be assimilated with that in the west, an assumption that is cast in doubt by the structural economic differences between the two parts of Germany.

Business organization

Membership in business organizations had some initial attractions, but these became steadily less compelling from 1991–2. For the Treuhand, wage stability and calculability were seen as prerequisites of investor confidence, central to a successful privatization programme. Strong employers' associations represented a pillar of order in the wage-bargaining arena, and the Treuhand therefore encouraged enterprises in its portfolio to subscribe (Wiesenthal 1995b: 15; Ettl 1995: 70). Industry associations also offered immediate economic benefits. The BDI, and more especially its affiliated sector associations like the VDMA in machine-building, established themselves as intermediaries for the transfer of technical and commercial expertise from the west (Berger 1995: 104). Technology transfer and commercial training may have served as membership incentives for Treuhand company managers embarking on modernization and unversed in entrepreneurial skills.

Membership trends are difficult to establish with accuracy amidst the upheaval in the corporate landscape brought about by privatization, liquidation, company restructuring and new business start-ups. Evidence from a number of sources, however, points towards a decline in employers' association membership from its peak in 1991 (Ettl and Heikenroth 1995; Schroeder and Ruppert 1996; Timmins 1997; French 1998; *Frankfurter Allgemeine Zeitung*, 25 August 1992; *Wirtschaftswoche*, 26 March 1993). The initial surge in recruitment meant that organizational density in the associations with a strong presence in the east was close to western levels. In 1991 the confederation of employers in the metals and electricals sectors (Gesamtmetall) claimed to represent companies employing 65 per cent of the industry workforce as against 69 per cent in western Germany (Gesamtmetall 1992: 37; 1991: 22–3). With a membership of some 420 companies employing a labour force of 150,000, the metals and electricals employers' association in Sachsen had a membership profile broadly similar to Gesamtmetall affiliates in the west (interview: VSME).

As in the trade unions, these initially high membership levels were unsustainable. The scale of decline is subject to regional and sectoral variation. In the metals and electricals sector, as can be seen from table 3.3, decline was particularly severe in Sachsen, where the VSME (Verband der Sächsischen Metall- und Elektroindustrie, Association of the Engineering and Electrical Industry in Sachsen) lost around 26 per cent of its member firms between 1992 and 1993, against average losses across eastern Germany of around 13 per cent. Membership also varies with ownership. Survey data shows that virtually all companies remaining under Treuhand administration in 1994 belonged to their employers' association, with membership declining sharply in the private sector. Here, firms under west German or foreign ownership were significantly more likely to subscribe than those under indigenous east German ownership. Alongside regional and sectoral variations, association membership varies significantly with company size, with an organizational density of 88 per cent amongst firms with a payroll of over 100, in contrast to 75 per cent in medium-sized companies, and a mere 37 per cent in small firms with fewer than fifty employees (Ettl and Heikenroth 1995). The relationship between company size and association membership points towards the explanation for membership decline and organizational weakness in the employers' associations. As we saw in chapter 2,

Table 3.3. *Employers' association membership: eastern Germany 1992–3*

| | Gesamtmetall | | | | | Regional confederation |
| | 1992 | | 1993 | | | 1994/5 |
	Member firms	Employed	Member firms	Employed		Member associations
Berlin-Brandenburg	287	59,445	269	49,088		67
Mecklenburg-Vorpommern	80	26,043	76	20,223		25
Sachsen-Anhalt	223	52,847	208	39,102		23
Sachsen	421	89,014	334	66,572		24
Thüringen	257	43,575	224	29,473		41
Total	1,268	270,924	1,111	204,458		

Sources: *Gesamtmetall* membership, Ettl 1995; cited Timmins 1997; *Land* confederation membership: author's interview data.

market transition is accompanied by a sharp decline in average company size. The preponderance of small and medium-sized firms in the post-communist economy is unconducive to employer organization. Below average membership levels in Sachsen have been explained in relation to the structure of the regional economy, in which small and medium-sized firms predominate (French 1998: 20).

The wave of company liquidations accompanying privatization thus provides only a partial explanation for membership decline. To be sure, corporate restructuring frequently led to company closure, but it often also entailed the breakup of former state enterprises into a number of smaller companies, which might have been expected to increase association membership. The inability of the associations to benefit from the growth of the private sector was related to their poor performance at recruiting amongst newly privatized companies and new company start-ups (interview: Nordmetall, Schwerin). Privatization and company restructuring faced the employers' associations with a rapidly shifting membership constituency, with many firms taking the opportunity to leave the employers' association. Survey data shows that, of the resignations from the VSME in Sachsen between 1991 and 1994, the overwhelming majority quit the association in the course of corporate restructuring during privatization. Of sixty-six firms surveyed, only four resignations were the result of liquidation (Schroeder and Ruppert 1996). Newly established firms, on the other hand, were resistant to association membership.

Bringing together the sector associations, the regional employer *confederations* vary in membership across the new *Länder*. In general, however, they are less broadly encompassing than in western Germany, with around twenty-five affiliated associations. The exception is Berlin-Brandenburg, which has sixty-seven affiliates reflecting the benefit of an established infrastructure in the western part of Berlin. Outside Berlin, whilst most major industrial sectors are represented in the confederation, the *Handwerk* (artisan trades) associations are conspicuous by their absence. As 'peak' organizations comprising sector associations rather than individual firms, their membership is less directly affected by corporate closures and has remained more stable.

The relative weakness of the employers' associations amongst SMEs is reflected in the competition it faces in this sector from the independent, east German UVs and the Bonn-based BVMW (Bundesverband Mittelständische Wirtschaft, Confederation of the Mittelstand Economy). UV membership varies widely from around 2,000 in Sachsen and Brandenburg to a mere 100 or 200 elsewhere (interviews: UV Norddeutschland, Thüringen, Erfurt, Sachsen-Anhalt, Rostock und Umgebung). For the most part, the UVs are composed of small firms; on average, member firms have a workforce of around twenty or fewer, and fewer than 10 per cent employ more than 100 (interviews: UV Norddeutschland, Thüringen). Their membership is heterogeneous, spanning the range of industrial and commercial sectors from construction and machine-building to the service sector and retailing. Most are management buyouts, reprivatized firms and newly established concerns, often those in financial trouble. Although seen by some as a transient feature of economic transformation, the larger UVs at least have a stable or expanding clientele. Following an aggressive recruitment campaign from its regional offices across the new *Länder*, the BVMW has a membership of over 9,500 predominantly small firms, representing almost one-third of its all-German membership (BVMW 1994). Oriented largely towards business consultancy, the relationship between the BVMW and its members is primarily one of a service provider and its customers (interview: BVMW, Rostock). Its presence alongside the UVs and the BDA-related employers' associations means that the SME company sector is one of the most competitive areas of the associational order.

Professional associations

By contrast with trade unions and employers' associations – in which despite some decline membership density remains relatively high – the professions are much less intensively organized. Estimates based on published sources and interview data indicate that around 35–40 per cent of the 42,000 doctors in the new *Länder* are members of a professional association, compared to around 60 per cent in western Germany. Amongst private practitioners, the Hartmannbund is the strongest of the associations, with around 6,200 members concentrated in the states of Sachsen and Thüringen, which have been the target of its recruitment drive (Hartmannbund 1991: 40; interview: Hartmannbund, Landesverband Mecklenburg-Vorpommern). Also based in private practice, the membership of the NAV-VB approaches 4,000, with a concentration of strength in Berlin reflecting its origins in the Charité hospital (NAV-VB, 1992: 18; *Der Niedergelassene Arzt*, 10 November 1993: 41–2; interview: NAV-VB, Landesverband Sachsen). The Marburgerbund has a membership of around 6,000 in the east, representing about 25 per cent of hospital doctors, as against 50 per cent in western Germany (interview: Marburgerbund, Landesverband Sachsen). All the doctors' associations have suffered membership decline since 1990–1, reflecting the financial difficulties experienced by newly established practices struggling with the burden of paying off start-up credit and the absence of a culture of *Berufspolitik* (vocational group politics).

In engineering, membership is even lower, the collapse of the KdT leaving engineers largely unorganized. Uniquely amongst organizations with their roots in the GDR, the KdT retained a mass membership after unification. Despite a steep decline from the pre-unification level of over a quarter of a million, KdT membership at its bankruptcy in 1994 stood at 65,000 (*Wirtschaft und Markt* 1994). As we have seen above, its survival as a mass organization was due to its successful advocacy on behalf of east German engineers in the struggle for professional recognition. Nevertheless, the KdT was a 'greying' organization, recruitment in schools and universities reaching a virtual standstill after unification. As successor organizations, the Engineers' Associations (Vereine der Ingenieure) were unable to recruit more than a rump of the KdT membership, collectively numbering around 4,500 members in 1994, concentrated mainly in Sachsen and Mecklenburg-Vorpommern. With around 40 per cent of their members in retirement, the new associations remain rooted in nostalgia for the old regime (interviews: Verein der Ingenieure und Wirtschaftler in Mecklenburg-Vorpommern; Verein der Ingenieure und Techniker in Thüringen; Verein der Ingenieure, Techniker und Wirtschaftler in Sachsen).

Unsurprisingly, given its attitude to the profession in the east, the Association of German Engineers (Verein Deutscher Ingenieure, VDI) found recruitment difficult, even amongst its target group of academically qualified engineers, its initial membership of 9,100 (VDI 1991: 10) sinking to around 8,500 (*Ingenieur Digest* 1994) before stabilizing. Organizational density is hard to assess with accuracy given the large number of small, specialist associations in the field, but it can be estimated at well under 10 per cent of the profession. A further indication can be drawn from comparison with western Germany, where the VDI has almost 120,000 members (VDI 1994).

Low levels of membership in professional organizations can be explained by two main factors. First, compared to trade unions and employers' associations, doctors' associations and the VDI receive less financial support from headquarters in the west, and lack the resource capacity to sustain extensive networks of regional organization. The poor recruitment performance of the professional associations underlines the key role of salaried officials in membership recruitment. Secondly, whilst trade unions perform demonstrable functions in the wage-bargaining arena, the activities of professional associations are less visible. In a society in which professional ethos is weakly developed, and in which attitudes towards associational activity tend towards the pragmatic, professional associations will continue to encounter recruitment difficulties.

Conclusion

With its genesis in institutional transfer from the west, the associational order in the new *Länder* replicates the German model, based on monopolistic sectoral organizations brought together in unitary confederations. This is not a model that can be expected to emerge spontaneously in post-communist society. In the countries of east/central Europe, socio-economic fragmentation and a diverse spectrum of interests are reflected in patterns of associational activity characterized by pluralist competition between a multiplicity of overlapping groups. Despite its monopolistic foundations, interest group activity in eastern Germany displays some of these tendencies in the challenge of the independent UVs to the BDA-affiliated employers' associations in the small-firm sector. Unitary systems of interest organization based on centralized and broadly encompassing groups may be too monolithic to accommodate the fragmented interest spectrum of post-communist society. A more pluralistic competitive and varied institutional design may be better adapted to this environment.

Support from the west means that organizational intensity is far greater than in the post-communist countries of east/central Europe where organization is crippled by the lack of resources (Ágh 1993). Nevertheless, resource constraints are reflected in organizational structures which are leaner than in the west. In contrast to the tripartite structure in the west, business organization rests on the twin pillars of the BDA-affiliated employer groups and the IHKs, with the BDI almost entirely absent. With the exception of the Gesamtmetall affiliates, sectoral employer organization is skeletal. Employer organization depends very heavily on a single sector, with the VME, constituting the organizational core of the *Land* confederations. Operating out of headquarters in the west, other sector associations have little organizational presence on the ground. A similar syndrome is evident in the trade unions. Whilst all the industrial trade unions have a presence in the workplace, only IG Metall and (to a lesser extent) ÖTV maintain a strong regional organization for co-ordinating shop-floor activity. The weakness of the other industrial unions is compensated by the presence of the DGB, which is a bigger player in trade union life than in the west. The professions struggle to sustain associational activity on the lines of the German model, professional associations of doctors and engineers representing little more than field agencies of organizations based in the west.

In sharp contrast to the weakness of sectoral organization, the regional presence of the employer and trade union confederations means that the territorial dimension is well developed. Endowed with considerable autonomy from parent organizations at national level, peak confederations in the *Länder* provide an infrastructure for the formation of regional interests and the representation of territorial identities. As we shall see in chapter 6, confederations based in regional capitals act as interlocutors with the *Land* government, serving as the focal point of regional corporatism. Regional officials also articulate relations between membership and national headquarters, overcoming the disjuncture between organizational centre and periphery that is a characteristic of trade unions and business associations in the countries of east/central Europe. The integration of the new *Länder* into the associational order of the Federal Republic is greatly facilitated by an institutional design incorporating a strong territorial dimension.

The German case suggests, however, that post-communist societies will be unable to sustain an associational order combining the sectoral and regional dimensions. Doubts about the sustainability of present levels of organization are fuelled by declining membership. As we have seen, membership decline is a common experience across the spectrum of interest group activity. Economic collapse accompanying market transition accounts for much of the effect. The downward plunge in trade union membership, however, was checked but by no means halted by labour market stabilization, and there are still no firm indications of where or when the bottom line might be drawn. As we saw in the previous chapter, labour market relations in the advanced post-communist economy provide an uncertain foundation for the mobilization of employee interests on solidaristic lines. Similarly, the structure of capital was seen to be unconducive to the collective representation of corporate interests within the broadly encompassing yet monolithic structures of the German model. Membership decline may thus be a function of the logic of collective action in post-communist society, and it is to this that we now turn.

4   Participation and the logic of collective action

This chapter examines the behavioural dimension of associational activity. It is motivated by one central question: is the social and cultural composition of post-communist society conducive to group participation and collective action? The question can be approached from the three social science perspectives outlined in the introduction, each focusing on somewhat different aspects of the socio-economic makeup of society. First, from the social psychological perspective, participation is taken to be a property of the democratic personality, in which a sense of personal effectiveness engenders perceptions of efficacy in public life. Post-communist society, it will be argued in this chapter, is unlikely to foster the sense of material security which has been seen as one of the essential prerequisites of the democratic personality. With its combination of opportunities and threats, market transition is reflected in a dual psychological response: either economic individualism and the pursuit of private material objectives, or a sense of powerlessness and anomie in the face of unfamiliar market forces. Survey data will be used alongside interview findings to investigate the effects of east Germany's accelerated market transition on psychological orientations towards participation in the associational arena.

A second approach equates democratic participation with the accumulation of social capital. In Almond and Verba's formulation, the roots of a civic culture lie in mutual trust and co-operation in social life spilling over into the political sphere. The resultant social capital takes the form of interpersonal and organizational skills that sustain participation in associational activity, generating a deep-seated attachment to social and political institutions. The civic culture is essentially a product of the evolution from parochial societies characterized by the dominance of primary relations, towards modern societies in which the self-confident citizen moves freely between the private and public spheres. In this chapter I shall assess the potential of post-communist society for social capital formation in terms of social co-operation, the acquisition of organizational skills, and institutional trust and allegiance.

As we saw in the introduction, rational choice theory explains the decision to participate in collective action in terms of incentive structures. Where benefits take the form of public goods freely available to all, the syndrome of free-riding will prevail. The rational actor will subscribe to collective action only in response to the offer of selective economic benefits available exclusively to members. The economic logic of the model has been modified by some to encompass those 'solidary incentives' deriving from group identification. Mobilization is facilitated where potential members of the group share a sense of collective identity. In resource mobilization theory, organizational support is also derived from networks of interpersonal relations between the potential members of the group. Rational choice theory, then, identifies the different logics of collective action in terms of distinctions between different types of membership incentive. Collective wage-bargaining is a weak incentive for trade union membership, since wage settlements are usually applicable to members and non-members alike, encouraging free-riding. Similarly the political activities of trade unions in representing their members' interests in the public policy process are freely available to all. By contrast, conflict insurance (job protection, workplace representation and legal advice) is selectively available to members only. Equally, the solidary benefits derived from social solidarity and identification with union objectives and ideology operate at the individual level and are exclusive to members.

This type of distinction provides the basis for a twofold typology of trade union membership. The American worker places primary value on his or her own economic interests, has an instrumental attitude towards membership benefits and ascribes little salience to political activity. Membership decisions are pragmatic, motivated by access to the protection, assistance and support of the union. By contrast, the motivations of the European trade union member derive from an 'historical matrix of politics, society and culture', emphasizing class solidarity rather than self-interest, and collective action rather than individualism (Moe 1980: 172–3). Although it is generally accepted that the model no longer corresponds with empirical reality, the European worker having gravitated towards his American counterpart, it nevertheless retains its utility as a typology for the analysis of trade union membership motivations in post-communist society. The insecurities associated with market transition may mean that the economic motivations associated with conflict insurance weigh more heavily, whilst, without the social and cultural underpinnings of group identification, solidary incentives are less likely to provide effective membership motivations.

For business groups, collective wage-bargaining provides stability and predictability in industrial relations, but the corollary is a loss of flexibility that may act as a membership disincentive. These groups also provide access to technical information and consultancy services available exclusively to members, usually the province of highly specialized trade associations. Empirical evidence points to access to information as a primary motive for business group membership (Moe 1980: 186). It also suggests, however, that political representation is a significant contributory factor, with membership motivations often rooted in identification with entrepreneurial values and common business interests. Against this background, I shall use survey and interview data to identify the incentive structure of group activity in post-communist society. In the absence of solidary incentives derived from group identification, and without supportive social networks, it will be argued, associational activity relies very heavily on instrumental motivation, exacerbating the problems identified in rational choice and resource mobilization theory.

Participation and collective action in post-communist society

Across eastern and central Europe, expectations that democratization would be accompanied by a burgeoning of political participation have been disappointed. Some have argued that, with liberalization, the 'invisible wall' between the private and public had been torn down, with a corresponding increase in participation (Kaplan 1993: 153). Most studies, however, suggest that, after an initial surge, political involvement subsequently receded. Electoral participation is low by western standards (Budge, Newton et al. 1997: 137). Beyond this, survey data is limited, and does not provide a strong basis for comparison. The data available, however, suggests quite wide cross-national variations. The highest levels of participation are found amongst Czechs, with 14 per cent claiming to be actively engaged in civic or political activity, against 10 per cent of Slovaks, and a mere 5 per cent of Poles (Rose 1992; Ammeter-Inquirer 1992).

Participation and political efficacy

Social psychology offers an explanation for relatively low levels of participation in terms of low perceptions of political efficacy reflecting the pervasive sense of economic insecurity in post-communist society. As can be seen from table 4.1, survey data suggests that perceptions of political efficacy in the countries of eastern and central Europe are generally lower than those in the west. Moreover, whilst perceptions of *external* efficacy (the responsiveness of the political system to the individual) are only

Table 4.1. *Political efficacy in Germany and east/central Europe*
% agreeing with statement

	Western Germany	Eastern Germany	Czech Republic	Hungary	Poland	Bulgaria	Russia
People like me don't have a say in government	68	84	78	86	90	78	–
Voting gets people like me a say in government	61	46	61	53	44	86	52
Elected officials lose touch quickly	88	91	87	86	91	88	92
Elected officials care what people think	91	32	31	33	25	24	20

Sources: Kaase 1994: 259; Budge, Newton et al. 1997: 138.

Table 4.2. *Indicators of economic development: Germany and east/central Europe*

	Hungary	Czech Republic	Slovak Republic	Poland	Romania	Bulgaria
Per capita GDP ($)	2,970	2,450	1,930	1,910	1,130	1,330
% families owning a car	49	58	47	34	29	41
% families deriving adequate income from regular job	34	58	46	43	43	29

Sources: per capita GDP, Lewis 1997: 9; car ownership and adequate income from one job: Rose and Haerpfer 1993: 21, 27.

marginally lower than western levels, the post-communist citizen has a quite markedly lower perception of *internal* efficacy (a sense of personal influence in politics).

If, as social psychology suggests, participation is related to perceptions of political influence, which in turn reflects economic security, we should be able to establish a systematic relationship between the data on political efficacy in table 4.1 and economic development. Table 4.2 gives comparative data on economic development across six east/central European countries using a threefold index based on per capita GDP, car ownership

Table 4.3. *Economic attitudes: Germany and east/central Europe*

% endorsing collectivist values

	Western Germany	Eastern Germany	Hungary	Czech Republic	Slovakia Republic	Poland	Romania	Bulgaria	ECE average[a]
Incomes should be made more equal	34	42	31	10	13	23	22	41	25
State should be responsible for material security	32	62	60	46	57	85	54	63	57
State ownership is best way to run an enterprise	10	14	24	17	27	31	48	47	33
Prefer secure job over well-paid job	83	88	73	48	37	67	69	65	60

[a] Includes ten countries.

Sources: east/central Europe; Rose and Haerpfer 1993, Germany; Rose, Zapf, Seifert and Page 1993.

and the percentage of households subsisting on the income from the main job without having to supplement this income from secondary employment elsewhere. Although the three indices do not always produce a consistent ranking, the broad pattern is clear, with Hungary and the Czech Republic standing out as the most economically developed, ahead of Slovakia and Poland in the middle rank, with Bulgaria and Romania lagging behind. Overall, the precondition of a sense of efficacy and participation in public life – that individuals are secure in the private sphere – is clearly not fulfilled in post-communist society.

As might be expected, there is some evidence linking levels of economic development with economic attitudes. As can be seen from table 4.3, economic attitudes are marked by a pronounced inclination towards collectivism over individualism, and a strong orientation towards economic security. Across the region, a majority (57 per cent) endorses the principle of *state* as opposed to individual responsibility for material security. Similarly a large majority (60 per cent) would prefer a secure job to a well-paid job. The Czech Republic stands out from this pattern with a majority (54 per cent) backing *individual* responsibility and a narrow majority (52 per cent) opting for high pay over job security. A comparison of economic aspirations between Czechs and Poles shows a significantly higher readiness amongst Czechs to consider changing jobs, getting a second job or working overtime as a strategy for economic improvement (Rose 1991: 38; Ammeter-Inquirer 1992: 17). A relatively higher level of economic security in the Czech Republic is reflected, then, in a strong orientation towards economic individualism.

The data in tables 4.1 and 4.2 shows little systematic evidence for a positive relationship between participation, political efficacy and economic development. To be sure, the Czech citizen has a slightly higher perception of political influence, corresponding to a relatively high level of economic development, a stronger orientation towards economic individualism than his east European neighbours and, as I observed at the beginning of this section, a predisposition towards participation. Beyond this, however, the data points rather in the opposite direction, towards a *negative* relationship between economic development and political efficacy. Hungarians, despite enjoying the highest per capita GDP of the countries shown here, rank amongst the lowest in terms of perceived political influence. Of the countries shown in table 4.1, however, the lowest perceptions of political efficacy are found in Poland, a middle-ranking country in terms of economic development. Fully 90 per cent of Poles are sceptical of their ability to influence government, whilst only 44 per cent believe in voting as a means of influence compared to 86 per cent of Bulgarians. High perceptions of political influence in Bulgaria contrast

Table 4.4. *Trust in public institutions: Germany and east/central Europe*
% expressing trust

	Western Germany	Eastern Germany	Hungary	Czech Republic	Slovakia Republic	Poland	Romania	Bulgaria	ECE average[a]
Military	40	40	44	40	48	59	76	54	47
Courts	56	44	46	38	31	35	45	15	33
Police	54	34	44	35	30	43	38	17	31
Government	32	27	21	57	32	25	27	13	26
Civil service	31	18	27	28	28	23	28	16	25

[a] Includes ten countries.
Sources: east/central Europe: Budge, Newton et al. 1997: 136; Germanay: Konrad–Adenauer-Stiftung Archive 9104; cited Langguth 1995.

sharply with a relatively low level of economic development. We must await conclusions from the east German case before attempting to explain these indications of an inverse relationship between economic development and political efficacy.

Social capital and civic culture

As we saw above, social capital is a product of co-operation and trust generated by social interaction in the public arena. What indications are there, then, that the liberalization of public life is accompanied by this pattern of social relations? Rose has argued in the Russian context that social co-operation takes place in the informal economy, on which a large majority of people depend in the face of economic collapse (Rose 1995: 36–7). His conclusion that this form of interaction generates 'informal social trust' is cast in doubt, however, by survey data suggesting that 70 per cent of Russians suspect the people around them of 'malevolence and hostility' (Wyman 1994: 52). The chaos of disintegrating economic and social infrastructures, it has been argued, breeds a syndrome of suspicion, hostility and hatred which destroys 'whatever social bonds have been left intact by totalitarian rule' (Sztompka 1993: 89). What all this suggests is that social trust is confined to primary personal relations, with suspicion and hostility prevailing in the wider social sphere.

In Almond and Verba's model of the civic culture, social co-operation and trust spill over into confidence and trust in social and political institutions. In post-communist society, social mistrust is reflected in low levels of institutional trust. As can be seen from table 4.4, the only public institution in which anything like a majority of eastern and central Europeans invest their confidence is the army. On a cross-regional average, the courts, police, government and civil service command the confidence of less than one in three post-communist citizens, with social and private institutions performing little better. Substantial cross-national variations are to be found, with the Czech Republic again standing out. With the exception of the army and the church, all the political and social institutions command above-average confidence amongst Czech citizens. In the general picture, however, social trust stops well short of social and political institutions.

Also in Almond and Verba's formulation, social capital is a generalized resource buttressing support for the political system. In eastern and central Europe, although newly democratic regimes attract widespread support, there is strong evidence that the attachment to democracy is a mirror image of the rejection of communism, and that it is motivated in large part by instrumental motives. As can be seen from table 4.5, Russia

Table 4.5. *Evaluations of political and economic systems: eastern Germany and east/central Europe*

% approval

	Eastern Germany	Hungary	Czech Republic	Slovakia Republic	Poland	Romania	Bulgaria	Russia	ECE average[a]
Political system									
Approve present	60	51	78	52	69	60	59	35	62
Approve past	32	58	23	50	38	33	51	51	42
Economic system									
Approve present	75	27	66	31	50	35	15	14	43
Approve past	36	75	42	74	52	60	66	61	61

Notes: Respondents were able to approve both systems, so totals may exceed 100.

[a] Includes ten countries.

Sources: Rose and Haerpfer 1995, tables 1 and 2; cited Wiesenthal 1996: 6.

is the only country where the present system fails to command majority support. Elsewhere some 62 per cent of east/central Europeans endorse the present regime, against 42 per cent who give a positive evaluation of the communist system. Support for the *political* system coexists with negative assessments of the economy. In some countries the majority compare the present economic system unfavourably with that in the old regime (Bulgaria, Hungary, Russia, Romania and Slovakia) whilst Poles divide evenly in popular perceptions of the new economy against the old. Only the Czech Republic stands out from this generally negative perception of the economic system.

The paradox of positive orientations to the political system in the face of scepticism towards the economy can be explained, it has been argued, by a 'legitimacy bonus' which stems from fear of the old communist system combined with hope for a satisfactory economic system in the foreseeable future (Mishler and Rose 1993: 24). Cross-national comparison shows that variations in support for democratic political systems are strongly correlated to differences in perceptions of economic performance (Rose and Mishler 1993: 25), indicative of instrumental attitudes towards democracy, characteristic of the 'output orientation' in Almond and Verba's formulation. It corresponds also to Sztompka's characterization of the pragmatism of post-communist political culture, with 'beliefs and loyalties treated opportunistically and instrumentally, valid as long as they produce benefits' (Sztompka 1993: 91).

Incentive structures and organizational resources

In chapter 2 it was concluded that market transitions in the countries of eastern and central Europe have not yet consolidated the structure of capital ownership or labour market relations. From the rational choice and resource mobilization perspectives, retarded social differentiation and the weakness of social cleavages are reflected in a scarcity of organizational resources, both in terms of the social networks which sustain collective organization, and the group identities which provide solidary incentives for participation. The scarcity of resources is compounded by their unequal distribution. In both the trade union and business arenas, reconstituted communist elements are able to access the network of their predecessors, advantaging them over their liberal rivals. The dominance of ex-communist trade unions across eastern and central Europe can be explained in these terms. In the large-scale enterprises remaining in the state sector, where mobilization benefits from the close-knit employee networks generated by mass employment, and where organizational infrastructures remain intact from the old regime, membership can be as high as 75 per cent. New unions, by contrast, lack 'infrastructure bases, networks and organizational skills' (Miszlivetz 1997: 30). One very striking feature of the associational landscape is the apparent inability of either old or new unions to penetrate the private sector where small firms predominate (Musil 1991: 385; Bamber and Peschanski 1996: 80–3; Myant 1994: 63).

The incentive structures of trade union membership appear to be primarily economic, with little evidence of solidary motivations born of group identification. Survey results amongst Polish workers show 'a labour movement mistrustful of its own class institutions, and confused over where its real interests lie', with overwhelming support for neo-liberal orientations towards employment relations and the market (Ost 1995: 184–8). Whilst the weakness of group values suggests that solidary or purposive incentives are unlikely to motivate trade union membership, the effectiveness of economic incentives like collective bargaining and conflict insurance is undermined by a widespread scepticism towards trade union representation. Only 8 per cent of Poles and 13 per cent of Russians express confidence in union representation in the workplace, whilst Czechs are almost equally sceptical (Musil 1991: 385–6). Nevertheless, for vulnerable workers in state enterprises with an uncertain future, the defensive function of trade unions may still be a membership motivation. Cross-national comparison shows that trade unions are strongest where there is most opposition to market transition. Above all, however, high levels of membership in the state sector are explained by the selective incentives associated with the role which the old unions retain in the distribution of social welfare benefits (Bamber and Peschanski 1996: 82). In general, however, the incentive structure for trade union mobilization is weak.

Business organization reflects the weakness of intercorporate networks in an economy divided between state and private sector, foreign and domestic capital, and large and small firms, as well as the ineffectiveness of solidary incentives in the absence of a collective identity in business circles. Intercorporate networks are largely confined to the 'directorate' of the state sector and the 'nomenklatura bourgeoisie' that has colonized large parts of the private sector. Reflecting the behavioural patterns of the old regime (Hankiss 1990: 83, 107), these elements continue to engage in informal modes of associational activity rooted in 'old-boy' networking, 'clan' relations, clientelism and corruption. In these circles, association is motivated primarily by the quest for influence over the distribution of state assets in the privatization process (Lomax 1997: 49). Associational activity in the small business sector, on the other hand, revolves largely around the offer of selective membership incentives in the form of business consultancy and legal advice (Stykow 1994: 12–15). Solidary incentives play little part in mobilization. As in the labour movement, membership motivations revolve primarily around pragmatic calculations of individual self-interest.

Participation and collective action in an advanced post-communist society

As in other post-communist countries, eastern Germany experienced a strong participatory surge accompanying the democratic revolution, which gradually evaporated thereafter. Electoral participation, although relatively high in cross-national comparison, declined steadily between 1990 and 1994, falling behind west German levels. The first democratic elections in the GDR in March 1990 attracted exceptionally high participation, with turnout at 93.4 per cent. In the Bundestag election of December 1990, turnout in the new *Länder* was 74.5 per cent as against 78.6 per cent in the west, falling to 72.9 per cent against 80.6 per cent in the west in 1994. Non-voting was particularly high amongst the young: in 1990 only 55.3 per cent of 18–24–year-olds voted, against 64.8 per cent in the west (Forschungsgruppe Wahlen 1990, 1994). Survey data relating to more diverse forms of participation point in a similar direction, 11.6 per cent of easterners reporting high levels of participation in 'conventional' forms of political activity (defined in terms of a range of indicators, from political discussion to party activity), as against 14.9 per cent in the west. Participation in 'unconventional', non-institutional activity (demonstrations, citizens' initiatives) was even lower, at 6.5 per cent against 10.9 per cent in the west (Kaase 1997: 17–19).

    Participation in economic interest groups displayed a similar pattern of upsurge followed by decline. Heavy recruitment across the associational order resulted in a rapid increase in group membership (as we saw in chapter 2) to a level comparable with or higher than that in the west. Interview data suggesting that high membership was matched by the level of engagement in associational activity is corroborated by survey data showing around one-third of trade union members engaged in organizational activity, as against one-quarter of their western counterparts. Involvement in vocational and occupational organizations was even higher at 68 per cent of the membership, as against 13 per cent in the west (Wessels 1992: 16–17). After the initial impetus of the democratic revolution, however, membership decline was paralleled by participation rates that fell away steeply to below western levels. By mid-1994, only 10 per cent of trade union members reported significant involvement in union activities, against 19.5 per cent in the west (IfEP, 1994). The remainder of this chapter is devoted to explaining this decline in participation in terms of the theoretical perspectives outlined above.

Participation and political efficacy

Eastern Germany might be expected to share the communist legacy of retarded civic competence that some have argued inhibits participation in post-communist society. As we saw in the introduction, the GDR espoused a particularly authoritarian variant of the state socialist model, placing very tight constraints on the scope for engagement in the public sphere. At the same time it buttressed the fragile legitimacy of the regime by the provision of a more comprehensive welfare state than in other post-communist countries. This syndrome of repressive paternalism might be expected to have left a dual legacy, the restriction of public life to the elite stifling any sense of individual efficacy, and the broadly encompassing welfare state encouraging a culture of dependency.

The residual effects of the communist legacy are, of course, overlaid by the experience of an economic transformation more rapid and thoroughgoing than elsewhere in east/central Europe. East Germans were uniquely privileged amongst the peoples of east/central Europe in having access to a 'ready-made state' (Rose and Haerpfer 1996, 1997; Wiesenthal 1996). Coupled to the economic locomotive of the Federal Republic, economic performance and personal economic circumstances are much more favourable than elsewhere in post-communist Europe. In terms of purchasing power, per capita income is around twice the level in the Czech Republic and over three times that in Poland. Eighty-six per cent of east Germans are able to derive a livelihood from their regular job. In 1993, 75 per cent of east Germans believed their economic situation was better than that in the old regime, in contrast to east/central Europe where 62 per cent reported a deterioration (Rose and Haerpfer 1993).

The relative openness of economic opportunity is matched by a strong achievement culture, and (contrary to popular perception in the west) a highly developed work ethic. Sixty-two per cent of easterners agreed with the statement that 'life is a challenge, in the face of which one has to use all one's efforts to achieve something', 17 per cent more than in the west (Noelle-Neumann and Kocher 1993: 36). Twenty-seven per cent rated work as 'the most important human activity', whilst 57 per cent regarded 'work as important for personal well-being' as against 9 per cent and 36 per cent respectively in the west (Meulemann 1997: 128).

Simultaneously, however, the rapidity of economic transformation entailed a severe 'exposure shock' as liberalization and privatization opened up the economy at a stroke to market forces. The reverberations of the impact can be seen in the first two years after unification in mass unemployment, a rapid turnover of managerial personnel, the devaluation of occupational skills and a regime of property restitution that often favoured westerners over eastern claimants (Wiesenthal 1996: 2). Adaptation to the demands of a radically new socio-economic system had an impact on all aspects of the individual's life. At the height of the democratic transformation, between 1989 and 1992, the birth rate in eastern Germany declined by 60 per cent, marriage by 65 per cent and divorce by 81 per cent (Kocka 1994: 185), reflecting the uncertainties of life in the face of market transition.

Socio-economic upheaval is reflected in a pervasive sense of social and psychological insecurity. Fears of social exclusion are expressed by 52 per cent of easterners, substantially higher than in the west (43 per cent). Seventy-three per cent are concerned about their vulnerability to social violence, as against 47 per cent in the west (Langguth 1995: 50). Social fears are reflected in a pervasive sense of psychological insecurity and anomie, evident in survey responses indicating uncertainty about the future and disorientation in the face of rapid social change. Over two-thirds of easterners register high anomie scores against around half in the west (Kaase 1997: 22). On a similarly constructed 'alienation' scale, 58 per cent of easterners registered high as against 25 per cent of westerners (Schöbel 1993: 8). Anomie is compounded by a weak sense of personal responsibility, the legacy of the GDR 'dependency culture'. Only 39 per cent of easterners believe that 'individuals should take responsibility for themselves', with 62 per cent ascribing social responsibility to the state, a reversal of attitudes in the west, where 68 per cent believe in personal as opposed to social responsibility (Rose and Haerpfer 1993; see also Roller 1992). In comparison to east/central Europeans, as can be seen from table 4.3, east Germans have a significantly more pronounced orientation to collectivism on all indicators except state ownership.

The combination of economic opportunity with social and psychological insecurity, it might be argued, produces conflicting responses. The first is characterized by economic individualism, a syndrome of 'lifeboat economics': by the pursuit of personal material security through single-minded engagement in the exploitation of emergent economic opportunities. Economic individualism might be expected to generate a sense of political efficacy, but it is also likely to lead to a preoccupation with the private sphere over participation in public life. The second response is the product of anomie and a sense of powerlessness in the face of the massive upheaval in private life accompanying socio-economic change. Perceiving social change as a threat, the anomic response is likely to lead to a passive withdrawal from public life. Thus both economic individualism and anomie lead, albeit by different routes, to a retreat into the private sphere which undermines the associational order.

Both of these tendencies can be recognized in interview responses to questions about psychological orientations to collective action:

Initially there was a tendency to come together . . . to do things collectively . . . because people were not used to being independent . . . then after a time everyone started thinking 'I can only achieve something for myself by working in my own company.'(Interview: UV Thüringen)

People withdraw into their own narrow circles, thinking 'I can rescue myself.' (Interview: Hartmannbund, Landesverband Mecklenburg-Vorpommern)

After the revolution [Wende] everyone was very dynamic and active . . . now they've become passive and depressive . . . people feel that they're powerless. (Interview: NAV, Sachsen)

Thus the dynamism of associational activity in the democratic revolution rapidly gave way either to economic individualism or to feelings of resignation and powerlessness in the face of social and political change.

Survey data also suggests that market transition is accompanied by declining perceptions of political efficacy. Initially, east Germans displayed a similar level of political efficacy to that found in the west. Between 1990 and 1994, however, the data shows declining perceptions of efficacy, running parallel to a decline in the importance ascribed to participation (Meulemann 1997: 129–30). Only around one in five believes that there are greater opportunities for political influence in the Federal Republic than in the GDR, with one in ten expressing the opposite view (Rose and Haerpfer 1993). Table 4.1 shows that, whilst levels of internal efficacy (beliefs in the responsiveness of the political system) are broadly similar in east and west Germany, the level of external efficacy (perceptions of the individual's capacity to influence politics) is significantly lower in the east. Cross-national comparison with the countries of east/central Europe produces more surprising results. As we have seen, in terms of per capita income and the ability to derive a livelihood from their main job, east Germans are uniquely privileged relative to citizens elsewhere in east/central Europe. Notwithstanding these economic advantages, however, they exhibit a high level of personal insecurity and a stronger orientation to collectivist values than their counterparts in other post-communist societies. Moreover, as can be seen from table 4.1, their perceptions of political influence are as low or lower than those in most comparator countries. Perceptions of personal influence are at their lowest in the economic sphere. Fully 40 per cent of easterners believe that personal influence in the workplace is less than in the previous regime, against only 14 per cent giving the opposite view. In relation to trade unions, 35 per cent believe that their influence is less than in the GDR, with only 11 per cent giving a positive response (Wiesenthal 1996: 7–8).

Thus the German case fails to support the expectations derived from the social psychological perceptive that higher levels of economic development in an *advanced* post-communist society might be accompanied by rising perceptions of personal efficacy and a participatory civic culture. Indeed, it points rather in the reverse direction, reinforcing the tentative conclusion drawn earlier in this chapter that political efficacy and economic development are negatively related in post-communist society. Market transition, then, is accompanied by a decline in perceptions of influence in the public sphere, explained in terms of the economic and psychological insecurity which it generates.

Civic culture and social capital

As in other post-communist societies, social capital formation may be expected to be inhibited by the disjuncture between the public and private spheres that was characteristic of communist society. Recoiling from authoritarian control in public life, individuals retreated into the private sphere creating a 'niche society' of private social networks (Misselwitz 1993: 106). A high priority on interpersonal relations is a residual legacy of this pattern of behaviour: 'easterners rate relations with family, friends, and people around them more highly than westerners (Bürklin 1993: 145). This emphasis on interpersonal relations might be expected to lead to a predisposition to prioritize the private sphere, and a reduced willingness to participate in the more impersonal sphere of public life.

Across the associational order, interview evidence suggests low levels of social capital. Trade union officials contrast the 'emancipated' works councillor in the west with his more passive counterpart in the east, whilst in business associations shortfalls in organizational skills, individual initiative and personal confidence are widely reported indicators of retarded social capital formation:

In the west they are very emancipated . . . and are able to deal with most matters as well as salaried officials. Here they simply don't have this experience. They are keen to learn but they often just don't have the time. (Interview: IG Metall, Bezirksleitung Berlin-Brandenburg)

There's a tendency to let others speak first . . . it's a lack of confidence really. (Interview: LVSA)

People learn very slowly to exercise their own initiative. For them to realize that shaping the future depends on them is a slow learning process. (Interview: LSI)

As workers are faced with the urgent need to re-skill in the private occupational sphere, however, the acquisition of civic skills assumes a lower priority. Even those who are prepared to participate in associational life remain heavily reliant upon salaried officials, often westerners well equipped with organizational resources derived from long professional experience.

Both trade unions and business associations report some evidence of 'social learning' as the cultural legacy of communism recedes parallel to the acquisition of the skills and the assertiveness associated with civic competence:

In my whole professional life I have never come across colleagues who are so willing to learn. (Interview: VSME, Dresden)

People are becoming more confident . . . they're saying 'We can do this just as well as the westerners.' (Interview: IG Metall, Verwaltungsstelle Magdeburg)

Managers in Treuhand firms were prepared to let the officials do everything. Now it's changing. People in privatized companies want to *do* things . . . to *change* things. (Interview: LVSA)

Not only is the learning process slow, however, it also appears to be restricted to a core of committed activists. More broadly, passivity remains the predominant characteristic of associational life.

As we saw in the introduction, social capital is generated by co-operation in interpersonal relations, spilling over into public life and engendering confidence and trust in social and political institutions. Survey data suggests relatively low levels of social trust, as the interpersonal bonds characteristic of communist society have been eroded in the more competitive environment of the market. Fifty per cent of easterners believed that their relations with their fellow citizens had deteriorated since the democratic revolution, with only 6 per cent reporting an improvement. Civic trust is also low, with less than 25 per cent of easterners expressing confidence in 'the public authorities' compared to over 40 per cent in the west. Trust in the police lies 20 percentage points behind western levels, with a similar trust deficit in relation to the courts (12 per cent), parliament (12 per cent), administration (13 per cent), government (5 per cent) and political parties (5 per cent). Only the army commands equal trust in east and west (Langguth 1995: 47). As can be seen from table 4.4, the level of trust invested in social and political institutions is broadly similar to the average for east/central Europe.

Support for democratic values is as high or higher than that in the west (Niedermeyer and von Beyme 1994; Dalton 1996; Kaase 1997: 7–11). In the face of this evidence of cultural assimilation, however, some observers questioned the strength of attachments to democratic values, suggesting that east Germans might merely be *Fragebogendemokraten* (opinion poll democrats), adroitly presenting pollsters with the 'correct' responses. Their tendency to identify democracy with a successful economic system indicates that their support of democratic norms may be based on a pragmatic assessment of the performance of the system (Dalton 1994: 491).

This interpretation is supported by data relating to attitudes towards democratic institutions. Whilst east Germans adhere, as we saw above, to democratic *values*, their satisfaction with democratic *institutions* was relatively low. Eurobarometer data shows 'satisfaction with the way democracy functions' significantly lower than in the west, at 49.4 per cent in 1990 (80.4 per cent in the west), falling to 39.1 per cent in 1991 (67.3 per cent), before steadying at 43.3 per cent in 1992 (65.3 per cent). Allensbach poll results for 1994 show only 31 per cent of easterners endorsing 'the form of democracy we have in the Federal Republic' with 28 per cent expressing the view that others were better, and 41 per cent uncommitted (Langguth 1995: 46, 53). Declining confidence in democratic institutions can be seen against the backdrop of economic decline in the east, suggesting that democratic allegiance derives from a pragmatic 'output orientation' geared to economic performance.

This conclusion is strengthened when the attitudes of east Germans are placed in comparative perspective. The 'legitimacy bonus' observed elsewhere in the region is absent in Germany. As we have seen (table 4.5), in most east/central European countries, endorsement of the political system outstrips evaluations of the economy. In the German case, the picture is reversed. Whilst 75 per cent of east Germans endorse the present economic system (compared with 43 per cent of east/central Europeans), only 60 per cent respond positively to the political system, marginally below the east/central European average of 62 per cent. The legitimacy deficit can be explained by the special circumstances of economic transformation in east Germany. With democratic stability embedded in the Federal Republic, east Germans can afford to take a more distanced view of the political system than their counterparts elsewhere in the region. Moreover, driven by images of western affluence, their economic aspirations are higher. East Germans are better off than Czechs, Poles and Russians, but they remain deprived by the standards of west Germans, their most immediate comparators. Thus the behavioural and attitudinal profile of east Germans reflects an instrumental, output orientation towards democratic and associational life. Allegiance to social and political institutions is closely correlated with perceptions of economic performance, measured against very demanding expectations derived from images of west German affluence.

Incentive structures and organizational resources

As we saw in the introduction, rational choice theory explains participation in collective action in terms of the organizational resources available to the group. In the absence of supportive social networks and collective identities, it was argued, interest groups in post-communist society are poorly endowed with the organizational resources that sustain collective action. Group mobilization can thus be expected to exhibit the sort of collective action problems identified in rational choice theory, with an incentive structure geared to individual economic benefits in which solidary incentives play little part. Across the spectrum of associational activity, organizational weakness can be related to a deficiency in those resources identified by collective action theory as prerequisites of successful group mobilization. Organized business suffers from the absence of the intercorporate networks characteristic of corporate governance in the German model:

The networks amongst firms which you get in the west have not yet developed here . . . there's been so much restructuring that everything's in a state of flux. (Interview: IHK, Schwerin)

The relationships which have evolved over forty years in the west simply don't exist here . . . businessmen and managers didn't know each other. We had to bring them together and introduce them . . . to build a feeling of group belonging . . . They have to be able to identify with a business class. (Interview: VWT)

Most employer and business organizations recognized this problem and had taken steps to encourage network formation, using specialist seminars or social functions to foster a sense of group belonging. In the absence of the interlocking networks of ownership and control characteristic of the German model of corporate governance, however, organized business lacks the sense of collective identity that motivates group mobilization: 'the entrepreneurial ethos is weak . . . business people have not yet begun to conceive of themselves as a class' (interview: VWT).

Militating against network formation is the structure of the corporate landscape, polarized between a handful of large companies and a proliferation of small firms in the indigenous *Mittelstand*. The importance of large companies as an organizational resource in both business groups and trade unions is well established, with a strong correlation between company size and participation in collective organization. Large companies are the mainstay of business groups; organizing a relatively small number of large companies involves lower transaction costs than mobilizing a much larger number of small firms (interview: Nordmetall, Hamburg). The sparsity of large firms in the post-communist economy thus inhibits organizational activity.

Trade unions benefit similarly from the reduced organizational costs involved in maintaining and servicing their membership in a large workplace. Moreover, trade unions derive an important organizational resource from the dense interpersonal networks generated by mass employment in large companies. Union officials are quick to relate organizational density to the 'bonding effect' of mass employment, and the difficulties of organizational maintenance amongst new business start-ups in the small firm sector:

Organizational density is highest where large numbers of people are employed in a single workplace . . . it's harder to organize in small and medium-sized firms . . . large numbers of people working together – that's what breeds solidarity. (Interview: DGB, Landesbezirk Sachsen)

In newly established firms, often with fewer than twenty workers, membership tends to be low . . . it's very difficult to organize here. (Interview: IG Metall, Bezirksleitung Berlin-Brandenburg)

The correlation between membership density and company size that we saw in chapter 3 can be explained in these terms. Declining union membership can be related to the sharp decline in average company size accompanying market transition. It may also be related to high levels of employment mobility consequent upon corporate instability. Members have to be re-recruited, and new organizational structures put in place. Endemic to market transition, 'job churning' means a constantly shifting union clientele, militating against membership consolidation. Across the associational order, then, interest groups suffer from the absence of the group networks and identities that support organizational activity in resource mobilization theory.

Resource deficiencies are compounded by weak incentive structures. From a rational choice perspective, it was argued in the introduction, the logic of collective action reflects the configuration of incentives and disincentives arising out of the structure of capital, employment relations and labour markets, and it is here that we should look to explain the membership profile of interest groups outlined in chapter 3. In the employers' associations, membership incentives revolve above all around wage-bargaining. German labour law binds firms to collective agreements concluded by the employers' associations. Large, high-profitability companies have most to gain from centralized collective bargaining in terms of industrial relations stability, wage-cost predictability and the regulation of wage competition. For SMEs facing tight budgetary constraints and seeking wage flexibility in the struggle for company survival, a legally binding framework of collective bargaining is an encumbrance, acting as a strong disincentive to association membership.

The disincentive effect of collective wage-bargaining on employers' association membership is reinforced by the weakness of labour markets in post-communist economies. Employers are better equipped to exploit the advantages bestowed by weak labour markets through individual bargaining than through collective agreements, which are less responsive to market forces (Streeck 1992a: 514):

Industrial relations have developed so dramatically against employees that wage agreements are quickly outpaced. Individual employers want to capitalize on their strength to reduce wage costs but they can't do this within the association. (Interview: IG Metall, Verwaltungsstelle Erfurt)

Interview evidence suggests that the drive for company flexibility is particularly strong in the post-communist economy, further accentuating the disincentive effect of collective bargaining:

In the west employers are more paternalistic; having invested in training they want to maintain worker loyalty and to discourage wage competition . . . In the east they're not interested in worker loyalty . . . they're interested in a flexible workforce. (Interview: IG Metall, Bezirksleitung Berlin-Brandenburg)

Wage flexibility does not necessarily mean driving down wages. For large companies and especially multi-nationals, the attraction of in-house bargaining lies rather in the scope it offers for more customized and differentiated pay structures reflecting 'corporate culture' and the profile of the labour force. Opel at Eisenach, for instance, rejects collective bargaining in favour of company agreements and a pay structure that bridges traditional distinctions between manual and white-collar workers. In small firms, on the other hand, abstention from association membership goes hand in hand with undercutting collectively agreed wage agreements.

Amongst small firms in the *Mittelstand* sector, the disincentive effect of collective bargaining is clearly shown in table 4.6. Virtually all large companies paid at or above collectively agreed rates in 1993, as against just one-third of firms with a payroll of fewer than fifty. Adherence to collective agreement also varies sharply between companies owned in east and west Germany. Nearly 90 per cent of companies based in the west paid wages in line with collective agreements, against 54 per cent of those under east German ownership. Amongst new business start-ups, the practice of undercutting agreed rates is endemic. Unsurprisingly, there was a strong correlation between adherence to collectively agreed wage rates and employers' association membership. Sixty-seven per cent of all firms outside the employers' association undercut agreed rates, rising to 77 per cent for small firms. Even amongst association members, 44 per

Table 4.6. *Adherence to collectively agreed wage rates in eastern Germany*
% firms surveyed

Company size (number of employees)	1–49	50–99	100–499	500+
1992(1993)	51(34)	77(71)	94(88)	100(98)
Ownership	West German/ foreign	East German	New business start-ups	
1992(1993)	92(89)	73(54)	31(0)	

Sources: IWH 1994; cited Ettl and Heikenroth 1995: 26.

cent of small firms breached agreements to which they were legally bound (Ettl and Heikenroth 1995: 27).

These tendencies reflect the erosion of institutionalized industrial relations that we saw in chapter 2. In the absence of flexibility in the institutional apparatus, there is a large-scale shift towards local bargaining, undermining the incentive structure of collective organization and facing the employers' associations with a dilemma. Embedded in centralized collective bargaining, they have a strong organizational interest in its maintenance. Within this system, however, they are unable to accommodate countervailing demands for flexibility from the small firm sector. Polarization between large and small firms in the wage-bargaining arena cuts across the sectoral solidarity that underpins collective action amongst employers. The exodus from the employers' associations and dominance of large companies in their membership profile that we observed in chapter 3 are thus explained by an incentive structure that has limited attractions for small firms.

The weakness of solidary incentives and the decentralization of wage-bargaining mean that selective membership incentives become increasingly important. Business groups offer a wide repertoire of specialist consultancy services and seminar series on 'marketing' or 'lean production' (interviews: UV Thüringen, Sachsen- Anhalt; Nordmetall, Schwerin; Verband der Mittelständische Wirtschaft, Rostock). Reflecting the concerns of their core membership in the large company sector, however, the BDA-affiliated associations are not well adapted to meeting the needs of small firms. Competing successfully for this clientele is the Bundesverband Mittelständische Wirtschaft (BVMW) which operates out of local, franchised, usually one-person offices and is almost exclusively occupied in this kind of activity. Consultancy services are also widely available outside the associational order on a commercial basis.

Unencumbered by the function of political representation, commercial consultancy is often available at a lower cost than through business associations, further weakening the incentive structures of the latter.

Employment relations also play a central role in the incentive structures of trade union membership. From the rational choice perspective, the wage-bargaining function of trade unions is a weak membership incentive; collective agreements confer their benefits upon members and non-members alike, encouraging free-riding. Nevertheless, it is not implausible to infer that east Germans invested in collective mobilization in the expectation of maximizing private rewards, encouraged by success in the wage-bargaining round of 1990–1. Bargaining success strengthened popular perceptions of identity between collective action and private welfare, evident in survey data showing over two-thirds of east Germans subscribing to the view that 'trade unions represent personal interests' against less than half of westerners (Wessels 1992).

As we saw in chapter 3, trade union membership was at its highest in large-scale enterprises under Treuhand administration. Here, the state funding of wage costs meant freedom from hard budget constraints; the trade-off between high wages and employment security and union membership represented a form of investment in wage maximization. Collective bargaining geared to wage maximization is less of an incentive to trade union membership in the newly emergent private sector, where hard budget constraints place a premium on wage flexibility in the interests of job security. Low levels of trade union membership in SMEs are related to the progressive decentralization and deregulation of wage-bargaining here. Localized bargaining undermines the rationale for union membership. The tendency towards management–works council agreements marginalizes trade unions in the wage-bargaining arena. Even where union officials are involved in company-level negotiations, there is a tendency to turn a blind eye to infringements of sectoral agreements. The hallmark of local bargaining is flexibility. With settlements geared to the profitability of the firm rather than industry-wide pay norms, centrally negotiated wage structures are of little relevance. In-house agreements reduce the bargaining depth of the trade unions, undermining an important part of the membership incentive structure.

Whilst decentralization and deregulation in industrial relations weaken the incentive structure of trade union membership, the weakness of labour markets in the post-communist economy has a countervailing effect. During privatization, the unions were party to negotiations over privatization, corporate restructuring and rationalization, with popular perceptions greatly exaggerating their capacity to protect employment. Thereafter, labour market volatility placed a premium on collective organization, trade unions providing conflict insurance in the form of legal assistance for employees involved in grievance procedures arising from redundancy or wrongful dismissal. Reliance on trade union representation also reflects a more hard-nosed managerial style in corporate life: 'in the west employers are more paternalistic . . . here they're more ruthless'. The involvement of the DGB in this kind of activity is reflected in the profile of its staff establishment; around 60 per cent of its officials are lawyers (interview: IG Metall, Bezirksleitung Berlin-Brandenburg). Thus the provision of conflict insurance services plays a key role in the incentive structure of trade union membership.

The predominance of economic motivations in the incentive structure of trade union membership underlines the importance of confidence in union representation. In 1990 the unions commanded widespread trust, with 82.6 per cent of members and 51.2 per cent of non-members expressing confidence in trade unions, against 88.3 per cent and 38.3 per cent in the west (Wessels 1992: 13). By 1994, much of this confidence had evaporated. Studies commissioned by the DGB (making no distinction between members and non-members) showed only 23 per cent evaluating trade union performance positively ('very good' or 'good'), against 48 per cent with reservations ('not so good') and 15 per cent unreservedly negative ('poor'). Evaluations of union performance were significantly more jaundiced than in the west, where, despite a negative trend following unification, opinion divided about evenly between approval and disapproval (IfEP 1994: 12).

Negative assessments of union performance in the east can be related to high expectations and exaggerated perceptions of the trade unions' capacity to deliver social and economic security:

People expect the *Verbände* [associations] to replicate the social security functions they performed in the GDR. (Interview: NAV, Sachsen)

There's an expectation that we can save jobs, or create new jobs. (Interview: IG Metall, Verwaltungsstelle Magdeburg)

People expect us to be able to regulate all aspects of life . . . care for the elderly, support for the unemployed . . . preventing firms from going under. (Interview: DGB, Landesbezirk Berlin-Brandenburg)

Exaggerated expectations are linked with an unwillingness to compromise on demands and interests. The expectation that trade unions should pursue the demands and interests of their members regardless of wider economic difficulties is expressed by 84 per cent of union members in the east, against 57 per cent in the west. Inflated expectations are reflected in disappointment, with only 56 per cent of union members reporting that their expectations had been 'fulfilled' or 'largely fulfilled', against 70 per cent in the west (IfEP 1994: 11). Trade unions come closer to fulfilling the expectations of their members than their counterparts in other east/central European countries, but dissatisfaction is still significantly more widespread than in western Germany. This syndrome of disappointed expectations and low levels of confidence in union performance may explain the readiness of trade union members in the east to consider renouncing union membership.

In the absence of a supportive social infrastructure providing solidary incentives for group membership, then, the decision to join hinges on individual economic motivations, accentuating the sort of collective action problems identified by rational choice theory. Research suggests that, where membership depends on this kind of motivation, group ties are tenuous (Visser 1994: 94–5). This expectation is confirmed by data suggesting that 54 per cent of union members in the east can conceive of renouncing membership as against 42 per cent in the west (IfEP 1994: 15).

Uninvolved in collective bargaining, professional associations offer few economic membership incentives. Membership motivations rely heavily on a sense of professional ethos, which is ill developed in post-communist society. In its absence, membership decisions are subject to pragmatic cost–benefit calculations:

The financial advisor comes along and says 'What's your expenditure . . . you pay DM350 to the Hartmannbund . . . What does it do for you? Has it realized your demands? No? So get out . . .' (Interview: Hartmannbund, Landesverband Mecklenburg-Vorpommern)

Interest representation tends to figure low in membership calculations, unless, as in the case of engineers and the KdT, the organization is demonstrably successful in defending the immediate material interests of its client group. Thus, the membership density of professional associations is significantly lower than in the west, and is subject to decline as doctors and engineers face up to the commercial rigours of private practice.

Conclusion

From the social psychological perspective, as outlined at the beginning of this chapter, a readiness to participate in social and political life is related to the individual's sense of effectiveness or efficacy, which may in turn be related to personal economic security. Evidence from the countries of east/central Europe, however, provides little support for this hypothesis.

The contrast between relatively high levels of political involvement in the more economically advanced Czech Republic and the passivity of the citizens in Poland provides some circumstantial evidence of a relationship between participation and economic development. There is, however, no systematic evidence of a positive relationship between participation, political efficacy and economy. In the face of a low level of economic development, Bulgarians exhibit markedly higher levels of political efficacy than their more affluent Hungarian counterparts.

Indeed, there is evidence of a *negative* relationship between the pace of economic transformation and the level of political efficacy. The German case may illuminate this apparent paradox. Despite access to consolidated democratic institutions, levels of political efficacy remain amongst the lowest of the post-communist countries, whilst rapid market transition has been accompanied by a steep decline in the perceptions of influence in the workplace and in trade union life. Thus the economic freedom of the market may come at the price of a sense of powerlessness and anomie in the face of the social forces it unleashes. The negative relationship between personal efficacy and economic development may thus be explained in terms of the economic insecurity generated by rapid market transition. Evidence from the German case suggests that the combination of opportunities and threats accompanying the market prompts a dual response: either economic individualism and the pursuit of private economic interests, or a passive withdrawal into anomie and isolation in the private sphere, neither of which is conducive to participation and associational activity.

Social capital is an elusive concept difficult to track empirically. The evidence available from the countries of east/central Europe, however, suggests that, whilst the strong interpersonal networks characteristic of communist society have broken down, there is little sign of the emergence of the syndrome of social trust and co-operation found in Almond and Verba's formulation of the civic culture. Certainly there is nothing to suggest an accumulation of social capital in the private sphere spilling over into public life. With no stable patterns of social co-operation to offset the competitiveness of the market economy, allegiances to social and political institutions are pragmatic and instrumental. A 'legitimacy bonus' in the aftermath of democratization means that endorsement of democratic political systems outstrips economic performance. Nonetheless, evaluations of the political system correlate closely with perceptions of improved economic performance in the future, suggesting a pragmatic, output orientation towards politics conforming to Almond and Verba's model of the subject rather than the civic culture.

Interview data from eastern Germany suggests that, even in an advanced post-communist society, social capital accumulation is slow and uneven. East Germans lack confidence in their role as actors in associational life, and, in so far as there is evidence of social learning, it appears to be confined to a relatively small corps of interest group activists. Levels of social trust are low, whilst trust and confidence in social institutions like trade unions are in decline. Germany deviates from its post-communist neighbours in experiencing a 'legitimacy deficit', whereby popular endorsement of the political system lags behind perceptions of economic performance. The behavioural and attitudinal profile of east Germans reflects an instrumental attitude towards social and political institutions, with allegiance closely correlated with perceptions of economic performance measured against the very demanding expectations derived from images of west German affluence.

Without the social infrastructures that the pluralist model takes for granted, interest groups are susceptible to the collective action problems identified in rational choice theory. We have seen how the potential for group mobilization is related to the availability of organizational resources in the form of supportive social networks and the distinctive group identities which provide solidary incentives for participation. Without these resources, group mobilization reflects a logic of collective action in which individual economic motivations predominate. In the post-communist societies of east/central Europe, the distribution of organizational resources is heavily skewed towards forms of activity with their roots in the old regime. This explains both the dominance of labour movements by the trade unions inheriting the organizational apparatus of their communist predecessors, and concentration of business organization in the networks of the 'nomenklatura bourgeoisie'. The incentive structures of collective action are weak. A pervasive scepticism towards trade union representation renders economic incentives ineffective, whilst the broadly based, generalist character of most business associations makes it difficult for them to use specialist services as selective membership incentives.

Despite the advancement of market transition in the German case, social structures provide only weak support for collective action, individual economic motivations predominating over solidary incentives. Trade union incentive structures conform more closely to the 'American model' of pragmatic individualism than to the 'European collectivist' type. In the absence of a cohesive managerial or entrepreneurial class, there is little evidence of a commitment to 'business values' underpinning group membership. In both employers' associations and trade unions, wage-bargaining is the key to the logic of collective action. Amongst employers, association membership calculations revolve around the tradeoff between stability and predictability on the one hand, and flexibility on the other, with strong evidence that small and medium-sized firms tend to opt for the latter. Similarly, centrally agreed collective wage agreements have little relevance to the employees of commercially weak companies where job security predominates over wage maximization. Thus the decentralization and deregulation of wage-bargaining undermines the logic of collective action in both employers' associations and trade unions. In the professional associations, the weakness of solidary membership motivations deriving from allegiances to vocational values means reliance on an incentive structure based on service provision. Indeed, we have observed the predominance of this type of incentive across the associational order.

Across the spectrum of organized interests, economic incentives figure more prominently in membership decisions than political motives. The advocacy role of interest groups in the political arena appears to exert little influence. Political representation is a public good, susceptible to the free-rider syndrome identified by Olson. Trade union membership appears to conform more closely to the American model of pragmatic individualism than to the European collectivist model. A similar conclusion emerges from the analysis of business group membership, with membership decisions revolving around wage-bargaining calculations, and little evidence of 'purposive political benefits' or a commitment to 'business values' playing a decisive role. The relative success of the business consultancy-oriented UVs and the BVMW is indicative of service provision as a membership incentive. In the professions, where the absence of economic incentives means that interest groups are reliant on allegiances to vocational values, a pervasive pragmatism prevails. Purposive motivations for collective action stem from an identification with the social and cultural values of the group. The weakness of group values in post-communist society means that the decision to subscribe to collective action is more likely to be based on economic pragmatism rather than group identification.

5   Group dynamics

As we saw in the introduction, the pluralist model of the associational order implies autonomous organization based on the volunteer involvement of the participants, with a professional staff merely serving the function of organizational maintenance. This conception of group dynamics was contrasted with the model postulated by exchange theory, in which associational activity is conceived in terms of the relationship between the professional leadership of the group offering benefits to a clientele in return for membership. Group leaders are thus seen as political entrepreneurs, and association is reinterpreted as a type of business activity, its defining characteristic being the essentially commercial relations between the group and its members. If, as we saw in the previous chapter, the decision to subscribe to an interest group is governed by instrumental cost–benefit calculations, the willingness to participate in organizational activity is likely to be lower than where membership motivations revolve around the solidary incentives associated with group identification. Group dynamics are thus likely to be characterized by mass passivity and professional domination, taking the form of the loosely coupled exchange relationship of the entrepreneurial model rather than the pluralist ideal of autonomous associational activity.

Empirical studies of the internal life of interest groups in the post-communist societies of east/central Europe are scarce, but what evidence there is supports the expectations outlined above. Trade union activity is strongly marked by the syndrome of mass passivity and elite domination. The reform of communist trade unions was a top-down process, led by an educated elite with a background in academic research institutes or the professions, whose union career was often interwoven with a career in politics (Myant 1994: 77–9). 'Divorced by education and social origins . . . from the social categories it purports to represent' (MacShane 1994: 348–9), the trade union leadership is seen by some as being composed of 'self-appointed bureaucratic fiefdoms . . . life support systems for their officials who make a living out of the pretence of representing workers' interests' (Lomax 1997: 50).

Emergent business associations also conform closely to the entrepreneurial model of interest representation in which individuals initiate organizations for commercial profit or to provide themselves with the organizational resources to launch political careers. Opportunities for this form of organization were plentiful amidst the chaos of economic transformation. Groups like RUIE (Russian Union of Industrialists and Entrepreneurs) and the National Association of Entrepreneurs in Hungary are thus subordinated to the political ambitions of their leaders. Often entering the electoral arena and acquiring the character of political parties, these groups tend to put the logic of influence before the logic of membership, militating against the consolidation of a mass membership base.

A passive membership

Across the associational order, interest group officials report very low levels of participation in organizational life. In business associations, passivity is related to the very heavy demands upon managers and entrepreneurs in firms undergoing restructuring and struggling for economic survival. The rigours of corporate management under these circumstances severely restrict voluntary commitments to associational life. Participation tends to be highest where the firm has achieved a measure of stability, and especially in larger firms with greater managerial capacity (interview: LSI). The weakness of group identification is also cited as a reason for the reluctance to assume responsibilities in public life: 'entrepreneurs have yet to grow into their role' (interview: VWT). Similarly in the professional associations, low participation rates may be explained by the weakness of the *Berufspolitik* tradition. 'People have no time for *Berufspolitik* . . . it's harder than in the west where there's a tradition . . . our members see no personal advantage to be derived from participation' (interview: Hartmannbund, Landesverband Mecklenburg-Vorpommern). Participation, then, is rooted in group identification; passivity may thus be seen as a reflection of the underdevelopment of social collectivities in post-communist society.

A similar picture of member passivity is evident in the trade unions, with engagement in organizational activity governed by instrumentalism: 'people are reluctant to become involved – they ask "what do I get out of it?"' (interview: IG Metall, Bezirksleitung Dresden). Here though, the picture is more complex, the intensity of participation varying widely from one form of activity to another. Officials report a markedly higher readiness to participate in activity bearing directly on 'bread-and-butter' issues, with action in support of wage-bargaining attracting exceptionally high levels of participation:

Our members here tend to emphasize traditional functions like collective bargaining . . . when you go beyond this you get a very small percentage who are prepared to be active. (Interview: DGB, Landesbezirk Berlin-Brandenburg)

When it comes to wage-bargaining, they are certainly not passive . . . we can mobilize people for demonstrations here, no problem . . . but it's harder in the east to mobilize people in support of another trade union . . . they say 'That's not my problem.' (Interview: IG Metall, Verwaltungsstelle Magdeburg)

The preoccupation with private concerns means that associational activity must be 'customized' to meet the material needs of specific social groups:

You target a specific group – for instance freelance journalists . . . and you say 'What can we do for you?' That works. You don't get people to come along for two days discussing things that don't concern them personally . . . it's very important here to have definite concrete issues. (Interview: IG Medien, Berlin-Brandenburg)

The predisposition towards forms of activity geared to specific material interests may reflect the 'commodity fetishism' of post-communist societies characterized by economic deprivation (Clark and Wildavsky 1990; Rose 1991: 43). Interview evidence provides some support for this interpretation:

People in the west can afford to be interested in culture and ideas. Here they have more immediate and material needs. When living standards reach the same levels we'll see that they're capable of developing more creativity . . . you can already see it at Siemens where the conditions are better and people are more secure. (Interview: IG Metall, Verwaltungsstelle Schwerin)

Pragmatic discrimination between different forms of activity is evident in the sharp contrast between high levels of works council (*Betriebsrat*) participation and the difficulty which union officials experience in the recruitment of shop stewards (*Vertrauensleute*). Easterners exhibit a much greater reluctance to assume this role than their western counterparts:

It's easier to get people to stand as *Betriebsräte* because they have a legal basis, and because they have more influence . . . over working time, overtime etc. . . . Management is bound to listen. As *Vertrauensleute* . . . there's no legal structure and it's hard to get management to take notice . . . They can have influence too, but first you have to build the structure and that's harder. (Interview: IG Metall, Bezirksleitung Dresden)

The contrast may be explained in terms of the perceived effectiveness of the respective roles and the conferral of status and prestige. There is also some evidence suggesting a preference for legally prescribed roles over more informal and ambiguous forms of participation.

Discrimination between different forms of activity is also evident in patterns of participation in public authority boards – labour market offices, industrial and welfare tribunals, health insurance boards etc. – on which employers and trade unions are represented. The widely reported readiness to accept labour court responsibilities was explained in terms of a strong popular belief in the law: 'people feel it gives them prestige'. Individuals are discriminating in their readiness to engage in public service activities of this kind: 'it depends on how influential and important the committees are' (interview: IG Metall, Verwaltungsstelle Erfurt). Interview data shows evidence of quite wide variation in the experience of group officials. Some officials report difficulty in finding volunteer representatives for public authority boards; others point emphatically in the opposite direction: 'There's an astonishingly high readiness to serve' (interview: IHK, Magdeburg); 'I'm amazed how many people have taken on these responsibilities in such a short time' (interview: IG Metall, Verwaltungsstelle Schwerin).

Amidst the general picture of passivity there are isolated instances of vigorous organizational life. Local variations in the intensity of participation can perhaps be explained by the personal factor. Lacking strong social foundations, activity is heavily dependent on the commitment and ability of a few key individuals:

Most of our members are active . . . we have quite a good attendance at business meetings and social functions . . . in some regions we often get 80 out of 120 members attending . . . and for some big events we might pull in a lot of non-members . . . we've had 400 at some of our big events . . . it varies a lot between regions . . . in some regions they only get around fifteen people to a social event. (Interview: UV Mecklenburg-Vorpommern)

This organization also reported above-average competition for elected office, in contrast to most other business associations. It may be significant that it possessed a strong organizational infrastructure, based on a professional staff of above-average proportions. Far from the ideal of autonomous organization in the classical model, this case points towards the orchestration of associational activity by a professional staff, consistent with the 'entrepreneurial' interest group postulated by exchange theory. The dominance of the associational order by interest group professionals is particularly pronounced in post-communist Germany, and it is to this that we now turn.

The professionalization of group activity

The genesis of associational life in east Germany through institutional transfer from the west entailed the rapid professionalization of interest representation. Whilst some officials were seconded on a temporary basis, many others remained permanently in the east, forming a functionary corps which was augmented by recruitment amongst easterners. Linked by a shared staff establishment, the Verband der Metall- und Elektroindustrie (VME) and the employer confederations in the *Land* capitals maintain around a hundred officials, backed by an administrative staff of around fifty. Berlin-Brandenburg is the largest, with twenty officials working out of the previously existing office in West Berlin, and the same number deployed in three regional offices in the eastern hinterland. Sachsen and Thüringen each have over twenty officials, Sachsen-Anhalt and Mecklenburg-Vorpommern around a dozen each. The smaller sector associations maintain only a skeletal staff, often with no more than one or two officials and a secretary in the *Land* office. The stronger of the independent UVs maintain a modest staff (Mecklenburg, for instance, has a staff of eight), whereas in Sachsen-Anhalt and Thüringen the office is run single-handedly by unsalaried officials combining their duties with the professional life of a business consultant.

Resourced by compulsory membership subscriptions and performing a range of quasi-public functions, the IHKs are exceptionally heavily staffed. The smallest of the chambers employ around fifty to sixty, whilst the largest have a personnel establishment approaching two hundred. When allowance is made for the lower level of economic activity in the east, staffing levels are similar to those in western Germany (the Hamburg chamber, for instance, has staff of 280). Around one-third of officials are engaged in vocational education activities, reflecting the principal function of the chambers.

The staff establishment of the employers' associations is dwarfed by that of the big industrial trade unions and the DGB. Across the new *Länder*, IG Metall employs almost 200 officials, divided between the *Bezirk* (regional) headquarters in Berlin-Brandenburg and Sachsen, and the district offices (*Verwaltungsstellen*). The DGB has an even larger establishment of over 300, made up of officials in the *Land* headquarters and district offices. In part, the size of trade union staff reflects a very heavy involvement in legal advice and representation in industrial tribunals following waves of mass redundancies. The DGB bears the larger part of this burden: around 60 per cent of its officials are lawyers. The Berlin-Brandenburg DGB handled nearly 23,000 labour law cases in 1991, an eightfold increase from the previous year (DGB Landesbezirk Berlin-Brandenburg 1993: 57). In post-communist society, the role of trade unions as service providers is accentuated, and their organizational structures are correspondingly staff-intensive.

Organizational activity in the professional associations relies on orchestration from headquarters in the west, backed by the voluntary commitment of *Land* chairmen who combine their duties with demanding careers in the field. Amongst doctors, the Marburgerbund has a chief executive and a small secretarial staff in all the new *Länder*, as does the Hartmannbund (with the exception of Mecklenburg-Vorpommern where it relies on unpaid, elected office-holders). The NAV-VB has only one chief executive, located in its Berlin office. Engineering associations place a similar reliance on unpaid volunteers. The VDI relies on its Düsseldorf headquarters, maintaining no more than a handful of field staff in the east, whilst the KdT successor associations rely exclusively upon unsalaried officers.

Chief executive dominance

The German attachment to formal legal structures as the bedrock of politics is reflected in an associational order in which democratic principles are codified in formal statutes. In virtually all organizations, sovereignty is vested in a membership assembly which delegates routine decision-making to an elected executive body, which in turn entrusts the day-to-day running of the organization to a salaried chief executive at the head of a professional staff. Employers' associations conform to this model, with an executive committee (*Vorstand*) elected by the member firms in the membership assembly (*Mitgliedsversammlung*). In the employer confederations, the assembly is indirectly constituted by the chairmen of the member associations, from amongst whom a praesidium and a president are elected. The sovereign body of the IHKs is the plenary assembly (*Vollversammlung*), meeting quarterly and consisting of between forty and seventy elected representatives. Electoral systems are structured to ensure that the composition of the plenary assembly reflects that of the membership, with seat quotas for sectoral groups (industry, exports, sole proprietors etc.). The executive organ of the chambers is the praesidium, with between five and ten members elected by the plenary assembly, and headed by a president.

For the most part, these formal structures of internal democracy remain lifeless. Contests for elected office are low-key, one chamber of industry and commerce reporting a voting rate of only 12 per cent in its plenary assembly election despite a postal ballot and a concerted publicity campaign. Competitive elections are rare, and some organizations experience difficulty in finding willing incumbents. Conflict is uncommon, and consensus is the dominant mode of decision-making. 'There is almost always a consensus in the *Vorstand*; sometimes agreement is reached *too* readily' (interview: LSI). Member firms tend to regard business associations as service providers, with salaried staff offering a range of services akin to business consultancy. If these services fail to match their needs, firms are more likely to reject the association than to pursue their interests through participation in its internal democratic processes. In terms of Hirschman's (1970) formulation, *loyalty* is dependent upon service delivery; should the organization fail to deliver, *exit* is an easier option than *voice*. The corollary of democratic inertia is the dominance of salaried officials, the most prominent of whom is the chief executive (*Geschäftsführer*). Elected officers are too fully occupied with the pressures of company management to play a hands-on role in associational life. The chairman or president may play role in external representation and in lobbying activities, but is rarely central in the internal life of the association: 'the president normally comes into the office once or twice a week' (interview: UVB). By contrast, the chief executive is pivotal. Although formally subordinate to the executive committee, in practice the elected leadership is steered by the chief executive. Policy decisions are pre-prepared by the chief executive in advance of *Vorstand* meetings, giving him a key role in opinion formation: 'I'll say what I think we ought to do and the decision will be taken unanimously' (interview: Nordmetall, Schwerin). Reliance on and deference to the chief executive is endemic to business association in eastern Germany.

The syndrome is even more pronounced in the employer confederations. Chief executives play the central role in mediating relations between the constituent associations, collectively constituting the advisory council (*Beirat*). Meeting more frequently than the elected executive committee, the advisory council is effectively the decision-making centre of the confederation. They also play a leading role in the specialist working groups which play an important part in opinion exchange and policy formation (interview: Vereinigung der Unternehmensverbände für Mecklenburg-Vorpommern). Moreover, close informal relations between the chief executives are an important lubricant in the confederal apparatus, especially in reconciling differences between associations:

We have a nice lunch together . . . it's an informal process but it normally works out . . . because the chief executive is the most influential figure within the Verband. (Interview: UVB)

Only if differences prove impossible to resolve on this basis will the elected chairman or president intervene. Otherwise the chief executive orchestrates confederal activity. This syndrome is exacerbated by the reliance of the *Land* confederations on the personnel establishment of the Gesamtmetall affiliates. The VME chief executive also serves the *Land* confederation, giving him a unique position in internal organizational life.

A similar tendency towards domination by salaried officials is evident in the trade unions. IG Metall's district offices incorporate participation through the representative assembly (*Vertreterversammlung*), composed of delegates elected in the workplace branches. Invested with formal sovereignty and meeting quarterly, the assembly is responsible for monitoring and steering union activities. Executive responsibilities are delegated to an elected management committee (*Ortsverwaltung*), composed of two salaried officials (*Bevollmächtigten*) and around a dozen 'lay' members. In practice, elections to the management committee attract little attention and, once in place, its members are rarely subjected to the scrutiny of the representative assembly. The two salaried officials inevitably dominate over the dozen or so 'lay' members, who are usually works councillors in local companies. Whilst works councillors in the west are often as accomplished as salaried officials, their counterparts in the east lack the organizational skills to play a major role in managing union business (interview: IG Metall, Bezirksleitung Berlin-Brandenburg). Thus the inherited structural constraints on participation are reinforced by the social and cultural characteristics of post-communist society, and the apparatus of participatory democracy is 'never really brought to life' (interview: IG Metall, Verwaltungsstelle Magdeburg).

Reliance on salaried officials is a function of the role in which trade unions are cast in post-communist society. A dependency culture is part of the residual legacy of the role which the GDR trade unions played in the delivery of social welfare provisions, fostering a tendency to see the union apparatus as a form of life support (*Lebenshilfe*). Union officials refer to the 'omnipotence syndrome' in which *dependency* is combined with *insistency*: 'they want everything done right away . . . they won't tolerate delay' (interview: IG Metall, Bezirksleitung Berlin-Brandenburg). One explanation for this syndrome is the projection of trade union power in the media:

Our top officials adopt the role of managers, occupying positions of power. So the members say 'What's my role since the men-in-suits are so powerful? What's the point in being active? My subscriptions pay his wages; he looks OK on TV; he can speak for me.' We've created a power image. In the west people see through it; they know it all depends upon them. Here people are more impressionable and susceptible to media influence. (Interview: IG Metall, Verwaltungsstelle Erfurt)

Passivity is thus a response to the power image projected by the trade unions, encouraging their members to cast themselves in the passive role of clients of the organization rather than participants in its internal life. Exaggerated expectations invested in the capacity of trade union officials to deliver their needs are a corollary of the low perception of personal efficacy which, as we saw in the previous chapter, is a characteristic of post-communist society.

Easterners and westerners

Institutional transfer inevitably meant that interest groups were established largely under the tutelage of functionaries seconded from the west. Despite a progressive permeation of the leadership and functionary corps of the associational order by indigenous elements, the top echelon remains dominated by westerners. Amongst the employers, the chief executives of the VME and regional employer confederations are generally westerners. The sole exception is Sachsen-Anhalt, where the functionary corps is exclusively eastern in composition. Amongst elected office-holders, easterners are better represented, although the picture is still uneven. The elected leadership inevitably reflects the managerial class from which it is drawn. It has been estimated that by mid-1992 around 50 per cent of corporate management positions in the new *Länder* were occupied by westerners (Ettl and Wiesenthal 1994). Nevertheless, in Sachsen, Sachsen-Anhalt and Thüringen, easterners constitute a substantial majority amongst elected office-holders. By contrast, in employer organizations spanning eastern and western *Länder*, westerners continue to predominate. Only in the IHKs, with their strong roots in the local economy, do easterners dominate the highest echelons of the functionary corps. Chamber officials are drawn about equally from the GDR managerial class and trade bureaucracy on the one hand, and new entrepreneurs on the other.

The professional leadership of the trade unions remains heavily dominated by westerners, although there is some evidence that the balance is being redressed. IG Metall's mixed (east–west) regions are staffed almost exclusively by westerners. Even in Dresden (its sole eastern region), 60 per cent of officials were westerners. In the local branch offices (*Verwaltungsstellen*), the principal executive official is invariably from the west, although easterners are increasingly predominant in the rest of the functionary corps. In the DGB, the *Land* chairman and the majority of officials in the *Land* bureaus are westerners, although at district (*Kreis*) level the functionary corps is composed predominantly of indigenous elements. Here, there has been a significant change since the first round of leadership elections in 1992. In the Sachsen-Anhalt DGB, for instance, five of seven of the (salaried) district chairmen are now easterners, an exact reversal of the previous position (DGB Landesbezirk Sachsen-Anhalt 1993: 7).

After an initial period of tensions and resentments, east–west relations in associational life have become more harmonious, especially where westerners have taken up residence in their adopted *Land* rather than commuting. Indeed, there is some evidence of a tendency for westerners to 'go native', identifying closely with their new constituency and advocating eastern interests with conviction. Nevertheless, the imbalance in organizational skills and experience between easterners and westerners inevitably exacerbates tendencies to elite domination and mass passivity in the associational order.

Conclusion

The German case confirms the tentative conclusions drawn from the countries of east/central Europe, of non-participatory interest groups supported largely by a professional leadership corps. Low levels of member participation can be explained in terms of the incentive structures of collective action in post-communist society, revolving above all around individual material benefits and with solidary incentives derived from group identification playing little part. Voluntary participation in associational life is related to the strength of entrepreneurial or managerial ethos, or identification with labour movement objectives. With little sense of group belonging, organizational commitment is weak. Interview data also provides an insight into the motivations behind participation. In every sphere of associational activity the readiness to participate is discriminatory, related to the form of activity. Officials emphasize the importance of targeting activities at the immediate material concerns of group members. There is some evidence that a rise in material standards may be accompanied by a more sociotropic orientation to participation, but in the absence of group identification it seems more likely that pragmatic cost–benefit calculations will continue to predominate.

The corollary of a passive membership is the dominance of interest group life by salaried officials whose role extends far beyond mere organizational maintenance. In business associations, the chief executive is the pivotal figure, orchestrating and steering organizational activity with the elected leadership operating in a secondary capacity. A similar syndrome is evident in the trade unions where activity revolves around officials in the district apparatus, whilst professional groups are often constituted simply as service agencies operating out of the west. Across the spectrum of group activity, leadership is delegated wholesale to the salaried officials with volunteer labour playing little part. Formal structures of democratic accountability are lifeless. If the professional leadership fails to fulfil expectations, the response is more likely to be exit than voice. Organizational activity thus conforms to the entrepreneurial model, oriented to the delivery of consultancy-type services, legal advice and vocational support, with interest representation playing a subordinate role.

In contrast to the pluralist ideal of autonomous organization, interest group activity in post-communist society conforms to the exchange model. Instead of representing an alternative form of social organization to the market, this type of activity is merely an extension of the market. It is questionable whether a system of interest representation constituted on these lines can serve the classical function of mediation between society and the state in public policy. Loosely constituted groups of the entrepreneurial type may lack the requisite internal cohesion and discipline to bind their members to policy bargains on corporatist lines, and it is to this aspect of group activity that we now turn.

6   Organized interests, the state and public policy

In the introduction, we saw how systems of interest representation are embedded in employment and labour market relations. Corporatist systems emerge out of interaction between employer and employee, structured through stable networks of exchange between employers' associations and trade unions. As exchange transactions intensify, employment relations cease to be private economy arrangements, becoming institutionalized in the public domain (Crouch 1993: 30). Accordingly, organized interests broaden the scope of their activities. If they are able to enter the political arena, their interaction develops into a network of 'generalised political exchange' (Crouch 1993: 3, 53; Marin 1990b; Traxler 1990), facilitating their incorporation into the public policy process. Corporatism thus goes hand in hand with institutionalized employment relations entrenched either in law, as in Germany, or in mutual agreement between employers' associations and trade unions as in the Scandinavian countries.

Democratization and market transitions in east/central Europe coincide with a shift in the west away from institutionalized systems of employment relations. Economic globalization and technological change place a premium on company flexibility, with industrial relations subject to transitional tendencies towards decentralization and deregulation. The pace of change has been subject to considerable cross-national variation. The paradigm case of de-institutionalization is the United Kingdom, where single-employer bargaining is now endemic (Millward et al. 1992), whilst at the opposite end of the spectrum, in the corporatist heartland of Scandinavia, institutional entrenchment has proved resistant to wholesale change. Despite modest concessions to company autonomy, multi-employer bargaining remains the norm (Wallerstein et al. 1997: 379–98), with liberalization subject to the surveillance of powerful employers' associations and centralized trade unions, a model of change characterized by 'centralized de-centralization' (Rehn and Viklund 1990: 311; Crouch 1994: 212). In Germany, as we saw in chapter 2, the post-Fordist revolution has been contained within traditional structures, with employers' associations and trade unions retaining a strong role, although there are strong pressures for more radical deregulation. Thus, despite cross-national variation, no country has been left untouched by these tendencies.

In chapter 2 it was argued that post-communist societies are unlikely to gravitate towards the type of institutionalized employment relations that provide the foundation for generalized political exchange on corporatist lines. As employment relations take shape in the course of market transition, there are strong indications that they are subject to precisely those forces of globalization and structural economic change that are driving the post-Fordist revolution in the west, and that decentralization and individualization are the dominant tendencies. In eastern Germany, we have seen, these tendencies appear in sharp relief, workplace regulations having been subverted by the dynamics of the post-communist economy, suggesting that this type of society is an inhospitable environment for corporatist interest mediation.

In the introduction I distinguished between the two faces of corporatism: as a system of interest mediation institutionalizing the social cleavage structure of capitalist society, and as a mode of policy-making incorporating the peak organizations of capital and labour into the policy process. The distinction is particularly revealing in the context of post-communist society. As a system of institutionalized class cleavages, corporatist *interest mediation* is unlikely to develop spontaneously in societies in which private economy relations are still too weak to generate a clearly defined pattern of social cleavages. The evidence of eastern Germany suggests that, although market transition is accompanied by a more differentiated society, its predominant characteristics are fragmentation, individualization and the absence of the broadly based, solidaristic class formations on which corporatism rests. One of the central arguments of this book is that configurations of economic interests reflect the structure of capital, employment relations and labour markets. With business interests reflecting the structure of capital – fragmented along the lines of corporate ownership, company size and profitability – and a similarly divergent spectrum of individual and collective interests in the labour market, the cleavage structure of post-communist society is hard to reconcile with the essentially bi-polar configuration of class interests postulated by the corporatist model of interest mediation.

Tendencies towards corporatist *policy-making*, on the other hand, reflect the intensity of state–society relations in the post-communist economic transformation. First, the state is architect of the economic order, creating the ground rules for the formation of capital through the privatization process. Secondly, the instability and underdevelopment of the post-communist economy intensify the engagement of the state in macro-economic management and structural policy (Bullmann and Schwanengel 1995: 194). Thirdly, the state is also called upon to manage the social consequences of economic transformation, balancing the conflict between economic discipline as a precondition of capital accumulation, and social peace as a prerequisite of democratic consolidation. In the absence of social foundations, however, corporatist policy-making is no more than a government strategy of institutional innovation, designed for ordering relations between state and economy and pre-empting social conflict by legitimizing transformation. It has been characterized variously as 'pre-emptive' or 'semi-corporatism' (Wiesenthal 1995c: 38–40; Stykow 1996: 1–4), or as 'tripartism without corporatism' (Reutter 1996).

Tripartism without corporatism

Across eastern Europe tripartite arrangements have been adopted by hard-pressed governments struggling for legitimacy in the face of the social tensions accompanying economic transformation (Héthy 1994). From its origins in Hungary in 1988, the model has been adopted in the Czech Republic, Slovakia, Bulgaria, Russia and Poland. Although subject to cross-national variations in the commitment of the parties to tripartite co-operation and in the results achieved, the institutional model varies little. Its centrepiece is a commission or council composed of representatives of government, the trade unions and business. Within this apparatus, the three partners conclude 'general agreements' governing a wide range of employment issues. Initially, these agreements focused on trade union rights and collective bargaining procedures, but, with the establishment of the ground rules of industrial relations, attention turned to the wider issues of wage regulation, social welfare provision and labour market support. Thus, whilst employment issues are at the centre of tripartism, the agreements often range much more widely across the public policy domain. However, whilst this form of tripartism bears a superficial resemblance to the corporatist model, the preconditions for the emergence of consolidated corporatist exchange are almost entirely absent.

The absence of social foundations is reflected in the organizational weakness of the social partners. Neither business nor the trade unions possess the requisite organizational strength and cohesion for the emergence of stable corporatist exchange. Business organization has hardly begun to enter the collective-bargaining arena from which corporatist exchange emerges, and its presence in tripartite institutions is often little more than symbolic. The organizational weakness of the trade unions is manifest in competition between rival union confederations, tenuous articulation between national headquarters and local branches, and weak membership ties. Organizational weakness undermines the unions' ability to sustain stable 'social contracts' with government. Identification with an unpopular government risks fragmentation and the loss of members to rival unions. Tripartite arrangements are thus susceptible to breakdown, consequent upon the withdrawal of trade unions for internal strategic reasons.

Eastern European tripartism is further weakened by the absence of the ideological bonds between trade unions and parties of the left which support corporatist relations in western Europe. Adopted for the most part by governments of the centre-right as a pragmatic manoeuvre for defusing social protest, tripartism reflects the weakness of party government (Waller 1994: 33; Myant 1994: 66). Lacking either social roots or a mass membership, governing parties are ill equipped to withstand the heavy demands which neo-liberal transformation strategies place upon their legitimacy. Retaining a mass membership base, trade unions provide the missing link with society. Excluded from the political arena, trade unions are in a position to mobilize opposition to government policy. Tripartism entails making policy concessions to the trade unions, but it also serves as a means of binding them to government policy, neutralizing their potential for opposition and securing social peace in the face of transformation conflicts. Governments thus find that the price of exclusion is higher than that of inclusion. Based largely on pragmatism, allied to a common commitment to an ill-defined conception of 'economic reform', relations between trade unions and government parties are tenuous, placing limits on the ability of the latter to 'take a free ride' on the tripartite principle (Wiesenthal 1995c: 38).

The stability of tripartite arrangements is also undermined by economic weakness. At the core of the corporatist bargain is a delicate trade-off, with the government offering policy concessions in return for restraint and discipline on the part of the trade unions. In practice, this trade-off is often undermined by sharply deteriorating economic performance, which constrains the ability of governments to fulfil their undertakings on incomes, employment and social policy. Tripartism is subject to frequent eruptions of conflict between governments treating their undertakings as no more than broad statements of intent, and trade union demands for the fulfilment of policy commitments. Conflict also arises over the scope of the arrangements, with trade unions complaining about the failure of government to include macro-economic policy in tripartite consultation (Héthy 1994: 324–5). Poland and Bulgaria exemplify the vulnerability of tripartism to periodic collapse following the withdrawal of the trade

unions (Thirkell et al. 1994: 113). The Russian experience further high-
lights the fragility of these kinds of agreement in the face of economic
weakness. Here, tripartism is merely symbolic, with government making
rhetorical commitments to social guarantees in return for rhetorical
pledges of support from the trade unions.

Stable tripartism has been restricted to the Czech Republic, where the
relative success of economic reconstruction reduced the intensity of
policy conflicts between the market economy and social solidarity. Economic success generated political stability, with a confident centre-right
government enjoying strong public support for neo-liberal strategies of
transformation. Conforming to the government's agenda, the trade
unions restricted themselves to pragmatic bargaining over the balance
between market and state in a 'social market' economy on western
European lines. Whilst political stability reduced government dependency on the trade unions, a 'social coalition' retained expedient attractions in discouraging an alliance between the unions and the social
democratic opposition (Myant 1994: 81). This stable constellation of
relations was rudely disturbed by the economic and political crisis of
1997. The entry of the social democrats into government after the following year's election may herald a realignment of the trade unions towards
the centre-left. Ultimately, though, corporatist interventionism is incon-
gruent with the liberal bias in the Czech strategy for economic transformation.

The fragility of tripartism in eastern Europe, then, reflects its shallow
social roots and the organizational weakness of the social partners. As we
saw above, consolidated corporatist systems are the product of dense
networks of political exchange emerging out of sustained and repetitive
interaction between the partners over a prolonged period of time. In the
absence of this type of generalized political exchange, tripartite arrangements are little more than a pragmatic bargaining manoeuvre characterized by outbreaks of political conflict, and lacking stability and durability.

Institutions without social foundations: corporatism in post-communist Germany

The German case is indicative of the limitations of institutionalized
collective bargaining in post-communist society. Preceding the emergence of the private economy, the first wage rounds in 1990–1 were
characterized by the subordination of economic rationality to the political
imperative of preserving social peace, resulting in pay settlements that
outstripped productive capacity and ultimately contributing to the collapse of the east German economy. With privatization, employment

relations and wage-bargaining were subjected to the forces of the market. As we saw earlier in this book, however, the fragmented spectrum of employer and wage-earner interests characteristic of the advanced post-communist economy is difficult to reconcile with the German model of institutionalized labour market relations. The resultant strains were evident in the exodus from the employers' associations as the straitjacket of legally binding wage agreements weakened the incentive structure of collective organization, and in outbreaks of industrial conflict as the employers took unilateral initiatives to revise earlier settlements. Far from providing the seedbed for stable exchange between capital and labour, institutionalized employment relations degenerated to open conflict.

Against this inauspicious background, government attempts to co-opt the employers' associations and trade unions into the management of the crisis in the transformation process were abortive. The government's adoption of a corporatist strategy in place of an initially neo-liberal approach was precipitated by the collapse of the east German economy, which left the state bearing the financial burden of uneconomic wage settlements in the form of labour market support and structural economic assistance. The Solidarity Pact was the culmination of a protracted series of bilateral talks with business and trade union leaders designed to secure business commitments to investment in the east as a quid pro quo for trade union acceptance of flexibility and restraint in wage-bargaining, which the government hoped to secure through assurances of structural support for the industrial core of the economy.

The failure of the pact to meet government aspirations reflected the organizational weakness of employers' associations and trade unions to reconcile their *functional* role in macro-economic management with their *representational* vocation of interest advocacy on behalf of a demanding membership. Ultimately then, the structural weakness of collective actors led them to prioritize organizational self-interest over wider social interests, the logic of membership taking precedence over the logic of influence. Malfunction in the relationship amongst organized interests, the state and public policy can thus be seen in terms of Schmitter's distinction between the two faces of corporatism, which underlines the weakness of tripartite policy-making in a context in which corporatist interest mediation lacks the requisite social underpinnings.

Theories of the transformation process in post-communist Germany have focused on the way in which the unification strategy of institutional *transfer* quickly evolved into a strategy of institutional *adaptation* (Lehmbruch 1991; Czada 1994: 252; Ettl 1995: 53–4). Institutional transfer, it is argued, reflects the 'politics of continuity' – the tendency of government and collective actors to rely on established and familiar institutions in a bid for mastery over unfamiliar and uncertain policy issues. In the alien environment of post-communist Germany, however, institutional and procedural arrangements drawn from the old Federal Republic produce unintended and adverse outcomes. Rapidly becoming unsustainable, the politics of continuity gave way to a process of adjustment, seeking new solutions to new problems in a bid for system stability (Gissendanner 1996: 469). As we shall see, however, the search for new formulas for relations amongst the organized interests, the state and public policy has proved elusive.

The limitations of institutionalized collective wage-bargaining

Institutional transfer extended the 'economic constitution' of the Federal Republic to the new *Länder*, establishing the principle of free collective bargaining (*Tarifautonomie*) in which trade unions and employers' associations are designated as bargaining partners. This blueprint for the new order had strong attractions for both trade unions and employers' associations, offering them a firm organizational foothold in the east and countering tendencies towards company-level bargaining already evident in the west. In the early stages of economic transformation, however, with the economy in the hands of the Treuhand, and with unions and employers still grappling with the task of organization-building, the economic underpinnings of industrial relations were absent. In this new context, the German model resembled an *Apparat ohne Unterbau* (apparatus without infrastructure) with wage-bargaining characterized by uncertainty and chaos (Schmid and Tiemann 1992: 150; Siebert 1992: 125–6; Bispinck 1991: 114) and the bargaining partners 'flying on instruments' into unknown territory (*Frankfurter Allgemeine Zeitung*, 28 April 1990).

Uncertainty was heightened by the politics of unification. Industrial relations in post-communist society are highly politicized, bound up as they are with the distribution of the social costs and benefits of economic transformation (Myant and Waller 1994). In Germany, politicization was particularly intense, as *political* citizenship created popular demands for commensurate steps towards *social* citizenship, and inclusion in the 'economic democracy of consumers' in the west. Wage convergence with the west was seen as providing a 'perspective for the future', countering the wave of economic migration which accompanied unification. Employers' associations were acutely conscious of the wider political significance of the settlement, regarding it as part of the process of economic and social integration. Whilst there was no *formal* brief from the government, it was clear informally that 'a settlement giving people in the east a perspective on . . . western levels of affluence would make a very welcome political contribution' (interview: Nordmetall, Hamburg). Thus the pay-bargaining rounds of 1990–1 were marked by the primary of politics over economic rationality.

For the employers, the problem of politicization was compounded by organizational weakness. Explanations for the persistence of sectoral wage-bargaining in the Federal Republic in defiance of transnational trends towards decentralization have centred on the strength and cohesion of the employers in relation to the trade unions. The collective strength of highly co-ordinated and disciplined employers' associations, it is argued, offsets the advantages of company bargaining. In the early post-communist economy, as we saw earlier in this book, employer organization remained weak. In engineering, Gesamtmetall had rapidly established a presence in the new *Länder*, built on an alliance with east German managers in enterprises under Treuhand administration. Supported by public subsidy, free of the hard budget constraints of the private sector, and often sharing common perspectives with their employees, enterprise managers were fully supportive of wage convergence with the west. Thus the coalition of Treuhand company managers, alongside employers' associations based in the west and holding little or no commercial stake in the east German economy, was inevitably reflected in agreements unrelated to commercial reality.

Since the 1990 wage round preceded unification, negotiations were conducted by easterners, officials from the rapidly disintegrating GDR trade unions on the one side and managers of Treuhand companies on the other, both monitored by union and employer officials from the west (*Handelsblatt*, 18 June 1990; *Suddeutsche Zeitung*, 16/17 June 1990). By the following year, the integration of wage-bargaining within west German structures was complete. In line with standard practice in the Federal Republic, bargaining opened in the metals sector, with a regional pilot agreement for Mecklenburg. Bargaining was conducted by westerners, with the employers represented by a two-man team of top negotiators from Nordmetall in Hamburg, and the union by a similarly experienced pairing from IG Metall's regional headquarters also in Hamburg. Although formally independent, the negotiators were in regular contact with Gesamtmetall and the BDA on the one side, and IG Metall's Frankfurt headquarters on the other.

From the outset, Nordmetall had formed close links with its east German counterpart, and had merged with the engineering employers in Mecklenburg at an early stage. Top Nordmetall officials had forged personal bonds of friendship with leading managers in the east. Moreover, they were of a generation that had a deep emotional investment in

German unification. Highly experienced negotiators, with a national reputation and nearing the end of their careers, they regarded the negotiations as a 'master class' which would make a lasting contribution to unification (*Der Spiegel*, 10 June 1991). In reality, however, they faced the impossible task of reconciling economic rationality with the political imperative of a socially acceptable settlement. Insiders refer to a deep sense of disorientation amongst the employers, with little assistance from Gesamtmetall or BDA headquarters:

I've never witnessed such a sense of disorientation among my western colleagues . . . we sought guidance from the BDA and from Gesamtmetall . . . we asked what we should do . . . and they shrugged their shoulders and didn't give us an answer . . . they didn't know what to say. Everyone's clever in hindsight but at the time no one was prepared to offer us any advice. (Interview: Nordmetall, Schwerin)

Conscious of their 'political mission', the Nordmetall negotiators re-nounced adversarial bargaining methods, encouraged by indications in the previous year's settlement that IG Metall were ready for 'conditional co-operation' (*Handelsblatt*, 2 July 1990). Under these circumstances, the standard procedures of industrial relations were suspended (Kleinheinz 1992: 20):

We had to seek new ways, and to try not to be so obsessed by power-play as in western negotiations . . . the tone of the negotiations was different . . . there was a readiness on both sides to put forward proposals the other side might be prepare to accept . . . both sides were taking political responsibility for the future. (Interview: Nordmetall, Hamburg)

The political imperative of maintaining 'social peace' meant that the employers were unusually reliant on the co-operation of the traditionally combative IG Metall, and were thus inclined to take the conciliatory stance of the union at face value. Phased wage convergence with the west was a concept put forward by the employers as a means of moderating the union's opening bid for an immediate wage increase of around 70 per cent. The proposal having been readily adopted by IG Metall, negotiations centred on the timescale for convergence, and Nordmetall's insistence on provisions for a revision of the settlement in the event of adverse economic developments. The implementation of the 'revision clause', however, was conditional upon union agreement, leaving the employers reliant upon the continuing readiness of IG Metall to pursue a co-operative course.

Caught up in unification euphoria, and with the normal routines of industrial relations in abeyance, the employers' bargaining position was thus characterized by the absence of the normal commercial considerations (Ettl 1995: 61–70; Schmid and Tiemann 1992: 152–3).

Productivity assessments played little part in the negotiations. Although the employers reiterated a rhetorical commitment to the principle of productivity-based wage-bargaining, this remained a ritual with little bearing on their negotiating position (Ettl 1995: 78). Departure from the principle was justified with reference to the special circumstances of unification (*Frankfurter Allgemeine Zeitung*, 11 March 1991). Inevitably, then, the wage settlement of 1991 was subject to the dictates of politics over economic rationality, and reflected the organizational weakness of the employers.

Whilst the 1990 agreement had made only a modest contribution to narrowing the wages gap, the phased wage agreement (*Stufentarifvertrag*) of 1991 set wages at around 60 per cent of west German levels, with a schedule of annual increments leading to convergence by 1994. The exclusion of supplementary agreements over working hours, holiday payments and bonuses meant that *real* wages would still lie some 20 per cent below western levels, but with productivity at around one-quarter of that in the west, the agreement meant an explosion of unit labour costs. Together with the acceleration of the Treuhand's privatization programme, the first stage of wage convergence in spring 1991 triggered a massive wave of redundancy and unemployment, as newly privatized companies engaged on brutal rationalization measures in the attempt to balance wage costs and productivity. Some observers have pointed to 'an unspoken understanding between employers and unions to use high wages . . . as a vehicle for rationalization and modernization', relying on a parallel increase in productivity through investment and the rapid introduction of new technology (Jakobi et al. 1992: 226). Such a strategy was flawed in two important respects. First, the influx of investment fell short of expectations, reflecting the counterattractions of lower labour costs offered by Germany's neighbours in east/central Europe, Secondly, the low level of indigenous east German capital accumulation meant that the growth of the *Mittelstand* sector of SMEs was slow. Acutely undercapitalized, this sector relied heavily on wage flexibility for survival. The failure of employment-generating growth can thus be attributed in both these respects to labour market dynamics resulting from the wage convergence with the west.

The settlement was subjected to concerted attack from business leaders, economists and the media, characterized as 'an unprecedented massacre of the employers' negotiators' (*Der Spiegel*, 10 June 1991), 'the biggest scandal in recent economic history' (*Die Welt*, 20 May 1991) and 'the worst mistake of the whole unification process' (*Der Spiegel*, 26 November 1992). Criticism focused on the short timescale for wage convergence. With wages outstripping productivity, it was argued, the inevitable consequences were uncompetitiveness, company closure and unemployment. However, the neo-liberal critique went further than this, attacking the core principles of the German model of 'solidaristic' wage-bargaining. The argument that standardized wage structures based on sectoral pay agreements distort labour markets by inhibiting the emergence of productivity-related wage differentiation was a familiar one in the west German context. Wage flexibility, it was maintained, was even more urgent in the context of the very sharp variations in productivity characteristic of the post-communist economy (Donges 1991; Härtel 1991, cited Flockton and Esser 1992: 293).

The degeneration of institutionalized wage-bargaining

Once the consequences of the wage explosion became apparent following the 1991 settlement, employers' associations in the new *Länder* began to mobilize in a bid for structural adjustment in wage-bargaining. In the metals industry, their objectives were twofold: first to slow the tempo of wage convergence by invoking the 'revision clause' contained in the 1991 agreement; secondly to adapt sectoral bargaining to prevailing economic circumstances introducing hardship agreements allowing insolvent firms to pay below prevailing wage rates. Upon the rejection of this initiative by IG Metall, the employers' association in Sachsen took the unprecedented step of unilaterally renouncing the terms of the agreement. A two-week strike was finally resolved, with the mediation of Sachsen minister-president Kurt Biedenkopf, in a compromise formula which failed to meet either of the employers' main objectives. The re-negotiated agreement retained the principles of phased wage convergence, although with a modest extension to the timescale. Over the broader issue of wage flexibility, the new settlement did little to adapt the German model of sectoral wage-bargaining to the economic realities of the new *Länder*.

Whilst the Biedenkopf formula contained a hardship clause, implementation was subject to agreement between the collective-bargaining parties rather than company-level agreement as the employers advocated. This was a victory for IG Metall, which had steadfastly rejected the employer's bid to use the provision as a lever to prise open the system of sectoral pay-bargaining. Entangled in procedural complexity, and subject to trade union prerogative, the hardship clause reflects the institutional and cultural rigidities of German industrial relations. Far from resolving the conflict, it has itself become a source of contention. The reluctance of companies to disclose commercially sensitive information and conflicting interpretations of the terms of the clause make agreement elusive. The limitations of the formula from the employers' point of view are evident from the infrequency of its implementation. In 1993 the employers' negotiator estimated that 50 per cent of its members in the east would qualify for hardship agreements (*Handelsblatt*, 17 May 1993). In the first twelve months of its operation, only seventy-eight appeals were upheld (Koch 1995: 154).

Mutual recriminations amongst the employers at the conclusion of the 1993 dispute were indicative of employer disarray in wage-bargaining. Closely identified with the *Mittelstand*, and a longstanding critic of the association's large-firm bias, Gesamtmetall's president was particularly outspoken in his condemnation of the 'capitulation' of the regional negotiators in Sachsen. Employer solidarity is difficult to maintain in the face of the conflict between the paramount *Mittelstand* interest in flexibility and the interest of larger companies in industrial relations stability. The internal divisions exhibited by the employers contrast sharply with the relative cohesion of the trade unions. The capacity of IG Metall to resist the employers' initiative stemmed from an ability to mobilize its members, with unexpectedly strong support for industrial action evident in strike votes of over 80 per cent. Thus the balance of strength remained heavily tilted towards the trade unions, and industrial relations continued to exhibit the asymmetry characteristic of the immediate post-unification years.

The failure of the employers' initiative to adapt the architecture of collective wage-bargaining merely served to increase the strains upon the structure. Frustrated in their bid for flexibility in the institutional apparatus, firms increasingly look for escape routes of their own, either through company agreements negotiated with regional trade unions or by direct negotiation with the works council. Tendencies towards local bargaining, as we saw in chapter 4, have weakened the incentive structures of collective action in employers' associations and trade unions. Thus the breakdown of institutionalized wage-bargaining is inextricably bound up with the organizational decline of the collective actors, weakening the foundations for corporatist relations between organized interests, the state and public policy.

The role of the state

In the German model of industrial relations, the role of the state is restricted largely to the shaping of favourable background conditions through structural policy designed to promote employment, or through more direct measures of intervention geared to rectifying temporary disturbances in labour market stability. In the new *Länder*, by contrast, both structural and labour market policy have been subject to unprecedentedly heavy demands (Flockton and Esser 1992), with structural policy administered through large-scale regional aid programmes and massive labour market support. Never designed to deal with mass unemployment, the state's labour market instruments met the full force of the employment crisis of 1991–2.

Initially, both Gesamtmetall and IG Metall looked to the state to confront structural economic problems, sharing the view that the employment fallout of an uneconomic wage settlements should be absorbed by the Treuhand (*Handelsblatt*, 28 June 1990, 2 July 1990). As privatization gathered momentum, however, Gesamtmetall changed its position, arguing that the company could no longer bear the burden of employment support (*Frankfurter Allgemeine Zeitung*, 6 April 1991; *Handelsblatt*, 6 May 1991). To ensure successful privatization, the government was obliged to release new owners from their legal obligation to honour existing employment contracts. Newly privatized companies were able to compensate for high wages by brutal rationalization and massive cuts in the payroll. German labour law meant that the Federal Labour Office now assumed heavy responsibilities for redundant labour. Thus both employers and trade unions were able to transfer the consequences of uneconomic wage settlements to the state as part of 'the cost of German unity'.

Wage-bargaining in the immediate post-unification period thus exhibited one of the classic problems of collective action: the tendency of collective actors to externalize the negative consequences of their actions, transferring the costs to other actors. The economic consequences of the 1991 wage settlement thus fell upon the state, with the government obliged to take responsibility for the gulf between productivity and the spiralling wage costs. Effectively the state assumed the role of 'third bargaining partner' (Bialas 1994: 51), obliged by the politics of unification to underwrite the costs of agreements in which it had no part. It was the need to control the consequences of this breakdown in collective action that led the government to embrace corporatist strategy.

Corporatism and economic transformation

The foundations of corporatism in eastern Germany can be located in the shift from neo-liberalism to interventionism accompanying the crisis of economic transformation in 1991–2. Initially conceived in neo-liberal terms, transformation strategy rested on the optimistic assumption that, with privatization, the dynamism of the west German economy would provide the impetus for economic renewal in the east. Rapid privatization was seen both as the motor of economic transformation and as a means of extracting the state from the economy. It was accompanied, however, by extensive programmes of structural economic development designed to cushion the social consequences of privatization. Economic transformation was therefore characterized by a tension between neo-liberalism and interventionism.

The tension between market and state ran through the operations of the Treuhand. Privatization entailed restructuring enterprises prior to their disposal into the private economy, with an investment outlay of some DM 170 billion in its first four years of activity. In this role the Treuhand thus became a thinly disguised instrument of industry policy, torn between commercial and social considerations. Despite its priority on privatization, it was unable to prevent itself becoming engaged in the salvage of commercially unsaleable enterprises occupying a strategic position in the regional economy. Preserving 'industrial cores' meant the reprieve from liquidation of potentially viable concerns, and their placement under management holding companies, financed by public–private partnership, for restructuring pending disposal into the private sector.

Adopting a neo-liberal strategy of fast, market-oriented privatization, the government had initially attempted to insulate the Treuhand from the political sphere by granting it quasi-autonomous status, subject only to the supervision of the finance ministry. As the social costs of rapid privatization became apparent, however, conflicts between economic, social and political objectives increased in intensity, exemplified by the giant ship-building conglomerate on the Baltic coast around Rostock. Converted into a holding company (Deutsche Maschinen- und Schiffbau, DMS) pending privatization, this cluster of uneconomic enterprises at the heart of the regional economy was entangled in a complex web of issues and interests. Immediate privatization on market principles would have led inevitably to the breakup, rationalization and liquidation of large parts of the sector. Privatizing DMS intact, on the other hand, entailed massive inducements to buyers in the form of public subsidy (Heseler 1993).

In the face of these alternative strategies, the Treuhand and federal government were subject to intense political pressure from the minister-president and economics and finance ministers of Mecklenburg-Vorpommern (themselves members of the supervisory board of the Treuhand), and from IG Metall officials mobilizing their members behind demands for state support to guarantee the survival of the sector. In the resultant clash between economic and political objectives, business interests played a marginal role. In the regional employer confederation, DMS represented the largest member firm, but its interest in self-preservation was at odds with the interest of other members in a more market-oriented strategy for economic regeneration and a wider distribution of state support. Torn between the competing interests of its members, the confederation had little option but to abstain from adopting a position, despite the crucial importance of the issue for the future of the regional economy (interview: Nordmetall, Schwerin). After a long period of political wrangling, DMS was finally given a subsidized privatization at a cost of some DM 6 billion, a rescue operation which subsequently collapsed when one of the participants, the west German ship-building firm Bremer-Vulkan, itself went into liquidation.

A similar nexus of relations amongst organized interests, the state and public policy was replicated across eastern Germany. The minister-presidents of the eastern *Länder* represented a strong pressure group on the management board of the Treuhand, with Sachsen premier Kurt Biedenkopf the leading spokesman for regional industry policy. Although not formally represented on the board, trade union leaders had access to top Treuhand officials, with bilateral meetings increasing in frequency from early in 1992. Parallel pressure was exerted by the Christian Democratic parliamentarians representing the eastern *Länder*, culminating in a meeting with the chancellor in January of that year (Kleinfeld 1992: 95–8, 103; Karrasch 1995: 110). Concerted pressure from trade unions and *Land* governments led to the agreement between the Sachsen economics ministry and the Treuhand in May establishing the ground rules for the reprieve of key companies in the regional economy (IG Metall, Sachsen 1993: 65). Reflecting a progressive change in federal government thinking, the agreement signalled a shift in Treuhand policy, reinforcing its industry policy function.

Flanking Treuhand privatization was a barrage of measures embedded in the networks of intergovernmental relations comprising the German system of co-operative federalism. Supported by massive financial transfers from Bonn, the joint task programmes on regional economic development (Gemeinschaftsaufgabe Verbesserung der regionalen Wirtschaftsstruktur and Gemeinschaftswerk Aufschwung Ost) provided the infrastructure for intervention. The apparatus of regional economic development incorporated the social partners with *Land* and municipal administration. Thus the regional agencies established to co-ordinate the activities of local employment enterprises (Gesellschaften für Arbeitsförderung, Beschaftigung und Strukturentwicklung, ABS) served to open up labour market policy to trade union participation. In structural policy, regional development units (Brandenburg's Aufbaustab Potsdam; BASIS in Sachsen) brought together business, trade unions, municipal administrations and labour offices in a bid to orchestrate specialist expertise from different spheres of economic activity, and to encourage private finance for public investment. The focal point of intervention in the *Länder* was the strategy for preserving 'industrial cores', developed by IG Metall, and first adopted in Sachsen in 1992 following the Treuhand/ economics ministry agreements. Sachsen's ATLAS model, Treuhand Companies Selected by the State for Stabilization (Ausgesuchte Treuhandsunternehmen vom Land angemeldet zur Sanierung), opened up industry policy to corporatist participation, with the selection of companies for reprieve and the formulation of restructuring plans undertaken by management team made up of Treuhand representatives, *Land* government, IG Metall, the DGB and the employers (Karrasch 1995: 109–10; Krumbein 1992: 218–19; Kleinfeld 1992: 100).

The development of the ATLAS model and its replication across the new *Länder* were facilitated by a progressive shift in government transformation strategy. Against the backdrop of de-industrialization, neo-liberal expectations of self-generating economic growth appeared hopelessly optimistic. Economic crisis was accompanied by acute political tensions, with a mounting tide of popular protest in the east and a spiralling budget deficit causing increasing concern in the west. Weakened by coalition differences and under mounting criticism from within his own party, the chancellor was ill equipped to withstand the political pressures which a neo-liberal strategy of deflation and monetary discipline would inevitably have entailed (Sally and Webber 1994: 22–3). With the recognition that economic take-off was a longer-term project than initially envisaged, political considerations demanded a strategy for managing the immediate social consequences of transformation. This strategic reorientation was signalled by the chancellor in a speech in November 1992 pledging that 'firms that have not yet been restructured should not be allowed to go under' (*Der Spiegel*, 23 November 1992). Financial backing for corporate rescue, however, was conditional upon reciprocal undertakings on the part of the trade unions, a classical manoeuvre in corporatist crisis management.

A corporatist strategy of crisis management had the support of an 'advocacy coalition' of diverse composition. For some time the BDA had advocated a new forum for labour market co-ordination in the new *Länder*, to include federal government ministries, *Land* and municipal governments, regional labour offices and the social partners. On a larger scale, the BDI president had suggested a 'national pact' in which the social partners would set out their respective contributions to economic reconstruction in the east (*Handelsblatt*, 15 December 1992). In a reversal of its previous neo-liberal stance, the economics ministry had issued a call for a new programme of concerted action based on the 1960s–70s model of bargained wage restraint (Kleinfeld 1992: 90–1). The SPD opposition reiterated its earlier demand for a joint programme of action in the east, a proposal which was echoed in the demand of the east German CDU for a concerted programme of economic reconstruction. Moreover, by mid-1992, as we shall see below, regional programmes of neo-corporatist crisis management were already underway in a number of the new *Länder*.

Macro-corporatism: from Kanzlerrunde to Solidarity Pact

The German response to the crisis of post-communist economic transformation reflects a corporatist bias in its political economy, which has led some to label the Federal Republic as a 'neo-corporatist democracy' (Hancock 1989; Sally and Webber 1994). This characterization has to be treated with a degree of caution. Prior to unification, the German experience of macro-level corporatism was restricted to concerted action (*Konzertierte Aktion*) between 1967 and 1977, a largely deliberative body geared to consensus-building rather than the conclusion of binding agreements. Nevertheless, it indicates a potential for co-operation between the social partners in the interests of economic and social stability.

The economic summits convened by the chancellor from the earliest stages of the unification process bore a close resemblance to *Konzertierte Aktion*. In addition to the chancellor and key government ministers, these *Kanzlerrunde* included the Treuhand and Federal Labour Office, along with around forty top officials from the 'peak' organizations of the Federal Republic's main economic interests. Once *Land* governments were constituted in October 1990, the minister-presidents of the new *Länder* took their place at the table. Little more than a loosely constituted forum for orchestrating the socio-economic dimension of unification, the meetings were never endowed with the official recognition implied by a formal title. Denied decision-making powers, the central function of the group was limited to consensus-formation, promoting mutual understanding over the objectives of economic transformation and mediating the claims of competing social groups (Kleinfeld 1992: 82–5).

The conduct of the *Kanzlerrunde* reflected these limited purposes. With the agenda set by the chancellor, meetings consisted largely of government information briefings, participants responding with position statements. Proceedings assumed a somewhat more discursive format with the introduction of the economic recovery programme, Gemeinschaftswerk Aufschwung Ost, signalling a more interventionist orientation in government policy, and a marginal increase in the involvement of the social partners in the policy process – although the absence of consultation in the formulation of the programme, however, is indicative of the limitations of the *Kanzlerrunde* from a neo-corporatist perspective.

The reorientation of government policy from neo-liberalism to crisis management was accompanied by an intensification of corporatist inter-action. Although the *Kanzlerrunde* continued to meet, the core negoti-ations were now conducted in bilateral talks in the chancellor's office, with government meeting key leaders of the trade unions and business separately. Bilateral top-level talks (*Spitzengespräche*) on these lines were not new, having taken place sporadically over the previous two years. From September 1992, however, they became the centrepiece of Kohl's attempt to negotiate a Solidarity Pact – a programme of government action linked to definite commitments of support by the social partners. Negotiations were more frequent than in the *Kanzlerrunde*, with over forty meetings within six months. They were also more focused, with the government presenting participants with a programme of demands and concessions prepared in advance by the chancellor's office (Sally and Webber 1994: 27–35).

Corporatist exchange in the *Kanzlerrunde* and Solidarity Pact talks centred on three contentious issues of economic transformation; the Treuhand privatization regime, wages policy and the investment contri-bution of private sector business. Excluded from the Treuhand manage-ment board (*Verwaltungsrat*), the trade unions were able to use the *Kanzlerrunde* as an alternative forum in which to press for changes in the privatization regime. Critical of its subordination to narrow commercial criteria, IG Metall demanded that the Treuhand should be geared much more closely to regional structure policy and the social consequences of company liquidation. Initially meeting a strong rebuttal from both Treu-hand and the chancellor, these demands were subsequently recognized in a series of understandings accompanying the government's progressive shift from neo-liberalism to crisis management. Solidarity Pact negoti-ations centred on the government's offer to make provision in the Treu-hand budget for the rescue of companies at the industrial core of the regional economy, conditional upon commitments to wage restraint on the part of the trade unions.

In contrast to the *Kanzlerrunde*, where the trade unions were largely successful in relying on the principle of free collective bargaining (*Tar-ifautonomie*) to exclude the issue from the agenda, incomes policy was central to the Solidarity Pact negotiations. In return for government undertakings on privatization, the unions were enjoined to accept greater flexibility in relation to the 1991 wage agreements in the east, and to exercise wage restraint in the face of deepening recession in the west. With its standing in the east based on a reputation as a fighting union, and with a membership already in deep decline, IG Metall had little scope for manoeuvre, but resolved its dilemma by combining a commitment to restraint in the *west* with a reiteration of the non-negotiability of agreed formulas for wage convergence in the *east*. Anxious to conclude an agreement ahead of the upcoming federal elections, Kohl had little option but to accept this limited bargain with the union.

Corporatist bargaining with business was equally limited in its results. From mid-1991, *Kanzlerrunde* meetings were punctuated by conflict over the contribution of west German business to economic reconstruction in the east. Business associations responded to requests for patriotic commitment in investment decisions and order placement by pointing to the high wage costs arising from the 1991 pay round. Sharply critical of the government's paralysis in the face of economic crisis in the east, business leaders condemned the sterility of *Kanzlerrunde*, underlining their dissatisfaction with a protest boycott (*Deutsches Allgemeines Sontagsblatt*, 11 September 1992). Although such an interpretation was strenuously denied, the resignation of the BDI president in autumn 1992 was widely seen as the result of deteriorating relations between industry and government (*Handelsblatt*, 4/5 September 1992). Despite these disturbances, however, Solidarity Pact negotiations were brought to a conclusion, drawing on entrenched routines of reciprocity between government and business in the Federal Republic. Government demands were pragmatically calibrated to commercial realities and the readiness of business to fulfil their requirements. Insurance was asked to put up DM 1 billion in housing investment, with an equivalent investment requested from the banks to float holding companies to finance the rescue of unsold Treuhand firms. For west German industry, the tasks were to boost the order books of companies in the east through targeted purchasing, and to support the labour market through the creation of apprenticeships. For the most part, business groups acceded to this catalogue of demands, although without sanctions to compel their members to comply they were reluctant to undertake quantifiable commitments (Sally and Webber 1994: 30–5).

Thus the outcome of the Solidarity Pact was largely symbolic, the investment commitments of business amounting to little more than normal commercial activities. Equally, the trade unions had given little away. Their incomes policy in the west would in any event have been subject to the constraints of rising unemployment; in the east, IG Metall continued to resist the employers' initiative on wage flexibility. Agreements with business and the trade unions were part of a wider political entente including the *Land* government and the opposition SPD in a strategic agreement which bound the parties to government policy, reducing the potential for conflict in the run up to the 1994 federal elections. In real terms, the most significant outcome of the Solidarity Pact was the government's industry policy commitment to a massive injection of public finance into companies, most of which would subsequently be disposed of to the private sector over the next two years, in a classic example of corporatist crisis management.

Meso-corporatism: regional crisis cartels

Regional crisis cartels are a variant of meso-corporatism, in which sectoral interests are reinforced by territorial solidarity in the face of industrial decline. It is at its strongest where the regional economy is concentrated in a single sector, linking the economic future of the region with the survival of the industrial core. A common interest in the preservation of the industrial core provides the focal point for cartels between trade unions, management and the *Land* government, transcending industrial relations issues and political partisanship. Crisis cartels typically perform three main functions: formulating survival strategies for the sector; concluding agreements over the distribution of the costs of industrial restructuring; and lobbying federal government for financial support. This type of meso-corporatist activity is most likely to emerge where there are strong regional networks of organized interest activity with access to a corresponding tier of subnational government. The German federal system provides optimal conditions for regional corporatism, as can be seen from the experience of cartel formation in the crisis-torn steel and shipbuilding sectors in the 1970s and 1980s (Esser and Vath 1985).

Interlocking interests between sectors and regions are endemic to post-communist economic transformation, the geographical concentration of industry in the socialist planned economy leaving a legacy of single-sector dependency. The syndrome was very pronounced in the new German *Länder*, with a giant chemicals complex around the Buna-Leuna region of Sachsen-Anhalt, ship-building in the coastal regions of Mecklenburg-Vorpommern, lignite mining around Cottbus in Brandenburg and machine-building in the Chemnitz region of Sachsen. Crisis cartels were thus a response to collapse of leading industrial sectors which stripped out the core of the region's economy.

Interest mediation and cartel formation reflected the structure of regional industry. The vast financial implications of restructuring gigantic industrial conglomerates in chemicals and ship-building required cartel formation at federal level. Sachsen-Anhalt's chemicals steering committee (Lenkungsausschub Chemie) thus included federal government ministers, Treuhand officials and the national chairman of IG Chemie along with the *Land* government. Similarly in Mecklenburg-Vorpommern, the rescue of ship-building was planned by the supervisory board of a holding company that included west German shipyard bosses and a banker alongside IG Metall officials based in neighbouring Hamburg. Only after key decisions had been made were programmes opened up to *local* economic actors. In the other *Länder*, where industrial concentration was less intense, corporatist interest mediation had a stronger regional dimension. In Brandenburg, the future of lignite mining was the remit of a *Land* government committee incorporating trade unions and enterprise management. Regional cartel formation was strongest, however, in Sachsen. Less monolithic than chemicals and ship-building, and with its pre-communist origins in *Mittelstand* ownership, machine-building was more easily privatized without recourse to massive federal government intervention. Nevertheless, Treuhand privatization resulted in large-scale de-industrialization, and left the sector in structural crisis. Regional corporatism in Sachsen took the form of an interest coalition between IG Metall and the *Land* government lobbying the Treuhand and Bonn for a change in the privatization regime, emphasizing the need to buttress the regional economy and labour markets against de-industrialization.

Underlying regional crisis cartels was an alliance between employers and trade unions, which, as we saw in chapter 2, emerged as a response to the unusual constellation of interests and organizational resources characteristic of post-communist economic transformation. For managers in Treuhand companies facing privatization, the organizational resources of the trade unions, and their capacity for mobilizing popular protest against Treuhand policy made them a valuable ally, especially in view of the weakness of industry and employer organization in Sachsen. IG Metall was strategically placed to form the interest association of Chemnitz machine-builders (Interessenverband Chemnitzer Maschinenbau, ICM), a cross-class interest cartel which, as we saw earlier, embodied the unusual interest spectrum in the post-communist economy. In contrast to other new *Länder*, where the union's apparatus was annexed to a neighbouring western region, the Sachsen IG Metall was endowed with organizational independence, strengthening its potential as a regional actor (interview: IG Metall, Bezirksleitung Dresden).

The organizational weakness of the employers was reflected in the structure of regional corporatism in Sachsen, built on an axis between IG Metall and the *Land* government. Far from being a forum for interest *mediation*, the Sachsen model was based on an interest *alliance*, the purpose of which was to put pressure on federal government to take responsibility for regional industry and labour markets, and to bear the larger part of the cost burden. A regional interest coalition was of political utility to both parties. For the Christian Democratic *Land* government under Kurt Biedenkopf, it was a pragmatic strategy for managing the electoral fallout from de-industrialization, transferring the political costs to federal government (Krumbein 1992: 216). For IG Metall, partnership with the *Land* government played a counterpart to its militancy in wage-bargaining, legitimizing and externalizing the costs of its high-income policy by transferring labour market responsibilities to federal government. The social partnership did not, however, encompass wage-bargaining, and IG Metall was therefore able to make policy gains without concessions to private-sector employer demands for pay restraint.

Relations between trade unions and the *Land* government were governed by a pragmatic willingness to compromise. Unencumbered by the neo-liberal inclinations of an FDP (Freie Demokratische Partei, Free Democratic Party) coalition partner, the Biedenkopf government was receptive to the interventionist policy initiatives of IG Metall. The pragmatism of the state premier was matched by the union, with official ideology playing little part in the flexible programme of the leadership: 'we're very undogmatic in our engagement with concrete issues . . . we have to be able to develop alternatives' (interview: IG Metall, Bezirksleitung Dresden). Thus, the union was flexible in its industry policy strategy, embracing private investors and banks alongside the Treuhand and the *Land* government (Krumbein 1992: 214, 217).

Union strategy was to build a broad-based coalition of interests with 'a creative dialogue geared to solving problems through collective policy initiatives' (interview: IG Metall, Bezirksleitung Dresden). The strategy was not unsuccessful: 'on a number of issues, the *Land* government has taken up ideas that the trade unions have advocated for some time' (interview: DGB, Landesbezirk Sachsen). Despite simmering wage conflicts, business organizations embodied the ethos of social partnership: 'there's a mutual exchange of views . . . that's why we're such close *Gesprächspartnern* [partners in dialogue]' (interview: LSI). Thus, despite its political character and asymmetrical composition, Sachsen's corporatist experiment was not without substance. It provided a framework for a creative dialogue in industry and labour market policy in which IG Metall initiatives were taken up by the *Land* government and subsequently adopted as a model for the other new *Länder*.

Sachsen shows that in a new political system and under the circumstances of economic transformation, neo-corporatist relations are less dependent on partisan affinities than in the west. Partisanship is less entrenched in the post-communist polity: 'we're open to a wider range of contacts than in the west' (interview: IG Metall, Bezirksleitung Dresden); 'institutions are less rigidly structured; ideology is not so ingrained' (interview: DGB, Landesbezirk Sachsen-Anhalt). Thus, in Sachsen-Anhalt, a Christian Democrat-led coalition made a rapid transition to corporatist crisis management, drawn into increasingly close contact with the trade unions through the structural collapse of the regional economy: 'initially the *Land* government adopted traditional conservative strategies . . . consultation came later when it became clear that these formulas didn't work' (interview: DGB, Landesbezirk Sachsen-Anhalt). However, whilst relations are not governed by partisanship, variations in the balance and intensity of regional corporatism nevertheless reflect political circumstances. In Brandenburg, a Social Democrat-led coalition including the citizens' group/environmental party Alliance '90 generated a distinctive pattern of corporatist relations, including the churches and environmental groups alongside economic interests in a broader conception of 'social partnership' than found elsewhere.

The limits to corporatist relations under the centre-right government were indicated by the experience of Thüringen, where an unstable Christian Democrat-led coalition was slow to adopt the sort of interventionist industry policy that served as the foundation of concerted action elsewhere. Alienation between the *Land* government and the social partners led to the formation of a common front between trade unions and the regional employer confederation, united in condemnation of government passivity. Taking its cue from Bonn after the Solidarity Pact of 1993, the *Land* government stepped up its engagement in regional industry and convened a series of 'economic summits' with unions and employers, but initiatives still lagged behind other *Länder*. Largely excluded from the policy arena, trade unions in Thüringen made more frequent use of mass mobilization as a means of bringing the government to the negotiating table.

The impact of partisanship was also evident in the changing dynamics of regional corporatism consequent upon turnover in party government after the *Land* elections of 1994. With centre-right governments replaced by CDU/SPD coalitions in Thüringen and Mecklenburg-Vorpommern, and by an SPD-led administration in Sachsen-Anhalt, the trade unions enjoyed a more sympathetic hearing: 'social democrats and trade unions think on the same lines in structure policy and over the consequences of privatization' (interview: IG Metall, Verwaltungsstelle Magdeburg; also interviews: DGB, Landesverband Mecklenburg-Vorpommern; IG Metall, Verwaltungsstellen Schwerin, Erfurt). Conversely, the employers found access more difficult with Social Democrats occupying key ministries (interview: LVSA). Partisanship is not the only political variable conditioning the policy process. Political stability is also a factor, with corporatist relations flourishing alongside a stable, single-party majority government with a clearly formulated strategy for regional development. Sachsen, and to a lesser extent Brandenburg, fulfilled these conditions. In Thüringen, by contrast, with an unstable government lacking a regional development strategy, corporatist relations failed to take root. In Sachsen-Anhalt, employer and business groups ascribed difficulties in their relations with the minority Social Democrat-led coalition formed in 1994 to political instability and policy uncertainty (interviews: LVSA; IHK, Magdeburg).

The dynamics of regional corporatism

Despite variations in the intensity of regional corporatism across the new *Länder*, there is a striking uniformity in the procedural and behavioural conventions of interlocution. The diffusion of the procedural norms was closely bound up with the process of institutional transfer. In large part, 'normative transfer' followed the transfer of personnel from the Federal Republic. As we saw in chapter 5, most leading officials in trade unions and business associations were westerners. Equally, in the higher echelons of public administration, some 57 per cent were civil servants seconded from similar appointments in the west (Glaeßner 1996: 192). Western actors brought with them the procedural and behavioural norms learned at the interface of public administration and organized interests in the Federal Republic. To be sure, the diffusion of these norms across the east–west divide in public administration was initially hesitant: 'the procedures and thought processes which are ingrained in a western political culture had to be learned' (interview: DGB, Landesbezirk Berlin-Brandenburg). Nevertheless, regional networks of corporatist exchange were established relatively quickly at both the bureaucratic and political levels.

At the political level, there are a range of forums for exchange between economic interest organizations and the *Land* government. Multilateral summits (*Spitzengespräche*) between top interest group leaders and the government occur quarterly, replicating the 'concerted action' formula of the *Kanzlerrunde*. These 'economic summits' are augmented by periodic bilateral talks between government and (respectively) the DGB and employers' confederation. At the political level, talks range over a very broad issue agenda, 'from vocational training to European policy and relations with the Czech Republic' (interview: LSI, Dresden), although the focus is usually on labour market, industry and economic policy issues. Between these set-piece summits, interest group chief executives meet economics ministers, minister-presidents and civil servants (*Staatssekretäre*) at regular (typically monthly) intervals on an informal basis to discuss more specific issues.

The most intensive interaction, however, takes place at the 'working level' of routine contact between senior interest group officials and section heads (*Abteilungsleiter*) in *Land* ministries. This sort of routine exchange is uniformly reported by trade union and employers' association officials across all five new *Länder*, and is seen as the bedrock of their relationship with the *Land* government. Informal dialogue with officials takes place on a weekly or even daily basis, providing channels for the exchange of information and views, and promoting a co-operative approach to routine policy-making. Interest group officials rate this kind of exchange more highly than formal representation in the committee apparatus of *Land* ministries (interviews: IG Metall, Verwaltungsstelle Magdeburg; DGB, Landesbezirk Mecklenburg-Vorpommern; LSI; Nordmetall, Schwerin).

A high level of policy expertise in most economic interest groups means that dialogue is conducted as between policy specialists, rather than between policy-maker and lobbyist. Technocratic exchange is largely independent of partisanship, and helps to offset difficulties arising from partisan conflict between interest groups and politically unsympathetic governments:

Political control over the [economics] ministry has changed, but we still have a dialogue at the working level. (Interview: Nordmetall, Schwerin)

We try to maintain co-operation on specialist issues [*Sachfragen*] . . . basically its about promoting the region, and we try to keep these issues above party politics. (Interview: IHK, Magdeburg)

Exchange between the *Land* government and economic interests, then, consists of a multiplicity of interactions at both the political and working levels, acquiring a quasi-institutional status. Embracing a wide range of policy issues, it is characterized by a technical style of interlocution, with the capacity to transcend partisanship. In all these respects, relations correspond closely to the concept of generalized political exchange in corporatist theory.

Organized interest and political parties

The organic linkages between organized interests and political parties that lie at the core of the classical model of corporatist interest mediation are missing from post-communist society. Party systems reflect the diversity and fragmentation of society. In the absence of socially structured partisanship, electoral choice is structured by the issues surrounding economic transition or the populist appeal of party leaders. The electoral profile of the parties in eastern Germany in an inversion of expectations derived from the west. In the first elections after unification, the Christian Democrats polled over 60 per cent of the manual-worker vote. Despite a tendency towards more 'normal' patterns of group partisanship in 1994, the centre-right continued to exercise attractions in this quarter until the collapse of the CDU vote in 1998. The Social Democrat electorate exhibits no clear profile, its electorate being distributed across the social scale. The experience of most western democracies suggests that socially structured partisanship is subject to long-term secular decline, and that residual traces of class voting are a legacy of a past from which post-communist society is irretrievably cut off.

The political profile of the parties in the new *Länder* also lacks sharpness of definition, their amorphous social composition operating against clear ideological positions. Political identities have not yet begun to crystallize, with ideological eclecticism particularly marked in the CDU. Despite initially espousing the western party's social market economy leitmotif, the CDU in the east harbours a strong orientation towards economic interventionism, although it displays more conservative inclinations on social issues. In the SPD it is possible to identify two broad cultural groupings. Those with a background in the church and civil rights movements out of which the party emerged embrace a liberal humanism that sits ill with the more conservative and pragmatic perspectives of more recent recruits drawn from the technical intelligentsia (Padgett 1996).

The axes between the trade unions and the SPD are much weaker than in the west. 'Relations are more flexible, looser, because ideological identities are not so hard and fast' (interview: IG Metall, Verwaltungsstelle Erfurt). First, the orientation of the majority of their members towards the centre-right parties leads most unions to resist too close an alignment with the SPD. Secondly, the bias of the party towards the technical intelligentsia is not conducive to strong union links. Thirdly, the policy orientation of the trade unions towards the rescue of the industrial giants at the core of the regional economy is at odds with the SDP's inclination towards promoting SMEs in the service sector. 'The SPD sees Magdeburg as a *Dienstleistungszentrum* [service provision centre]; it doesn't care about the problems of the industrial cores' (interview: IG Metall, Verwaltungsstelle Magdeburg). Finally, anxious to disassociate itself from GDR socialism, the SPD has deliberately renounced organizational activity in the works councils in which party–union relations are based in the west. In the absence of strong ties to the SPD, trade unions sometimes lean towards the ex-communist PDS. With its strategic objective of permeating civil society to compensate for its political isolation, the PDS places a priority on relations with organized interests. Although the DGB is strongly against co-operation, the PDS has been able to establish relations in particular sectors by mobilizing its membership within the union. Thus the union of trade, banking and insurance workers, HBV, recognizes the PDS and SPD equally, whilst the PDS also has links with the teachers' union (GEW). The public sector union (OTV) is sympathetic in some regions, as are some IG Metall regional offices.

Organized business is similarly remote from the centre-right parties: 'party loyalties are less ingrained . . . there's less fear of talking to people across party lines' (interview: Nordmetall, Schwerin); 'There's little connection between the *Verbände* [associations] and the parties . . . in the west it's often quite a close relationship . . . here it's virtually non-existent' (interview: LVSA). The CDU is 'rather distant from the thinking of business in the east' (interview: LSI). Its business auxiliary organizations have only a tenuous presence in the new *Länder*. Its economic council (*Wirtschaftsrat*) is centrally administered from Bonn, whilst the middle-class association (*Mittelstandsvereinigung*) is weak. For their part, business group officials emphasize the importance of remaining above partisanship: 'I have talks with the *Mittelstandsvereinigung* and with the economic committees [*Wirtschaftsgremien*] of the FDP; but I'm not bound to a party . . . that's a source of strength' (interview: UV Sachsen-Anhalt). Professional associations are also more distant from party politics. Less conservative than in the west, the professions are less closely tied to the centre-right parties: 'the FDP provides a sort of political home for doctors . . . but they divide fairly evenly between the parties' (interview: NAV-VB, Sachsen). Across the associational order, an aversion to partisanship is explained as a reaction against the role of the party in the previous regime.

Organized interests, then, are less politicized than in the west. Although at leadership and functionary levels interest groups have links to their 'political allies', the absence of common social roots means that the relationship is peculiarly inorganic. Weak partisanship and blurred political identities mean that there is more potential for cross-partisan alliances of the sort that we have seen operating in regional corporatism. On the other hand, corporatist structures lack the solid foundations provided by entrenchment in the overlapping networks of party–interest group relations. In an open political market, relations remain opportunistic and pragmatic, with temporary, ad hoc alliances rather than the stable and persistent patterns of exchange characteristic of the corporatist model. Moreover, without the legitimation provided by partisan alignments, economic interests will tend to remain outsiders in the political process, the associational order remaining subordinate to politics and marginal to the parliamentary arena.

Conclusion

Although continuity with the Federal Republic provided a stable foundation for wage-bargaining in the immediate post-unification period, institutional transfer backfired in a number of important respects. A pervasive politicization meant that economic rationality was subordinated to the politics of unification. Subsequent settlements geared to wage convergence with the west proved unsustainable under deteriorating economic circumstances. Organizational weakness undermined the capacity of employers' associations to re-negotiate the deal, reducing their appeal for employers who were better able to exploit favourable labour market conditions through company-level bargaining. The role of the state in labour market support allowed the bargaining partners to externalize the negative consequences of their actions, leaving the state to bear the burden of uneconomic wage settlements – a classic dysfunction of collective action. The response of the state was to fall back on corporatist solutions, but the failure of the Solidarity Pact merely served to underline the unsustainability of corporatism without social foundations.

The centrality of the state in post-communist economic transformation intensifies interaction between private interests and the public policy process. Corporatist arrangements offer a means of linkage between the two domains, increasing the repertoire of techniques for managing the transformation process. Schmitter's distinction between the two faces of corporatism, however, indicates its limitations in post-communist society. In the absence of the institutionalized social cleavages that form the bedrock of corporatist *interest mediation*, tripartite systems of *policy-making* lack social foundations. Little more than an attempt by hard-pressed governments to co-opt economic elites to the public policy process, the eastern European experience indicates the shallowness and instability of tripartism without corporatism.

Post-communist Germany shares some of the characteristics of this syndrome. Macro-corporatism reflected the political economy of the Federal Republic more than social relations in the east. This is not to say that eastern interests were not represented. An interest alliance of *Land* government and trade unions lobbied hard for federal government support for collapsing regional economy. *Kanzlerrunde* and Solidarity Pact negotiations, however, were conducted along the lines of east–west resource dependency rather than bargaining between capital, labour and the state characteristic of the corporatist model. The outcome also failed to conform to corporatist expectations. In the Solidarity Pact, government undertook to underwrite industry policy without reciprocal wage concessions by the trade unions or significant investment commitments on the part of business.

Narrower in scope and less dependent on broadly based social interest, meso-corporatism may be better adapted to post-communist society. In the German case, the regional variant of meso-corporatism flourished alongside industry and labour market programmes administered within the intergovernmental networks of co-operative federalism. With their organizational structures running parallel to the federal system, trade unions and employer confederations made ready partners for *Land* government. Far from emerging from the interplay of *competing* interest, however, regional crisis cartels were based on a *common* interest in preserving industrial cores and promoting the regional economy. Meso-corporatism may therefore be seen as a situational response to the upheaval of economic transformation, reflecting also the transfer to the new *Länder* of procedural and behavioural norms learned in the west. The weakness of institutionalized industrial relations that we observed in the previous chapters casts some doubt on the sustainability of corporatist exchange as a formula for a rational economic development in post-communist society.

Conclusion

This book began by outlining a number of hypotheses, generated from group theory, concerning the sort of associational order we might expect to see emerging from post-communist society. Group theory locates the origins of association in the issues and cleavages arising in economic life, with interest group configurations reflecting the structure of capital, employment relations and labour market dynamics. Post-communist societies in the early stages of market transition, it was suggested, were insufficiently differentiated to generate associational activity on pluralist lines. Whilst market transition could be expected to break up the monolithic structures of communist society, it was unlikely to generate the sharply defined cleavages and cohesive social formations that gave birth to associational activity in industrial society. Instead, I postulated a pervasive process of social dealignment and the emergence of rather fluid and atomized societies in which the conditions for interest group formation would be singularly unfavourable.

With politics and society in east/central Europe still in flux, the outline of associational order has yet to emerge in sharp relief. Nowhere have we found even the semblance of a stable, fully functioning interest group system. In some countries, of course, interest group formation is prejudiced by the economic instability and chaos accompanying market transition. Elsewhere it is retarded by the slow pace of political and economic transformation, which leaves society relatively undifferentiated, with an economic elite dominated by a reconstituted nomenklatura and a few successful commercial magnates coexisting uneasily with an impoverished mass. Even in the 'leading' post-communist countries like the Czech Republic, Hungary and Poland, where market transition and democratic consolidation are most advanced, emergent socio-economic structures are unconducive to associational collectivism.

Privatization, it has been argued, has not generated a clearly defined structure of capital ownership. Significant parts of the state sector have been either left untouched, or merely subject to commercialization under the ownership of state investment funds. The widespread form of voucher privatization leads to a dispersed distribution of capital and a weak property structure which retards class formation. Privatization by direct sale, on the other hand, is often subject to foreign acquisition, the resultant domination of the post-communist economy by international capital being reinforced by direct foreign investment. Indigenous capital is restricted largely to the small-firm sector, where rapid privatization and new business start-ups have led to a proliferation of activity. This hybrid structure of capital ownership is reflected in the pluralistic diversity of business organization.

Employment relations vary widely across east/central Europe, reflecting the diversity of economies in transition. In companies where privatization has left pre-existing management structures intact, the communist legacy of repressive paternalism remains strong, and role differentiation is ill defined. Economic transformation tends to generate alliances across class lines, with a common front between managers and workers sharing common interests in company survival and perceiving themselves as victims of system change. Where ownership relations are more sharply defined, and especially in companies under foreign ownership, industrial relations are characterized by decentralization, managerial autonomy and individual pay contracts. This is not a model of employment relations that can be expected to generate the sort of collective group interests and identities on which the associational order rests.

The characteristics and tendencies we have observed in the economies of east/central Europe are even more pronounced in eastern Germany's *advanced* post-communist society. Whilst the upheaval of market transition is now receding, there is little evidence of the emergence of the stable patterns of economic interdependency that promote collective association. Despite – or perhaps because of – the rapidity and depth of market transition, socio-economic relations are marked by fragmentation, individualization and the absence of the social infrastructures that support collective action. Economic transformation in eastern Germany, of course, has coincided with far-reaching changes in economic life in the west. The response to inertia in the German model has taken the form of 'restructuring from below' in an attempt to open up the parochialism of the insider system of corporate governance to the influences of the global economy, and to break free of the network of rules governing the factory floor and wage-bargaining arena. As we have seen, these tendencies are greatly accelerated by the structure of capital and labour markets in the east.

The German case suggests that polarization between large- and small-scale capital is endemic to the post-communist economy. The accumulation of indigenous capital is slow. Privatization left the overwhelming majority of large companies in west German hands, with only a substratum of small and medium-sized firms, created through reprivatization and management buyouts, under indigenous ownership. Although new business start-ups have proliferated, their growth is retarded by capital shortages and reliance on credit. Concentrated in the service sector, food processing and construction, indigenous capital is weak in the manufacturing sectors in which German employer organization has its centre of gravity. Polarized between large west German companies and small indigenous entrepreneurs, the structure of the post-communist economy is thus unconducive to the sense of co-operative interdependence that binds collective business organization together. As we saw in the introduction, the polarization of the corporate landscape between large and small firms operates against the collective definition of corporate interests. Without a strong *Mittelstand* to mediate the interests of large and small firms, business organization lacks cohesion and unity. The diversity of the corporate landscape in post-communist society is reflected in interest conflicts that undermine the foundations of organizational activity. Economic transformation itself generates interest conflicts, as we saw in the case of the Rostock ship-builders, between competing models of privatization. More enduring, however, are those conflicts arising out of the structure of capital. Geared primarily to the large-company sector in which their centre of gravity is located, employers' associations are generally unresponsive to demands for flexibility articulated by small and medium-sized concerns.

The proliferation of small firms makes the post-communist economy unfavourable territory for trade union organization. Trade unions draw strength and solidarity from mass employment in large-scale industrial plants The deconcentration of employment into small firms militates against the formation of the collective identities and interests on which trade union organization rests. Labour movement solidarity is also undermined by the fragmented spectrum of employee interests arising from heterogeneous segmented labour markets. Earning capacity and security of employment are subject to sharp variation with income differentials wider than in western Germany, reflecting the sharp unevenness of productivity and profitability between sectors and firms. The problem is compounded by conflicts between wage-earners and the unemployed. In post-communist society, the 'wages–employment dilemma' is a central issue of economic reconstruction, sharpened by the scale of unemployment. The resultant fragmentation of individual and collective interests undermines institutionalized forms of employment relations, accelerating tendencies towards decentralization and deregulation.

The persistence of relatively stable industrial relations in western Germany reflects a capacity for bargained adjustment in the face of economic change. The challenge of globalization has been met at least in part by employers and trade unions collaborating to exploit the scope for flexible adjustment in works council bargaining. Amongst employers in the west, however, there is a growing perception that this sort of defensive adaptation has exhausted its potential, and they are looking for more offensive strategies. In the post-communist economy, tendencies towards adaptation from below are exacerbated by the commercial pressures on insolvent firms in the small-company sector, and are exhibited in abstinence from employer-association membership and the prevalence of in-house wage agreements that undercut sectoral pay settlements. Institutionalized collective bargaining, it may be concluded, is too inflexible to stand up to the pressures generated by a developing post-communist economy. With variations in productivity and profitability reflected in fragmented labour markets, industrial relations are difficult to contain within centralized structures. Employers' associations and trade unions are buckling under the competing pressures of function and representation, unable to reconcile their role in an institutionalized system of collective bargaining with the imperative of representing the broad spectrum of business interests found in post-communist society. Sensitive to local variations in productivity, profitability and labour markets, company-level industrial relations are more attuned to the more differentiated landscape of the post-communist economy than the corporatist model of institutionalized collective bargaining. The emerging pattern of employment relations in eastern Germany correspond much more closely to the fluidity and decentralization of the pluralist model.

The professional groups that have been examined here were unusual in generating indigenous organizational activity in the aftermath of the collapse of the GDR. Group mobilization focused upon key issues: restructuring health care in the case of doctors; the recognition of qualifications in the case of engineers. Once these issues were resolved, however, neither of these groups was sustainable, and both were assimilated into the professional life of the Federal Republic. Associational activity amongst the professional strata lacks social and cultural foundations. Professionals in medicine and engineering have the transferable skills to adapt to a market environment; the commercialization of the professions, however, presents many of them with the unfamiliar challenge of private practice. For east German professionals, without the ethos of their counterparts in the west, exposure to the commercial rigours of private practice generates a competitive individualism that is deeply antithetical to group solidarity.

The evidence presented in this book suggests that the differentiated spectrum of interests in post-communist society is difficult to contain within unitary structures of interest representation. The kaleidoscopic mosaic of business organization found in the countries of east/central Europe is indicative of the difficulties involved in reconciling the cleavages between state and private sectors, domestic and foreign capital, and large and small firms. Within the competitive mêlée of capital clubs and business circles, no organizational design is discernible. Sectoral or trade associations are almost unknown, and most large associations are generalist in character. Region exerts a stronger force as the foundation of business organization than sector, reflecting the persistence of regional networks inherited from the communist economy. Confederations, where they exist, are loosely constituted, enlisting individual company membership alongside their affiliated associations. In the trade unions organizational fragmentation is endemic, with bifurcation between old and new unions compounded by political differences and personal rivalries. Squeezed between a proliferation of craft and occupational unions on the one hand and general unions on the other, industrial unions are weak, whilst the particularism of enterprise activity has emasculated the confederations. Thus the organizational principles of centralization and articulation are entirely alien to the post-communist labour movement.

Characterized by hierarchy and order, the institutional design of economic interest groups in eastern Germany reflects the legacy of their origins in the west, based on the principle of strong sectoral organization and relatively loose confederations. The strength of the German model of trade union organization, it has been argued, lies in the *articulated* structure of the industrial unions, with regional and local networks mediating between the leadership and the grass-roots. With membership in decline, only the largest of the industrial unions can sustain this level of organization. The smaller unions are subject to acute resource deficiencies, and the burden of organizational maintenance in the east has contributed to the process of union merger and the emergence of multi-branch unions. Even in IG Metall, which has the strongest presence in the east, the weakness of the shopfloor apparatus limits organizational depth and reduces its capacity for articulation. Its local offices have the potential to act as the focal point of organizational life, but, as we have seen, they tend to act as centres for service delivery rather than member mobilization. To some extent, the organizational weakness of the industrial unions is compensated by the presence of the DGB. Inhibited from playing its traditional role as political representative of the labour movement, however, by the divergent orientations of the industrial unions towards issues like the wages–employment dilemma, the DGB is confined in large part to service provision. Thus weakened on its own turf, the German model is unlikely to provide the blueprint for trade union organization in the countries of east/central Europe where resource constraint and political divisions are particularly acute.

Formally, business organization in the east replicates the tripartite model of western Germany, with employer interests represented separately from the product-specific interests of industrial sectors, and with commerce organized in the chambers. In practice, however, the BDI delegates its representation through the BDA, whilst the local chambers resemble an extension of public administration rather than centres of autonomous associational activity. The BDA itself relies heavily on a single sector association, the Gesamtmetall affiliates supplying the infrastructural wherewithal for the regional confederations. Undermined by the movement away from institutionalized collective bargaining, the BDA employers' associations face competition in the small-firm sector from the indigenous UVs (entrepreneur associations), and from the Bonn-based Association of the *Mittelstand* Economy (BVMW), both of which are more oriented towards the delivery of consultancy services. The dynamics of the post-communist economy exacerbate the organizational problems of accommodating the divergent perspectives of large and small business within unitary structures. The institutional design of the associational order reflects economic relations, the hierarchy and order of the German model being subject to tensions arising from the bipolar structure of capital. Ultimately, the American model of 'untidy competition' may be the one towards which business gravitates.

If the organizational design of interest group systems is related to their socio-economic foundations, so too is the level of participation in organizational activity. Heterogeneous labour markets, as we have seen, provide unfavourable conditions for the mobilization of employee interests, whilst the structure of capital is similarly unconducive to associational collectivism in corporate life. We might therefore have expected membership in trade unions and business associations to lie below western levels. This expectation is not borne out by the available survey data, which shows a relatively high level of trade union membership in the countries of east/central Europe. The distribution of membership, however, is indicative of a syndrome of organizational weakness that can be expected to intensify as market transitions run their course. Membership is heavily concentrated in the state sector, where the old unions have been able to rely on an organizational apparatus inherited from the previous regime. New unionism has failed to take off, and remains restricted to isolated occupational groups strategically placed to assert their bargaining strength. In the emergent private sector, trade unions show little sign of being able to establish organizational foundations. Business association membership, despite the proliferation of groups, also appears to be low in the private sector. German trade unions display symptoms of organizational sclerosis comparable with those of their east European counterparts. Membership is heavily concentrated in the public sector, and in large, privatized firms in old industrial sectors. It is notably weaker in newly established companies, small firms and the service sector. Steep membership decline reflects the effects of deindustrialization, which has cut large swathes through the industrial heartland of the labour movement. Amongst German employers, association membership is directly correlated with company size.

In chapter 4 I addressed the question of group participation from three social science perspectives. Comparative data from the countries of east/ central Europe yielded no evidence of a systematic relationship between participation, political efficacy and economic development as postulated by the social psychological approach to the question. Contrary to expectations that high levels of material security would be reflected in increased perceptions of political efficacy, we found that citizens in some countries where market transition has been slowest had relatively high perceptions of their ability to influence politics. The tentative conclusion drawn from this evidence was that there may be a *negative* relationship between the pace of economic and political transformation and individual perceptions of influence. Thus, for all their failings, familiar structures may be more conducive to perceptions of influence than the unfamiliar, and often rather distant, apparatus of democracy.

The German case supports this conclusion. Despite the advancement of market transition and access to a consolidated democratic system, perceptions of individual influence in politics in eastern Germany are comparatively low. More interestingly from the perspective of this book, there is a perception that influence in the economic arena – the workplace and in trade unions – has declined with the transition to a market economy. Alongside evidence of a pervasive sense of powerlessness and anomie amongst east Germans, this suggests that low perceptions of competence and efficacy reflect the economic insecurity generated by rapid market transition. The combination of opportunities and threats accompanying the market economy appears to elicit a dual response: powerlessness and anomie coexist with economic individualism and a strong achievement orientation. Neither of these responses, however, is likely to lead towards associational activity.

Instead, we have found a fragmentation and individualization in private economy relations which strike at the heart of the associational order. Following in the footsteps of early democratic theory, the concept of social capital locates the mainspring of association in the bonds engendered by interdependency in the private sphere, generating patterns of social co-operation and trust that spill over into public life with private and public interwoven in a seamless network linking the individual, civil society and the state. In the harshly competitive environment of the post-communist economy, old interpersonal bonds have broken down without being replaced by the more impersonal networks of interdependency and co-operation characteristic of democratic civil society. There is little to suggest an accumulation of social capital in the private sphere spilling over into allegiance to social and political institutions. Across the countries of east/central Europe, institutional trust is relatively low. Evaluations of democratic politics are closely correlated with economic expectations, a pragmatic orientation towards politics conforming, in Almond and Verba's terms, to a subject, rather than a participant, civic culture.

The expectation that, with its stable economic life and a ready-made interest group system, eastern Germany might have been expected to demonstrate stronger tendencies towards social capital accumulation than its eastern neighbours was not supported by interview evidence. Despite the opportunities for role modelling provided by the strong presence of west Germans in associational life, social learning is slow, confined to a small corps of interest group activists. There is equally little evidence of a more developed associational order reflected in confidence and trust in social and political institutions. Confidence in social institutions, with the exception of the military, lies well below west German levels, broadly on a par with the east European average. Unlike its eastern neighbours, where democratic institutions enjoy a legitimacy bonus, east Germany shows a legitimacy deficit, with evaluations of democracy lagging behind perceptions of economic performance. I have accounted for this relation with the very demanding expectations generated by images of west German affluence. Even in the advanced post-communist society, then, the notion of social capital generated in associational life and spilling over into support for democratic political institutions appears fanciful.

The most telling of the three perspectives on participation that I have deployed above is rational choice theory. This is also the approach that adapts most readily to the main theoretical project of this book, which was to relate associational activity to its socio-economic foundations. Group mobilization, it was argued in the introduction, reflects the incentive structures and organizational resources of collective action, which are in turn rooted in economic relations. In chapter 2, we saw how the structure of post-communist society provides a weak foundation for interest group activity, lacking the close-knit social networks and distinctive group identities that support collective organization in resource mobilization theory by generating solidary incentives for participation. In the absence of solidary incentives, economic membership motivations predominate and collective action is vulnerable to the problems identified in rational choice theory.

This model has proved its utility in explaining the persistence in the countries of east/central Europe of forms of associational collectivism rooted in the old regime in terms of access to inherited resources: trade unions inheriting the organizational apparatus of their predecessors, or the dominance of associational activity in the corporate sphere by a reconstituted nomenklatura drawing on the resources of old networks. It explains the retarded development of business group activity in terms of the fragmented structure of capital, with cleavages between state and private sector, domestic and foreign capital, and small and large firms, operating against the formation of those intercorporate linkages, and distinctive group identities, which support associational activity in the corporate sphere. Reliant, in the absence of solidary motivations, upon economic incentives, the broadly based groups which predominate in business organization are insufficiently specialized to address the specific needs of their clientele. The organizational weakness of the labour movement has been explained as a reflection of heterogeneous labour markets and the individualization of employment relations which militate against the sort of class identities from which solidary membership motivations are derived. On the other hand, the effectiveness of economic incentives is undermined by a widespread lack of confidence in trade union representation.

In the German case, we have found a similar logic of collective action, although groups are somewhat better equipped for providing the economic incentives upon which collective action depends in the absence of the supportive social networks and group identities underpinning solidary membership motivations. The key to understanding the logic of collective action in the east German context is wage-bargaining, the dynamics of which explain both the initial recruitment success of the trade unions and employers' associations, and their subsequent membership decline. For employers, especially in the small-firm sector, the dynamics of the post-communist economy place a premium on flexibility over the stability and predictability of collective bargaining. The willingness of employers to subscribe to collective bargaining, moreover, is dependent upon the benefits derived from organizational strength in relation to the trade unions. Organizational weakness, evident in the wage rounds of 1990–2, undermines the logic of collective action amongst employers, especially in weak labour markets. For employees, on the other hand, the insecurity of employment in commercially weak companies engenders a predisposition towards informal company-level deals which undercut collectively agreed settlements but safeguard jobs. Accelerating the deregulation of employment relations, then, the dynamics of the post-communist economy undermine the logic of collective action that revolves around centralized wage-bargaining.

The weakness of solidary membership motivations and the reduced role of collective wage-bargaining in the incentive structures of both trade unions and employers' associations lead to a increasingly heavy reliance upon the selective membership incentives associated with service provision – 'conflict insurance' in the trade unions, consultancy services in business associations, technical information and advice in the professions. Recruitment in professional associations like the Hartmannbund and the VDI relies on their reputation as the voice of the profession, and on technical services and advice. The underdevelopment of vocational ethos in eastern Germany, however, means that political representation counts for little in membership motivations, whilst the weakness of organizational networks at the regional and local level creates problems of service delivery. Associational activity in the professions is thus caught up in a vicious circle of organizational weakness and low recruitment in which Olson-type collective action problems are acute. Across the spectrum of interest group activity, interview evidence suggests that group members apply a rigorous cost–benefit analysis to the services that membership confers. Expectations are high, and failure to satisfy often results in exit from the organization. This conclusion corresponds to the results of research elsewhere that suggests that, where group affiliation depends on economic incentives, membership ties are weak.

The weaknesses which we have seen in the socio-economic foundations of the associational order exacerbate the sort of collective action problems identified in the rational actor model. Without the solidary incentives derived from group identification, collective action depends heavily on the provision of selective membership incentives. As in Olson's formulation, political representation is merely a byproduct of their primary group function of servicing their members. Maintaining the intensive networks of political lobbying, however, entails an outlay which has to be underwritten by membership subscriptions. Where member services are available more inexpensively elsewhere on a commercial consultancy basis, and where membership decisions revolve around acute cost–benefit calculations, the economic logic of collective action is intensified.

A logic of collective action embedded in an incentive structure heavily skewed towards service provision is reflected in internal group dynamics. In the introduction, I contrasted the pluralist ideal of *autonomous* associational activity with the *entrepreneurial* model postulated by exchange theory in which a professional interest group leadership undertakes to provide services to a loosely constituted clientele on quasi-commercial lines. The limited evidence available from east/central Europe suggests that interest group activity here corresponds to this model. In the business arena, group leadership is often personalized, and the mobilization of support via the offer of services to members is primarily a means to acquire influence with which to launch a political career. Trade union leaderships have been depicted similarly as 'bureaucratic fiefdoms' geared to political influence. In Germany the picture is somewhat different. Although not without political influence, business association or trade union leadership is not a springboard to a political career. Whilst not driven by political opportunism or commercial profit, however, German interest groups are subject to professional domination, and their activities can be interpreted in terms of the interests of their leaders in organizational maintenance. Responding to the high priority placed on member services, German interest groups have reinvented themselves as service providers.

This syndrome is particularly strong in eastern Germany. With little sense of group belonging, members' commitment to participation in group activity is weak. The readiness to participate is governed by a pragmatic discrimination, varying from one form of activity to another, and is strongest in those activities geared to the immediate material concerns of group members. Participation in the democratic life of the organization is weak, with leadership functions effectively delegated to salaried officials. Deference to the latter, however, is combined with high expectations as to performance and a readiness to exit if not satisfied. Passivity may be related to the weak formation of social capital in post-communist society, but with little indication of increased activism over time it might be interpreted as a symptom of the post-modern syndrome of instrumentality in social and political life outlined in the introduction. Whatever the source of this passivity, the dynamics of internal group life correspond closely to the entrepreneurial model, the exchange of services for membership resembling an extension of the market rather than an alternative form of social organization.

The expectation that interest group politics in the post-communist societies will progressively converge with the pluralist model is difficult to sustain in the light of what we have seen in this book. As we saw in the introduction, the early theorists of civil society set out to reconcile societal pluralism and the egotism of private interests with social cohesion and solidarity. Their answer lay in the socializing effects of conflict and interdependency arising out of the social division of labour, generating a multiplicity of competing but mutually dependent interests that bound society together through its own internal divisions. Pluralist analysis developed a more refined analysis of associational activity embedded in configurations of interests reflecting the structure of capital and employment in industrial society. With intercorporate relations, labour market dynamics and the delivery of professional services increasingly subject to global forces, however, and with a correspondingly more diverse and differentiated spectrum of interests, the associational order in the advanced capitalist societies is much more loosely constituted and fluid.

Where in this shifting configuration of economic and social relations might we locate post-communist society? The countries of east/central Europe have taken different trajectories of political and economic transformation. In parts of the region, the transition to the market economy is insufficiently advanced to precipitate the patterns of social differentiation underlying interest group formation. Elsewhere, however, post-communist economies have already been penetrated by international capital, technological change and modern communications.

To be sure, penetration is uneven, and society remains poised between modernity and backwardness. As these economies are drawn within the ambit of the wider European and global economy, it is likely that they will be subject to those forces driving social change in the advanced capitalist countries. Eastern Germany's advanced post-communist society exhibits pronounced tendencies in this direction. Characterized by fragmentation, individualization and social dealignment, it is inhospitable territory for the type of associational collectivism in which the German model of interest organization is rooted.

Social dealignment, it has been argued, is reflected in the behavioural attitudinal profile of the post-communist citizen, which conforms closely to the 'democratic pathology' identified by contemporary social theory, as we saw in the introduction, as a characteristic of post-modern society in the west. The evidence of the German case points towards the underdevelopment of the 'democratic personality' as defined by social psychology, the weakness of allegiances to social and political institutions consequent upon the retarded accumulation of social capital, and the predominance of an economic logic over sociotropic orientations to collective action. All of this is clearly recognizable from the 'black post-modern scenario' in which apathy and anomie coexists with economic individualism, and in which pragmatic citizens calculate the costs and benefits of collective action, making them unreliable participants in group activity.

The entrepreneurial model of group mobilization through a quasi-commercial exchange between a professionalized leadership and a clientele membership, on the other hand, is difficult to reconcile with the more optimistic vision of post-modern association characterized by autonomy, participation and solidarity. Entrepreneurial interest group activity on the exchange model points to the commercialization rather than the 'democratization of everyday life'. This form of association is far removed from Parsons's 'societal community', de Tocqueville's 'art of association' or Durkheim's notion of professional ethics as the antidote to the egotism of the market. Whilst group theory takes association to be an alternative form of social organization to market relations, the exchange model simply extends the market to encompass association. Loosely coupled and anonymous, the entrepreneurial organization is ill equipped to serve the function of social integration attributed to interest group activity by classical pluralism. It may nevertheless offer a form of organization for atomized societies that lack the social prerequisites to sustain an associational order of the classical type.

The associational order in the advanced capitalist countries, of course, exhibits many of the characteristics that have been attributed in this book to post-communist society. Indeed, much of the conceptual apparatus I have employed derives from the observation of interest group degeneration in the west. Undermined by economic change and social dealignment, however, interest groups in the west nevertheless retain many of the residual features inherited from their historical and social origins. Lacking this social and cultural heritage, associational activity in post-communist society can be expected to be more susceptible to the forces of economic change. Paradoxically, then, societies in which social modernity was until recently stifled by communism may now be on the road to post-modernity. In this book, we have examined associational activity in east Germany's advanced post-communist society as a 'fast-forward' study to predict how group activity in east/central Europe might be expected to develop. The results suggest that, contrary to conventional expectations of convergence with the pluralist model, these societies might actually 'leap-frog' the west in their assimilation with the post-modern model of interest group politics. Indeed, in so doing, they may provide a window on the future, providing us with a foretaste of interest group politics in the twenty-first century.

References

Aarts, K. 1995, 'Intermediate Organisations and Interest Representation', in H.-D. Klingemann and D. Fuchs (eds.), *Citizens and the State*, vol. I of *Beliefs in Government*, Oxford University Press, pp. 187–213.

Ágh, A. 1993, *The Social and Political Actors of Democratic Transition*, Budapest Papers on Democratic Transition 75, Department of Political Science, Budapest University of Economics.

Almond, G. A. and Coleman, J. S. (eds.) 1960, *The Politics of the Developing Areas*, Princeton University Press.

Almond, G. A. and Verba, S. 1963, *The Civic Culture: Political Attitudes and Democracy in Five Nations*, Princeton University Press.

Ammeter-Inquirer 1992, *Poland: Results of a Survey of Economic and Political Behaviour*, Studies in Public Policy 201, Glasgow: Centre for the Study of Public Policy, University of Strathclyde.

Anderson, C. W. 1979, 'Political Design and the Representation of Interests', in Schmitter and Lehmbruch 1979, pp. 271–98.

Arato, A. 1981, 'Civil Society Against the State: Poland 1980–1981', *Telos*, 47: 23–47.

Arato, A. and Cohen, J. L. 1984, 'Social Movements, Civil Society and the Problem of Sovereignty', *Praxis International*, 4: 266–83.

Atkinson, M. M. and Coleman, W. D. 1985, 'Corporatism and Industrial Policy', in Cawson 1985b, pp. 22–44.

Baglioni, G. 1990, 'Industrial Relations in Europe in the 1980s', in Baglioni and Crouch 1990, pp. 1–41.

Baglioni, G. and Crouch C. (eds.) 1990, *European Industrial Relations: The Challenge of Flexibility*, London: Sage.

Bamber, G. J. and Peschanski, V. 1996, 'Transforming Industrial Relations in Russia: A Case of Convergence with Industrialised Market Economies?', *Industrial Relations Journal*, 27, 1: 74–88.

Bastian, J. 1997, *So viel Bündnis war noch nie: The Institutional Architecture of an Alliance for Jobs in Germany*, Discussion Papers in German Studies: Institute for German Studies, University of Birmingham.

BDA/BDI 1990, *Pressemitteilung*, Cologne, 28 February.

Beck, U. 1986, *Risikogesellschaft*, Frankfurt am Main: Suhrkamp.

Bendix, R. 1964, *Nation-Building and Citizenship*, New York: Wiley.

Benzler, S., Bullmann, U. and Eißel, D. (eds.) 1995, *Deutschland-Ost vor Ort: Anfänge der Lokalen Politik in den neuen Bundesländern*, Opladen: Leske and Budrich.

Berend, I. T. 1995, 'Alternatives of Transformation: Choices and Determinants – East-Central Europe in the 1990s', in Crawford 1995a, pp. 130–49.

Berger, U. 1994, *Strategies of the Federal Association of German Industry in the Transformation of the East German Economy*, Budapest Papers on Democratic Transition 85: Hungarian Centre for Democracy Studies Foundation.

1995, 'Engagement und Interessen der Wirtschaftsverbände in der Transformation der ostdeutschen Wirtschaft: Industrieverbände im Spannungsfeld von Mitgliederinteressen und Gemeinwohl', in Wiesenthal 1995a, pp. 95–125.

BfB 1994, *BfB Jahrbuch 1994*, Bonn: BfB.

Bialas, C. 1994, *Gewerkschaftlicher Organisationsaufbau und Transformation der Lohnpolitik im Prozeß der deutschen Einheit: Die IG Metall in den neuen Bundesländern 1990–1993*, Research Report AGTRAP 1, Berlin: Max-Planck-Gesellschaft.

Bialas, C. and Ettl, W. 1992, *Wirtschaftliche Lage und soziale differenzierung im Transformationsprozeß: Zwischenbilanz der sozio-ökonomischen Transformation der neuen Bundesländer für die Analyse der entstehenden Interessenmittlungsstruktur*, Working Paper AG TRAP 92/1, Berlin: Max-Planck-Gesellschaft.

Bispinck, R. 1991, 'Tarifpolitik und Arbeitskänmpfe 1990', in M. Kittner (ed.), *Gewerkschaftsjahrbuch 1991*, Cologne: Bund Verlag, pp. 90–156.

1993, 'Collective Bargaining in East Germany: Between Economic Constraints and Political Regulations', *Cambridge Journal of Economics*, 17: 309–32.

Bluhm, K. 1995, 'Regionale Unterstutzungsnetzwerke in der ostdeutschen Industrie: Der Interessenverband Chemnitzer Maschinenbau', in Wiesenthal 1995a, pp. 160–93.

Boll, B. 1994, 'Interest Organisation and Intermediation in the New Länder', *German Politics*, 3: 114–28.

Bosch, G. and Knuth, M. 1993, 'The Labour Market in East Germany', *Cambridge Journal of Economics*, 17: 295–308.

Brown, A. H. 1984, 'Political Power and the Soviet State: Western and Soviet Perspectives', in N. Harding (ed.), *The State in Socialist Society*, London: Macmillan, pp. 51–103.

Brusis, M. 1994, *Korporatismus als Transformationskonsens: Der Fall Ungarn in osteuropäischen Vergleich*, Working Paper AG TRAP 94/3, Berlin: Max-Planck-Gesellschaft.

Budge, I., Newton, K., et al. 1997, *The Politics of the New Europe: Atlantic to Urals*, London and New York: Longman.

Bullmann, U. and Schwanengel, W. 1995, 'Zur Transformation territorialer Politikstrukturen, Landes- und Kommunalverwaltungen in den neuen Bundesländern', in Benzler, Bullmann, and Eißel 1995, pp. 193–224.

Bürklin, W. 1993, 'Perspektiven für das deutsche Parteiensystem: Politische Konfliktlinien und die sozialdemokratische Kultur', *Daedalus*, 123: 137–54.

BVMW, unpublished membership data, Bonn.

Cameron, D. R. 1984, 'Social Democracy, Corporatism, Labour Quiescence, and the Representation of Economic Interest in Advanced Capitalist Society', in J. H. Goldthorpe (ed.), *Order and Conflict in Contemporary Capitalism*, Oxford: Clarendon, pp. 143–99.

Campbell, A. 1962, 'The Passive Citizen', *Acta Sociologica*, 6: 9–21.

Cawson, A. 1985a, 'Introduction. Varieties of Corporatism: The Importance of the Meso-Level of Interest Intermediation', in Cawson 1985b, pp. 1–21.

Cawson, A. (ed.) 1985b, *Organised Interests and the State: Studies in Meso-Corporatism*, London: Sage.

Chirot, D. 1980, 'The Corporatist Model and Socialism', *Theory and Society*, 2: 363–81.

Clark, J. and Wildavsky, A. 1990, *The Moral Collapse of Communism: Poland as a Cautionary Tale*, San Francisco: ICS Press.

Clarke, S. 1994, 'Trade Unions, Industrial Relations and Politics in Russia', in Waller and Myant 1994, pp. 133–60.

Clarke, S. and Fairbrother, P. 1994, 'Post-Communism and the Emergence of Industrial Relations', in Hyman and Ferner 1994, pp. 368–98.

Cohen, J. L. and Arato, A. 1992, *Civil Society and Political Theory*, Cambridge, MA: MIT Press.

Cox, T. and Vass, L. 1994, 'Civil Society and Interest Representation in Hungarian Political Development', *Journal of Communist Studies and Transition Politics*, 10: 153–79.

Crawford, B. (ed.) 1995a, *Markets, States, and Democracy: The Political Economy of Post-Communist Transformation*, Boulder: Westview Press.

1995b, 'Post-Communist Political Economy: A Framework for the Analysis of Reform', in Crawford 1995a, pp. 3–43.

Crouch, C. 1993, *Industrial Relations and European State Traditions*, Oxford: Clarendon.

1994, 'Beyond Corporatism: The Impact of Company Strategy', in Hyman and Ferner 1994, pp. 196–222.

Czada, R. 1994, 'Schleichweg in der "Dritte Republik": Politik der Vereinigung und politische Wandel in Deutschland', *Politische Vierteljahresschrift*, 35: 245–70.

1996, 'The Treuhandanstalt and the Transition from Socialism to Capitalism', in A. Benz and K. H. Goetz (eds.), *A New German Public Sector: Reform, Adaptation and Stability*, Aldershot: Dartmouth, pp. 93–118.

Dalton, R. 1994, 'Communists and Democrats', *British Journal of Political Science*, 24: 469–93.

1996, 'A Divided Electorate?', in Smith, Paterson and Padgett 1996, pp. 35–54.

de Tocqueville, A. 1988, *Democracy in America*, ed. J. P. Mayer, New York: Harper and Row.

Desai, R. and Orenstein, M. 1996, 'Business Associations and the State in the Czech Republic with Some Remarks on the Situation in Poland', in H. Wiesenthal (ed.), *Organised Business Interests as Outcomes and Agents of Socio-Economic Transformation in East/Central Europe*, Research Report AG TRAP 7, Berlin: Max-Planck-Gesellschaft, pp. 15–31.

Deubner, C. 1984, 'Change and Internationalization in Industry: Towards a Sectoral Interpretation of West German Politics', *International Organization*, 38: 501–35.

DGB Landesbezirk Berlin-Brandenburg 1993, *Geschäftsbericht 1990–1993*, Berlin: DGB.

DGB Landesbezirk Sachsen-Anhalt 1992, *Geschäftsbericht 1990–1992. Aufbruch statt Abbruch: Für eine lebenswerte Zukunft in Sachsen-Anhalt*, Magdeburg: DGB.

1993, *Geschäftsbericht 1992–1993. Aufbruch statt Abbruch: Für eine Zukunft mit Arbeit*, Magdeburg: DGB.

DGB Landesbezirk Thüringen 1994, *Geschäftsbericht 23 Mai 1992–22 Januar 1994*, Erfurt: DGB.

Donges, J. B. 1991, 'Arbeitsmarkt und Lohnpolitik in Ostdeutschland', *Wirtschaftsdienst*, 4: 283–91.

Dunlop, J. T. 1958, *Industrial Relations System*, New York: Reinhart and Winston.

Durkheim, E. 1964, *The Division of Labour in Society*, trans. G. Simpson, New York and London: Free Press/Collier Macmillan.

Dyson, K. H. F. 1981, 'The Politics of Economic Management in West Germany', in W. E. Paterson and G. Smith (eds.), *The West German Model: Perspectives on a Stable State*, London: Frank Cass, pp. 38–57.

Egorov, V. 1996, 'Privatisation and Labour Relations in the Countries of Central and Eastern Europe', *Industrial Relations Journal*, 27: 89–100.

Eichener, V. Kleinfeld, R., Pollack, D., Schmid, J., Schubert, K. and Voelzkow, H. (eds.) 1992, *Problem der Einheit: Organisierte Interessen in Ostdeutschland*, vols. I and II, Marburg: Metropolis.

Eichener, V. and Voelzkow, H. 1992, 'Bahauptung einer ostdeutschen Altorganisation gegen die Konkurrenz ans dem Western: Berufständische Organisationen der Ingenieure', in Eichener et al. 1992, vol. I, pp. 249–65.

Ekiert, G. 1991, 'Democratisation Processes in East Central Europe: A Theoretical Reconsideration', *British Journal of Political Science*, 21: 205–31.

Erdmann, Y. 1992, 'Aufbau und Entwicklung von ärzteverbände in Ostdeutschland', in Eichener et al. 1992, vol. II, pp. 319–55.

Esser, J. and Vath, W. 1985, 'Overcoming the Steel Crisis in the Federal Republic of Germany', in W. Meny and V. Wright (eds.), *The Politics of Steel: The European Community and the Steel Industry in the Crisis Years 1974–1984*, Berlin: De Gruyter/European University Institute, pp. 123–58.

Ettl, W. 1995, 'Arbeitgeberverbände als Transformationsakteure: Organisationentwicklung und Tarifpolitik im Dilemma zwischen Funktionalität und Representativität', in Wiesenthal 1995a, pp. 34–94.

Ettl, W. and Heikenroth, A. 1995, *Strukturwandel, Verbandsabstinenz, Tarifflucht: Zur Lage ostdeutscher Unternehmen und Arbeitgeberverbände*, Working Paper AG TRAP 95/3, Berlin: Max-Planck-Gesellschaft.

Ettl, W. and Wiesenthal, H. 1994, *Tarifautonomie in de-industrialisierten Gelände: Report und Analyse eines Institutionentransfers im Prozeß der deutschen Einheit*, Working Paper AG TRAP 94/3, Berlin: Max-Planck-Gesellschaft.

Etzioni, A. 1961, *A Comparative Analysis of Complex Organisations*, New York: Free Press.

Fichter, M. 1993, 'A House Divided: German Unification and Organised Labour', *German Politics*, 2: 21–39.

Fichter, M. and Kubjuhn, M. 1992, 'Die Gewerkschaften im Einigungsprozeß: Ausdehnung mit alten Organisationsstrukturen und neuen Intergrationsproblemen', in Eichener et al. 1992, vol. I, pp. 159–73.

Fichter, M. and Reister, H. 1996, 'Gewerkschaften: Organisation und Politik in den neuen Bundesländern', in O. Niedermeyer (ed.), *Intermediäre Strukturen in Ostdeutschland*, Opladen: Westdeutscher Verlag, pp. 1–27.

Flockton, C. 1996, 'Economic Management and the Challenge of Reunification', in Smith, Paterson and Padgett 1996, pp. 211–32.

Flockton, C. and Esser, J. 1992, 'Labour Market Problems and Labour Market Policy', in Smith, Paterson, Merkl and Padgett 1992, pp. 281–300.

Forschungsgruppe Wahlen 1990, *Bundestagswahl 1990: Eine Analyse der ersten Gesamtdeutschen Bundestagswahl am 2 Dezember 1990*, Mannheim: Forschungsgruppe Wahlen.

1994, *Bundestagswahl 1994: Eine Analyse der Wahl zum 13 Deutschen Bundestag am 16 October 1994*, Mannheim: Forschungsgruppe Wahlen.

French, S. 1998, *Necessity or Opportunity?: The Undermining of Multi-Employer Bargaining in the New Länder*, Discussion Papers in German Studies: Institute for German Studies, University of Birmingham.

Fuchs, D. 1993, *A Metatheory of the Democratic Process*, Berlin: Wissenschaftszentrum Berlin für Sozialforschung.

Frydman, R. and Rapaczynski, A. 1994, *Privatization in Eastern Europe: Is the State Withering Away?*, Budapest: Central European University Press.

Gabriel, O. W. 1995, 'Political Efficacy and Trust', in J. van Deth and E. Scarbrough (eds.), *The Impact of Values*, vol. III of *Beliefs in Government*, Oxford University Press, pp. 357–89.

Gebuhr, K. 1993, *Von Konspiration bis Fusion: Ein Chronik des Rudolf-Virchow-Bundes, Sonderausgabe aus Anlaß der Bundesversammlung 1993 des NAV–Virchowbund von 12 bis 14 November im Universitätsklinikum Charité Medizinische Fakultät der Humboldt Universiät zu Berlin*, Berlin: Rudolf-Virchow-Bund.

Gesamtmetall 1991, *Geschäftsbericht*, Cologne: Gesamtmetall.

1992, *Arbeitgeberverband Gesamtmetall*, Cologne: Gesamtmetall.

Gissendanner, S. 1996, 'Transfer or Transformation?: What the German Social Science Literature Has to Say About Unification and Its Systemic Effects', *German Politics*, 5: 460–84.

Glaeßner, G.-J. 1996, 'Regime Change and Public Administration in East Germany: Some Findings from a Research Project in Brandenburg and Saxony', *German Politics*, 5: 185–200.

Grant, W. 1993, 'Business Associations in Eastern Europe and Russia', *Journal of Communist Studies*, 9: 86–100.

Grant, W., Paterson, W. and Whitston, C. 1987, 'Government–Industry Relations in the Chemical Industry: An Anglo-German Comparison', in S. Wilks and M. Wright (eds.), *Comparative Government–Industry Relations in Western Europe, United States and Japan*, Oxford: Clarendon, pp. 35–60.

Grant, W. and Streeck, W. 1985, 'Large Firms and the Representation of Business in the UK and West German Construction Industry', in Cawson 1985b, pp. 145–73.

Hall, J. and Ludwig, U. 1995, 'German Unification and the "Market Adoption" Hypothesis', *Cambridge Journal of Economics*, 4: 491–507.

Hancock, M. D. 1989, *West Germany: The Politics of Democratic Corporatism*, Chatham, NJ: Chatham House.

Hankiss, E. 1990, *East European Alternatives*, Oxford: Clarendon.

Härtel, H.-H. 1991, 'Lohnpolitik im vereinten Deutschland', *Wirtschaftsdienst*, 1/91: 7–10.

Hartmannbund 1991, *Jahresbericht, 1991*, Bonn: Hartmannbund.

Hausner, J., Pedersen, O. K. and Ronit, K. 1995, 'Evolution of Interest Representation and Development of the Labour Market in Post-Socialist Countries', in Hausner, Pedersen and Ronit (eds.), *Evolution of Interest Representation and Development of the Labour Market in Post-Socialist Countries*, Cracow Academy of Economics/Friedrich Ebert Stiftung, pp. 363–414.

Hayward, J. 1995, 'Organised Interests and Public Policies', in J. Hayward and E. C. Page (eds.), *Governing the New Europe*, Cambridge: Polity Press, pp. 224–56.

Hegewisch, A., Brewster, C. and Koubek, J. 1996, 'Different Roads: Changes in Industrial and Employee Relations in the Czech Republic and East Germany Since 1989', *Industrial Relations Journal*, 27: 50–64.

Heseler, H. 1993, 'Sectoral Restructuring: The East German Shipyards on the Path to the Market Economy', *Cambridge Journal of Economics*, 17: 349–63.

Héthy, L. 1991, 'Towards Social Peace or Explosion?: Challenges for Labour Relations in Central and Eastern Europe', *Labour and Society*, 16: 347–58.
  1994, 'Tripartism in Eastern Europe', in Hyman and Ferner 1994, pp. 312–36.

Hirschman, A. O. 1970, *Exit, Voice and Loyalty: Responses to Decline in Firms, Organizations and States*, Cambridge, MA: Harvard University Press.

Hough, J. 1979, *The Soviet Union and Social Science Theory*, Cambridge, MA: Harvard University Press.

Hughes-Hallett, A., Ma, Y. and Mélitz, J. 1996, 'Unification and the Policy Predicament in Germany', *Economic Modelling*, 13: 519–44.

Huntington, S. P. 1991, *The Third Wave: Democratization in the Late Twentieth Century*, Norman: University of Oklahoma Press.

Hyman, R. 1994, 'Introduction: Economic Restructuring, Market Liberalism and the Future of National Industrial Relations Systems', in Hyman and Ferner 1994, pp. 1–14.

Hyman, R. and Ferner, A. (eds.) 1994, *New Frontiers in European Industrial Relations*, Oxford and Cambridge, MA: Blackwell.

IfEP 1994, *Trendbarometer 94: Zusammenfassende Trendanalyse und Präsentationsunterlagen, Juni 1994*, Cologne: IfEP.

IG Metall 1995, *Metall: der Monatsmagazin der IG Metall*, 4.

IG Metall Sachsen 1993, *Geschäftsbericht 1992–1993, 3 Ordentliche Bezirkskonferenz 9/10 July 1993*, Dresden: IG Metall Bezirksleitung Dresden.

Ingenieur Digest: Das Magazin für Technik und Wirtschaft, October 1994: 12.

Ingenieur Nachrichten: Zeitschrift des Ingenieurtechnischen Verbandes eV für Thüringen, 4, 1994: 000.

Inglehart, R. 1971, 'The Silent Revolution in Europe: Intergenerational Change in Post-Industrial Societies', *American Political Science Review*, 65: 991–1017.

IWH 1994, *Unternehmensbefragung im Ostdeutschen Verarbeitenden Gerwerbe: Un-*

tersuchung im Auftrag der Max-Planck-Gesellschaft, 'Arbeitsgruppe Transform-ationsprozeße in den neuen Bundeslandern', Halle: IWH.

Jakobi, O., Keller, B. and Müller-Jentsch, W. 1992, 'Germany: Codetermining the Future?', in A. Ferner and R. Hyman (eds.), *Industrial Relations in the New Europe*, Oxford: Blackwell, pp. 218–68.

Jenkins, J. C. 1983, 'Resource Mobilization Theory and the Study of Social Movements', *American Review of Sociology*, 9: 527–53.

Jordan, G. 1993, 'The Pluralism of Pluralism: An Anti-Theory?', in Richardson 1993, pp. 49–70.

Kaase, M. 1994, 'Political Culture and Political Consolidation in Central and Eastern Europe', *Research on Democracy and Society*, 2: 233–74.

1997, 'Consensus, Conflict and Democracy in Germany', *German Politics*, 6: 1–28.

Kaase, M. and Newton, K. 1995, *Beliefs in Government*, vol. V of *Beliefs in Government*, Oxford University Press.

Kädtler, J. and Kottwitz, G. 1994, 'Industrielle Beziehungen in Ostdeutschland: Durch Kooperation zum Gegensatz von Kapital und Arbeit?', *Industrielle Beziehungen*, 1: 13–38.

Kaplan, C. S. 1993, 'New Forms of Political Participation', in A. H. Miller, W. M. Reisinger and V. L. Hesli (eds.), *Public Opinion and Regime Change: The New Politics of Post-Soviet Societies*, Boulder: Westview Press, pp. 153–67.

Karrasch, P. 1995, 'Gewerkschaftliche und gewerkschaftsnahe Politikformen in und mit der Kommune – Leipziger Erfahrungen', in Benzler, Bullmann, and Eißel 1995, pp. 99–120.

Keane, J. (ed.) 1988a, *Civil Society and the State: New European Perspectives*, London: Verso.

1988b, 'Despotism and Democracy: The Origins and Development of the Distinction Between Civil Society and the State 1750–1850', in Keane 1988a, pp. 35–71.

Kimber, R. 1993, 'Interest Groups and the Fallacy of the Liberal Fallacy', in Richardson 1993, pp. 38–48.

Kirschner, L. and Sommerfeld, U. 1991, 'Rechtssoziologische Aspekte betrieb-licher Mitbestimmung und in der ehemalige DDR', *Zeitschrift für Rechts-soziologie*, 12: 32–56.

Kiss, Y. 1994, 'Privatisation Paradoxes in East Central Europe', *Eastern European Politics and Societies*, 8: 122–52.

Kleinfeld, R. 1992, 'Zwischen Rundem Tisch und Konzertierter Aktion: Kor-poratistische Formen der Interessenvermittlung in den neuen Bundesländ-ern', in Eichener et al. 1992, vol. I, pp. 73–134.

Kleinheinz, G. 1992, 'Tarifpartnerschaft im vereinten Deutschland: Die Be-deutung der Arbeitsmarktorganisationen für die Einheit der Arbeits- und Lebensverhaltnisse', *Aus Politik und Zeitgeschichte*, B 12/92: 14–24.

Kloc, K. 1994, 'Trade Unions and Economic Transformation in Poland', in Waller and Myant 1994, pp. 125–32.

Koch, K. 1995, 'The German Works Council and Collective Bargaining: Devel-opments Since Unification', *German Politics*, 4: 145–56.

Kocka, J. 1994, 'Crisis of Unification: How Germany Changes', *Daedalus*, 123: 173–93.

Krumbein, W. 1992, 'Situativer Korporatismus', in Eichener et al. 1992, vol. I, pp. 211–24.

Kumar, K. 1993, 'Civil Society: An Inquiry into the Usefulness of an Historical Term', *British Journal of Sociology*, 44: 375–95.

Lane, C. 1994a, 'Is Germany Following the British Path?: A Comparative Analysis of Stability and Change', *Industrial Relations Journal*, 3: 187–98.

   1994b, 'Industrial Order and the Transformation of Industrial Relations: Britain, Germany and France Compared', in Hyman and Ferner 1994, pp. 167–95.

Lane, R. 1959, *Political Life*, Glencoe, IL: Free Press.

Langguth, G. 1995, *In Search of Security: A Socio-Psychological Portrait of Today's Germany*, Westport, CT and London: Praeger.

Lanzalaco, L. 1992, 'Coping with Heterogeneity: Peak Associations of Business Within and Across Western European Nations', in J. Greenwood, J. R. Grote and K. Ronit (eds.), *Organised Interests and the European Community*, London: Sage, pp. 173–206.

Lasswell, H. D. 1948, *Power and Personality*, New York: Norton.

Lehmbruch, G. 1982, 'Introduction: Neo-Corporatism in Comparative Perspective', in Lehmbruch and Schmitter 1982, pp. 1–28.

   1991, 'Die deutsche Vereinigung: Strukturen und Strategien', *Politische Vierteljahresschrift*, 32: 21–44.

Lehmbruch, G. and Schmitter, P. C. (eds.) 1982, *Patterns of Corporatist Policy-Making*, Beverly Hills and London: Sage.

Lewis, P. G. 1997, 'Theories of Democratization and Patterns of Regime Change in Eastern Europe', *Journal of Communist Studies and Transition Politics*, 13: 4–25.

Lipset, S. M. 1959, *Political Man*, Baltimore: Johns Hopkins University Press.

   1994, 'The Social Requisites of Democracy Revisited', *American Sociological Review*, 59: 1–22.

Lomax, B. 1997, "The Strange Death of Civil Society in Post-Communist Hungary', *Journal of Communist Studies and Transition Politics*, 13: 41–63.

MacShane, D. 1994, 'The Changing Contours of Trade Unionism in Eastern Europe', in Hyman and Ferner 1994, pp. 337–67.

Mahnkopf, B. 1991, 'Vorwärts in der Vergangenheit?: Pessimistische Spekulationen über der Zukunft der Gewerkschaften in der neuen Bundesrepublik', in A. H. Westphal, H. M. Heine and U. Busch (eds.), *Wirtschaftspolitische Konsequenzen der deutschen Vereinigung*, Frankfurt am Main: Campus, pp. 265–86.

Marginson, P. and Sisson, K. 1994, 'The Structure of Transnational Capital in Europe: The Emerging Euro-Company and Its Implications for Industrial Relations', in Hyman and Ferner 1994, pp. 15–51.

Marin, B. (ed.) 1990a, *Generalized Political Exchange*, Frankfurt am Main: Campus Verlag.

Marin, B. 1990b, 'Generalized Political Exchange: Preliminary Considerations', in Marin 1990a, pp. 37–66.

Marody, M. 1992, 'From Social Idea to Real World: Clash Between New Possibilities and Old Habits', in K. Z. Poznanski (ed.), *Constructing Capitalism: The Re-emergence of Civil Society and Liberal Economy in the Post-Communist World*, Boulder: Westview Press, pp. 159–78.

Mayntz, R. 1990, 'Organisierte Interessenvertretung und Föderalismus: Zur Verbandestruktur in der Bundesrepublik Deutschland', in T. Ellwein, J. J. Hesse, R. Mayntz and W. F. Scharpf (eds.), *Jahrbuch zur Staats- und Verwaltungswissenschaft*, Baden-Baden: Nomos Verlagsgesellschaft, pp. 145–57.

Melucci, A. 1988, 'Social Movements and the Democratisation of Everyday Life', in Keane 1988a, pp. 245–60.

Meulemann, H. 1997, 'Value Changes in Germany After Unification: 1990–1995', *German Politics*, 6: 122–39.

Millward, N., Stevens, M., Smart, D. and Hawes, W. R. 1992, *Workplace Industrial Relations in Transition*, Aldershot: Dartmouth.

Ministerium für Arbeit, Soziales, Gesundheit und Frauen des Landes Brandenburg 1994, *Gesundheitswesen im Umbruch: Gesundheitsreport des Landes Brandenburg 1994*, Potsdam: MfASGF.

Mishler, W. and Rose, R. 1993, *Trajectories of Fear and Hope: The Dynamics of Support for Democracy in Eastern Europe*, Studies in Public Policy 214, Glasgow: Centre for the Study of Public Policy, University of Strathclyde.

Misselwitz, H.-J. 1993, 'DDR: Geschlossene Gesellschaft und offenes Erbe', in W. Weidenfeld (ed.), *Deutschland. Eine Nation – Doppelte Geschichte*, Stuttgart: Verlag, Wissenschaft und Politik, pp. 103–18.

Miszlivetz, F. 1997, 'Participation and Transition: Can the Civil Society Project Survive in Hungary?', *Journal of Communist Studies and Transition Politics*, 13: 27–40.

Moe, T. M. 1980, *The Organisation of Interests: Incentives and the Internal Dynamics of Political Interest Groups*, Chicago University Press.

Moore, B. Jnr 1966, *Social Origins of Dictatorship and Democracy: Lord and Peasant in the Making of the Modern World*, Harmondsworth: Penguin Books.

Musil, J. 1991, 'Responses of the State and the Social Partners to the Challenges of Restructuring and Privatisation', *Labour and Society*, 16: 381–99.

Myant, M. 1994, 'Czech and Slovak Trade Unions', in Waller and Myant 1994, pp. 59–84.

Myant, M. and Waller, M. 1994, 'Parties and Trade Unions in Eastern Europe: The Shifting Distribution of Political and Economic Power', in Waller and Myant 1994, pp. 161–81.

NAV-VB 1992, *Jahresbericht 1990–1991*, Cologne: NAV-VB.

Neumann, S. 1956, 'Towards a Comparative Study of Political Parties', in Neumann (ed.), *Modern Political Parties: Approaches to Comparative Politics*, Chicago University Press, pp. 395–421.

Niedermeyer, O. and von Beyme, K. (eds.) 1994, *Politische Kultur in Ost- und Westdeutschland*, Berlin: Akademie Verlag.

Noelle-Neumann, B. and Kocher, R. (eds.) 1993, *Allensbacher Jahrbuch für Demoskopie 1984–1992*, Munich and Allensbach: Verlag für Demoskopie.

Nove, A. 1995, 'Economics of Transition: Some Gaps and Illusions', in Crawford 1995a, pp. 227–45.

Offe, C. 1985, 'The New Social Movements: Challenging the Boundaries of Institutional Politics', *Social Research*, 52: 817–68.

1991, 'Capitalism by Democratic Design: Democratic Theory Facing the Triple Transition in East Central Europe', *Social Research*, 58: 865–92.

1992, 'German Reunification as a "Natural Experiment"', *German Politics*, 1: 1–12.

Olson, M. 1965, *The Logic of Collective Action: Public Goods and the Theory of Groups*, Cambridge, MA: Harvard University Press.

Ost, D. 1995, 'Labour, Class and Democracy: Shaping of Political Antagonisms in Post-Communist Society', in Crawford 1995a, pp. 177–203.

Padgett, S. 1996, 'Parties in Post-Communist Society: The German Case', in P. Lewis (ed.), *Party Structure and Organization in East-Central Europe*, Cheltenham: Edward Elgar, pp. 163–86.

Panebianco, A. 1988, *Political Parties: Organisation and Power*, Cambridge University Press.

Parsons, T. 1969, *Politics and Social Structure*, Glencoe, IL: Free Press.

Pelczynski, Z. A. 1988, 'Solidarity and the Rebirth of Civil Society in Poland 1976–1981', in Keane 1988a, pp. 361–80.

Piore, M. J. and Sabel, C. F. 1984, *The Second Industrial Divide*, New York: Basic Books.

Pollert, A. and Hradecka, I. 1994, 'Privatisation in Transition: The Czech Experience', *Industrial Relations Journal*, 25: 52–63.

Poznanski, K. Z. 1995, 'Political Economy of Privatization in Eastern Europe', in Crawford 1995a, pp. 204–26.

Priewe, J. 1993, 'Privatisation of the Industrial Sector: The Function and Activities of the Treuhandanstalt', *Cambridge Journal of Economics*, 17: 333–48.

Putnam, R. D. 1993, *Making Democracy Work: Civic Traditions in Modern Italy*, Princeton University Press.

Pye, L. W. 1990, 'Political Science and the Crisis of Authoritarianism', *American Political Science Review*, 84: 3–19.

Pye, L. and Verba, S. (eds.) 1965, *Political Culture and Political Development*, Princeton University Press.

Rehn, G. and Viklund, B. 1990, 'Changes in the Swedish Model', in Baglioni and Crouch 1990, pp. 300–25.

Reutter, W. 1996, 'Tripartism Without Corporatism: Trade Unions in Central and Eastern Europe', in A. Agh and G. Ilonszki (eds.), *Parliaments and Organised Interests: The Second Steps*, Budapest: Hungarian Centre for Democracy Studies, pp. 59–78.

Richardson, J. J. (ed.), 1993, *Pressure Groups*, Oxford University Press.

Roller, E. 1992, *Ideological Basis of the Market Economy: Attitudes Towards Distribution, Principles and the Role of Government in Western and Eastern Germany*, Berlin: Wissenschaftszentrum Berlin für Sozialforschung.

Rose, R. 1991, *Between State and Market: Key Indicators of Transition in Eastern Europe*, Studies in Public Policy 196, Glasgow: Centre for the Study of Public Policy, University of Strathclyde.

1992, *Czechs and Slovaks Compared: A Survey of Economic and Political Behaviour*, Studies in Public Policy 198, Glasgow: Centre for the Study of Public Policy, University of Strathclyde.

1995, 'Russia as an Hour-Glass Society: A Constitution Without Citizens', *East European Constitutional Review*, 4: 34–42.

Rose, R. and Haerpfer, C. 1993, *Adapting to Transformation in Eastern Europe: New Democracies Barometer II*, Studies in Public Policy 212, Glasgow: Centre for the Study of Public Policy, University of Strathclyde.

1995, 'Democracy and Enlarging the European Union Eastwards', *Journal of Common Market Studies*, 33: 427–50.

1996, 'The Impact of a Ready-Made State: Die privelegierte Position Ostdeutschlands in der postkommunistischen Transformation', in H. Wiesenthal (ed.), *Einheit als Privileg: Vergleichende Perspektiven auf die Transformation Ostdeutschlands*, Frankfurt am Main and New York: Campus, pp. 105–40.

1997, 'The Impact of a Ready-Made State: East Germans in Comparative Perspective', *German Politics*, 6: 100–21.

Rose, R. and Mishler, W. T. E. 1993, *Reacting to Regime Change in Eastern Europe: Polarization or Leaders and Laggards*, Studies in Public Policy 210, Glasgow: Centre for the Study of Public Policy, University of Strathclyde.

Rose, R., Zapf, W. S., Seifert, W. and Page, E. 1993, *Germans in Comparative Perspective*, Studies in Public Policy 218, Glasgow: Centre for the Study of Public Policy, University of Strathclyde.

Rutland, P. 1992, *Business Elites and Russian Economic Policy*, London: Royal Institute of International Affairs.

Salisbury, R. H. 1969, 'An Exchange Theory of Interest Groups', *Midwest Journal of Political Science*, 13: 1–32.

1979, 'Why No Corporatism in America', in Schmitter and Lehmbruch 1979, pp. 213–30.

Sally, R. and Webber, D. 1994, 'The German Solidarity Pact: A Case Study in the Politics of the New Germany', *German Politics*, 3: 18–46.

Saunders, P. 1993, 'Citizenship in a Liberal Society', in Turner 1993a, pp. 57–90.

Schmid, J. and Tiemann, H. 1992, 'Gewerkschaften und Tarifverhandlungen in den fünf neuen Bundeslandern, Organisationsentwicklung, politische Strategien und Probleme am Beispiel der IG Metall', in Eichener et al. 1992, vol. I, pp. 135–58.

Schmidt, M. G. 1982, 'Does Corporatism Matter?: Economic Crisis, Politics and Rates of Unemployment in Capitalist Democracies in the 1970s', in Lehmbruch and Schmitter 1982, pp. 237–58.

Schmitter, P. C. 1979a, 'Modes of Interest Intermediation and Modes of Societal Change in Western Europe', in Schmitter and Lehmbruch 1979, pp. 63–94.

1979b, 'Still the Century of Corporatism?', in Schmitter and Lehmbruch 1979, pp. 7–52.

1981, 'Interest Mediation and Regime Governability in Contemporary Interest and North America', in S. Berger (ed.), *Organising Interests in Western Europe*, Cambridge University Press, pp. 287–330.

1982, 'Reflections on Where the Theory of Neo-Corporatism Has Gone and Where the Praxis of Neo-Corporatism May Be Going', in Lehmbruch and Schmitter 1982, pp. 259–80.

Schmitter, P. C. and Lehmbruch, G. (eds.), 1979, *Trends Toward Corporatist Intermediation*, Beverly Hills and London: Sage.

Schneider-Lenné, E. R. 1992, 'Corporate Control in Germany', *Oxford Review of Economic Policy*, 8: 11–23.

Schöbel, C. 1993, *Sozialisation in unterschiedlichen Systemen: Zum Profil der Persönlichkeitstypen in West- und Ost-Berlin*, Berlin: Wissenschaftszentrum Berlin für Sozialforschung.

Schroeder, W. and Ruppert, B. 1996, 'Austritte aus Arbeitgeberverbänden: Motive–Ursachen–Ausmaß', *WSI Mitteilungen*, 49: 316–29.

Siebert, H. 1992, *Das Wagnis der Einheit*, Stuttgart: DVA.

Silvia, S. J. and Markovits, A. S. 1995, 'An Ounce of Prevention?: The Reform of the German Trade Union Federation', *German Politics*, 4: 66–73.

Simmel, G. 1955, *Conflict and the Web of Group Affiliation*, London: Collier Macmillan.

Skilling, G. G. and Griffiths, F. 1971, *Interest Groups in Soviet Politics*, Princeton University Press.

Smith, G., Paterson, W. E., Merkl, P. and Padgett, S. (eds.) 1992, *Developments in German Politics*, vol. I, London: Macmillan.

Smith, G., Paterson, W. E. and Padgett, S. (eds.), 1996, *Developments in German Politics*, vol. II, London: Macmillan.

Staniszkis, J. 1984, 'Martial Law in Poland', *Telos*, 54: 87–100.

Stein, R. (ed.) 1992, *Charité 1945–1992: Ein Mythos von innen*, Berlin: Argon.

Streeck, W. 1984, *Industrial Relations in West Germany*, London: Heinemann.

  1992a, 'Inclusion and Secession: Questions on the Boundaries of Associational Democracy', *Politics and Society*, 20: 513–20.

  1992b, *Social Institutions and Economic Performance: Studies of Industrial Relations in Advanced Capitalist Economies*, London, Newbury Park, New Delhi: Sage.

Streeck, W. and Schmitter, P. C. 1992, 'From National Corporatism to Transnational Pluralism: Organized Interests in the Single Market', in Streeck 1992b, pp. 197–231.

Stykow, P. 1994, *Formen der Representation von Wirtschaftsakteuren in Rußland: Eine Fallstudie*, Working Paper AG TRAP 94/7, Berlin: Max-Planck-Gesellschaft.

  1996, *Organised Interests in the Transformation Process of Eastern Europe and Russia: Towards Corporatism?*, Working Paper AG TRAP, Berlin: Max-Planck-Gesellschaft.

Szablowski, G. and Derlien, H.-U. 1993, 'East European Transitions: Elites, Bureaucracies and the European Community', *Governance*, 6: 304–24.

Szabó, M. 1991, 'Changing Patterns of Mobilisation in Hungary Within New Social Movements', in G. Szoboszlai (ed.), *Democracy and Political Transformation*, Budapest: Hungarian Political Science Association, pp. 298–322.

Sztompka, P. 1993, 'Civilisational Incompetence: The Trap of Post-Communist Societies', *Zeitschrift für Soziologie*, 22: 85–95.

Taylor, C. 1975, *Hegel*, Cambridge University Press.

Thirkell, J., Atanasov, B. and Gradev, G. 1994, 'Trade Unions, Political Parties and Governments in Bulgaria, 1989–1992', in Waller and Myant 1994, pp. 98–115.

Tiemann, H., Schmid, J. and Lober, F. 1993, 'Gewerkschaften und Sozialdemokratie in den neuen Bundesländern', *Deutschland Archiv*, 26: 40–51.

Timmins, G. 1997, *German Unification and Organized Labour: An Investigation into the Impact of Post-Communist Transition in the Former German Democratic Republic on the 'West German Model' of Industrial Relations*, unpublished PhD thesis, University of Huddersfield.

Tóth, A. 1994, 'Great Expectations – Fading Hopes: Trade Unions and System-Change in Hungary', in Waller and Myant 1994, pp. 85–97.

Traxler, F. 1990, 'Political Exchange, Collective Action and Interest Governance: Towards a Theory of Industrial Relations and Corporatism', in Marin 1990a, pp. 67–88.

Turner, B. (ed.) 1993a, *Citizenship and Social Theory*, London: Sage.

1993b, 'Introduction', in Turner 1993a, pp. 1–19.

Verband Deutscher Maschinen- und Anlagenbau (VDMA) 1993, *Maschinen- und Anlagenbau Ostdeutschland und Berlin*, Frankfurt am Main: VDMA.

Verein Deutscher Ingenieure (VDI), 1991, *Geschäftsbericht*, Düsseldorf: VDI.

1994, *VDI Presseinformation*, Dresden, 30 August.

Visser, J. 1994, 'European Trade Unions: The Transition Years', in Hyman and Ferner 1994, pp. 80–107.

Walker, J. L. 1983, 'The Origins and Maintenance of Interest Groups in America', *American Political Science Review*, 77: 390–406.

Waller, M. 1992, 'Groups, Interests and Political Aggregation in East Central Europe', *Journal of Communist Studies and Transition Politics*, 8: 128–47.

1994, 'Political Actors and Political Roles in East/Central Europe', in Waller and Myant 1994, pp. 21–36.

Waller, M. and Myant, M. (eds.), 1994, *Parties, Trade Unions and Society in East-Central Europe*, London: Frank Cass.

Wallerstein, M., Golden, M. and Lange, P. 1997, 'Unions, Employers' Associations and Wage Setting Institutions in Northern Europe, 1950–1992', *Industrial and Labour Relations Review*, 50: 379–401.

Wenger, M. 1995, *Bankrot und Aufbau: Ostdeutsche Erfahrungen*, Baden-Baden: Nomos Verlagsgesellschaft.

Wessels, B. 1992, *Bürger und Organisationen – Ost- und West Deutschland: Vereint und doch verschieden?*, Berlin: Wissenschaftszentrum Berlin für Sozialforschung.

Wiesenthal, H. 1993, *Blockaden, Asymmetrien, Perfektionsmängel: Ein Vergleich der Representationschancen sozialer Interessen im Transformationsprozeß*, Working Paper AG TRAP 93/5, Berlin: Max-Planck-Gesellschaft.

(ed.) 1995a, *Einheit als Interessenpolitik: Studien zur sektoralen Transformation Ostdeutschland*, Frankfurt am Main and New York: Campus Verlag.

1995b, *From Inefficient Universalism to Prosperous Particularism?: About Functions Performed by Early Business Interest Associations in East Central Europe, Russia and Eastern Germany*, Working Paper AG TRAP 95/6, Berlin: Max-Planck-Gesellschaft.

1995c, *Representation of Functional Interests in West and East European Democracies: Theoretical Co-ordinates and Empirical Assessment*, Research Report AG TRAP 5, Berlin: Max-Planck-Gesellschaft.

1996, *Post-Unification Dissatisfaction: Or, Why Are So Many East Germans*

Dissatisfied with West German Political Institutions?, Working Paper AG TRAP 96/6, Berlin: Max-Planck-Gesellschaft.

Wiesenthal, H., Ettl, W. and Bialas, C. 1992, *Interessenverbände im Transformationsprozeß: Zur Representations- und Steuerungsfähigkeit des Verbändesystem in der neuen Bundesländer*, Working Paper AG TRAP 92/3, Berlin: Max-Planck-Gesellschaft.

Wilke, M. and Müller, H.-P. 1991, *Zwischen Solidarität und Eigennutz: die Gewerkschaften des DGB im deutschen Vereinigungsprozeß*, Melle: Verlag Ernst Knoth.

Wilson, G. K. 1993, 'American Interest Groups', in Richardson 1993, pp. 131–44.

Wirtschaft und Markt: Das ostdeutsche Magazin für Unternehmer, August 1994: 26.

Wyman, M. 1994, 'Russian Political Culture: Evidence from Public Opinion Surveys', *Journal of Communist Studies*, 10: 25–54.

Index

All-Poland Alliance of Trade Unions
(OPZZ), 35, 74, 77
All-Union Central Council of Trade
Unions (Russia), 35
Alliance '90 (Bündnis '90), 46, 159
Almond, G., 12–13, 98, 105–7, 123, 173
anomie, 98, 111–12, 123–4, 172, 177
anti-communist opposition, 5, 28–38, 77
Arato, A., 4, 6, 17
artisan trades, 59, 93
Association of Hungarian Manufacturing
Industry (MGYOSZ), 79
association, art of, 18, 178
ATLAS, *see* Ausgesuchte
Treuhandsunternehmern vom Land
angemeldet zur Sanierung
Ausgesuchte Treuhandsunternehmern
vom Land angemeldet zur Sanierung
(ATLAS), 151–2

Balkans, 9, 23, 28, 54
BASIS, *see* Beratungsstelle für
arbeitsorientierte Strukturentwicklung
in Sachsen
BDA, *see* Bundesvereinigung der
Deutschen Arbeitgeberverbände
BDI, *see* Bundesverband der Deutschen
Industrie
Beck, U., 8
Beratungsstelle für arbeitsorientierte
Strukturentwicklung in Sachsen
(BASIS), 151
Berlin, 47, 94, 130, 131
Betriebsegoismus, 57, 63
Biedenkopf, K., 147, 151
Bonn, 151, 159, 163
Brandenburg, 47, 151, 156, 157, 159
Bremer-Vulkan, 151
Bulgaria,
anti-communist opposition, 33, 77
democratic transformation, 23
participation, 101–4, 123

social capital in, 104, 106–7
trade unions, 35, 74, 77
tripartism, 139–41
Bundesverband der Deutschen Industrie
(BDI),
membership, 82
membership incentives, 90–1, 119
organization, 40–1, 81, 171
Bundesverband Mittelständische
Wirtschaft (BVMW),
competition with BDA affiliates, 119–20
membership, 93, 94
membership incentives, 119, 125, 171
organization, 60
Bundesvereinigung der Deutschen
Arbeitgeberverbände (BDA),
competition with *Unternehmerverbände*,
42, 60, 170
establishment in eastern Germany, 40–1
membership, 82
membership incentives, 119
organization, 60–2, 80, 171
and wage-bargaining, 144–7
see also individual constituent confederations
Bündnis für Arbeit (Alliance for Jobs), 67
business groups,
confederations, 79, 93, 96–7, 170
east-central Europe, 23–4, 36, 37, 53–5,
76–7, 79, 107, 127, 170
easterners and westerners in, 160
elected officials, 129, 131
emergence in eastern Germany, 29–30,
37, 39–42
entrepreneurial model of, 36, 127, 129,
132
inter-organizational competition, 96,
119, 171
local organization, 74, 79
membership, 8, 77–8, 97
membership incentives, 99–100, 108–9,
116–22, 124–5, 132
organizational cohesion/fragmentation,

55, 59, 76–7, 116–17, 142, 168, 170
participation in, 127–9, 131–2, 135
and political parties, 163
regional organization, 79, 93, 96–7, 170
salaried staff, 129, 132, 135
sectoral organization, 55, 59–61, 74, 79,
  93, 96, 170
and the state, 20, 78–9, 142–4
and wage-bargaining, 117–22
see also individual groups; employer
  associations
BVMW, *see* Bundesverband
  Mittelständische Wirtschaft

capital,
  structure of, 1, 7, 9, 16, 52–3
  east-central Europe, 70–1, 107, 167–8
  Germany, 58–61, 167–8
Cawson, A., 6, 20–2
CDU, *see* Christlich Demokratische Union
chambers of commerce,
  under communist regimes, 31
  post-communist, 77
  see also Industrie- und Handelskammern
Charité hospital, Berlin, 47, 94
Charter 77, 32–4
chemicals industry, 81–2, 156
Chemnitz, 57–8, 156, 157
Christlich Demokratische Union (CDU),
  151, 153, 157, 158–9, 161–3
citizenship, 3–4, 12, 143
CITUB, *see* Confederation of Independent
  Bulgarian Trade Unions
civic culture, 13–15, 98, 105–7, 113–16,
  123, 173
Civic Forum (Czechoslovakia), 33–4
civil society, 3–5, 17–18, 28–38, 50–1,
  173, 176
civilizational incompetence, 14, 107
CMKOS, *see* Czech–Moravian
  Confederation of Trade Unions
Cohen, J., 4, 17
collective action,
  American model of, 73, 124, 171
  and group membership, 16, 18–19, 169
  incentive structures in, 15–17, 19, 26,
    99, 106–9, 116–22, 124, 132, 135,
    148, 173–5
  and membership motivations, 18–19, 26
  pragmatism in, 18–19, 121–2, 127, 177
  problems of, 149, 174
  theories of, 9, 11–19, 51, 117, 124
co-management, 57–8
commodity fetishism, 128
Confederation of Independent Bulgarian

Trade Unions (CITUB), 35, 74, 77
construction industry, 59, 70, 77, 168
corporatism, 6–8, 19–23, 27, 30, 73,
  137–43, 163, 169
  and economic transformation, 149–53
  and interest mediation, 3, 20–2, 138,
    142, 164
  macro-, 20–3, 153–6, 164
  meso-, 21–3, 156–60, 164–5
  and organizational articulation, 10–11,
    79, 140, 170–1
  and organizational centralization, 10–11,
    75–6, 79, 140, 170–1
  and policy-making, 3, 20–2, 138–41,
    142, 149–53, 164
and social structure, 22–3, 137–9
corruption, 31, 36, 77, 108
Cottbus, 156
Croatia, 77
Crouch, C., 7, 8, 11, 22, 137
CSKOS, *see* Czech and Slovak
  Confederation of Trade Unions
Czech and Slovak Confederation of Trade
  Unions (CSKOS), 35, 74
Czech–Moravian Confederation of Trade
  Unions (CMKOS), 74
Czech Republic,
  anti-communist opposition, 5, 32–7
  business groups, 55, 76–7
  democratic transformation, 23–4, 32–7,
    166
  market transition, 9, 54–6, 166
  participation, 100, 101–4, 123
  regime change, 28–9
  social capital, 104–7
  trade unions, 35, 74
  tripartism, 139–41
Czechoslovakia, 24, 28, 32

Danube Circle (Hungary), 31–2
democracy, support for, 106–7, 114–15
Democratic League of Independent Trade
  Unions (Hungary), 35, 75
democratic theory, 3–5, 11, 19–20, 172
democratic transformation, 23–4, 28–9,
  31–7, 109, 111, 166
  elite exchange theory of, 23–6, 28–9
  see also individual countries
Deutsche Maschinen- und Schiffbau,
  150–1
Deutscher Gewerkschaftsbund (DGB),
  and corporatist relations, 158–9
  establishment in eastern Germany, 44–6
  and industrial action, 64–5
  membership, 87–90, 117

membership expectations, 121, 130
organization, 84–5
organizational cohesion/fragmentation,
    61–2, 67, 84
political role of, 84, 85
salaried staff, 130, 134
Deutscher Industrie und Handelstag
    (DIHT),
establishment in eastern Germany,
    42–3
membership, 82
organization, 82–3
DGB, *see* Deutscher Gewerkschaftsbund
DIHT, *see* Deutscher Industrie und
    Handelstag
division of labour, 5, 6, 176
Dresden, 47, 82, 134
Durkheim, E., 4–5, 178

Eisenach, 60, 118
electrical industry, 59
employer associations,
    and collective identity, 116–17
    and corporatist exchange, 160–1
    elected officials, 131–2
    emergence in eastern Germany, 39–43
    interview research in, 26
    and macro-corporatism, 153–6
    membership, 90–4, 116–17, 174
    membership incentives, 99–100,
        116–22, 124–5
    and meso-corporatism, 156–60
    organization, 59–61, 80–1, 96, 169
    organizational cohesion/fragmentation,
        63, 148, 169
    and political parties, 163
    salaried staff, 130, 132–5, 148
    social foundations, 59–61
    and wage-bargaining, 63–5, 144–8
    see also individual associations; business
        groups
employment relations, 1, 6–8, 52–3,
    137–8, 141–2, 167, 169
    east-central Europe, 55–6
    Germany, 57–8, 61–5
engineering associations, 46–7, 49–50, 58,
    67
engineering industry, 49–50, 59, 91, 169
entrepreneurial model, of interest
    representation, 3, 19, 24, 36, 50, 127,
    129, 136, 176, 177–8
Erfurt, 45
Etzioni, A., 18
exchange theory, 2–3, 18–19, 27, 126,
    136, 176, 178

FDGB, *see* Freier Deutscher
    Gewerkschaftsbund
FDP, *see* Freie Demokratische Partei
Federal Labour Office, 153
Federation of Independent Russian Trade
    Unions (FNPR), 35, 75–6
FNPR, *see* Federation of Independent
    Russian Trade Unions
food processing industry, 59, 168
Freie Demokratische Partei (FDP), 158,
    163
Freier Deutscher Gewerkschaftsbund
    (FDGB), 43–4, 46

GDR, *see* German Democratic Republic
German Democratic Republic (GDR),
    civil society in, 38
    democratic transformation, 109, 111
    organizations, 30, 38, 45, 133, 143,
        169
    regime change, 29–30
German model, 25–6, 58–9, 61–3, 67, 77,
    96–7, 116, 142, 143, 147, 148, 170–1,
    177
German unification, 25, 29–30, 37, 44, 50,
    66, 90, 111, 146–7, 149, 153, 161,
    164
Gesamtverband der metallindustriellen
    Arbeiteberverbände (Gesamtmetall),
establishment in eastern Germany, 40–2
    membership, 91–4
    organization, 80, 96, 144, 171
    organizational cohesion/fragmentation,
        148
    salaried staff, 132, 148
    and wage-bargaining, 63–5, 144–8
GEW, *see* Gewerkschaft Erziehung und
    Wiβensaft
Gewerkschaft Erziehung und Wiβenschaft
    (GEW), 46, 88
Gewerkschaft Handel, Banken,
    Versicherung (HBV), 162–3
    membership, 88
Gewerkschaft Öffentlichen Dienste,
    Transport und Verkehr (ÖTV),
    establishment in eastern Germany, 46
    membership, 85, 88–9
    organization, 85–6
    and political parties, 163
globalization, 8, 67, 137, 169, 177
group interests, 52–3, 59–61
group mobilization, 2, 28–37, 169, 173
group theory, 2–3, 166

Hamburg, 157

Hartmannbund, 175
   establishment in eastern Germany, 48
   membership, 86, 94–5
membership incentives, 122, 127, 175
membership participation, 112, 127
organization, 67–9, 86, 94
organizational cohesion/fragmentation,
   67–9
salaried staff, 131
HBV, *see* Gewerkschaft Handel, Banken,
   Versicherung
health care, 47–8, 67–9
Hegel, G., 4, 11
Helsinki accords, 32
Hungary,
   anti-communist opposition, 5, 31–7
   business groups, 36, 55, 76–7, 79, 127
   democratic transformation, 23–4, 31–7,
      166
   market transition, 50, 54–6, 166
   participation, 101–4, 123
   social capital in, 104–7
   regime change, 28–9
   trade unions, 34–5, 74–5
   tripartism, 139–41

ICM, *see* Interessenverband Chemnitzer
   Maschinenbau
IGCPK, *see* Industriegewerkschaft
   Chemie, Papier, Keramik
IG Medien, *see* Industriegewerkschaft
   Medien
IG Metall, *see* Industriegewerkschaft
   Metall
IGBE, *see* Industriegewerkschaft Bergbau,
   Chemie, Energie
IHK, *see* Industrie- und Handelskammern
incentive structures,
   business associations, 15–17, 90–1,
      99–100, 116–22, 124–5, 132, 148,
      171
   and collective action, 15–17, 19, 26, 99,
      106–9, 116–22, 124, 127, 132, 135,
      148, 173–5
   in post-communist society, 100, 107–15
   professional associations, 49–50, 69–70,
      95, 122, 175
   trade unions, 15–17, 89, 99–100, 108–9,
      116–22, 124–5, 130, 148
income differentials, 65, 110, 168
Independent Federation of Labour
   –Podkrepa' (Bulgaria), 35, 74, 77
indigenous organizational initiatives, 38,
   51
industrial relations,

east-central Europe, 18, 51, 55–6, 139
   Germany, 17, 57–8, 61–5, 117–22,
      141–8, 163–4, 168–9, 174–5
Industrie- und Handelskammern (IHK),
   and corporatist relations, 161
   elected officials, 131, 134–5
   establishment in eastern Germany, 42–3
   membership, 82
   organization, 43, 82–3, 116, 131
   salaried staff, 130, 134–5
Industriegewerkschaft Bergbau, Chemie,
   Energie (IGBE), 84
Industriegewerkschaft Chemie, Papier,
   Keramik (IGCPK), 88
Industriegewerkschaft Medien (IG
   Medien), 88, 128
Industriegewerkschaft Metall (IG Metall),
   58, 64, 66–7
   and corporatist relations, 150, 152,
      154–5, 158–9
   elected officials, 85
   establishment in eastern Germany, 44–6
   membership, 83, 87–90, 117
   membership expectations, 121, 133–4
   membership incentives, 89, 130
   membership participation, 113–14,
      127–9, 132–3
   organization, 58, 84–5, 144, 157, 170
   and political parties, 159, 162–3
   political role of, 85
   salaried staff, 130, 132, 134
   and the state, 149
   and wage-bargaining, 118, 144–5, 147–8
   and works councils, 64, 128
Inglehart, R., 12
institutional transfer, 29–30, 38–9, 44, 61,
   129–31, 134, 142–3, 160
institutional trust, 103–5, 114, 173
intercorporate networks, 108, 116
Interessenverband Chemnitzer
   Maschinenbau (ICM), 57–8
Italy, 14

Kammer der Technik (KdT),
   collapse of, 86–7, 95
   in GDR, 48–9
   membership, 49, 86, 95, 130
   membership incentives, 49–50, 69–70,
      95, 122
   organization, 49–50, 86–7
   salaried staff, 130–1
   social foundations, 69–70
   and VDI, 49
Kanzlerrunde, 153–4, 164
KdT, *see* Kammer der Technik

Keane, J., 4
Keynesianism, 21–2
Kohl, H., 154, 155

labour markets, 1, 7–8, 52–3, 65–7, 71, 87,
    118, 120–1, 168–9
Landesverband der Sächsischen Industrie
    (LSI), 41, 61, 82, 113, 114, 127,
    158
Landesvereinigung der Arbeitgeber- und
    Wirtschaftsverbände Sachsen-Anhalt
    (LVSA), 59, 113, 114, 160, 163
Lane, C., 11–12
Lasswell, H., 11–12
Lehmbruch, G., 142
Leipzig, 38, 39, 47
LSI, see Landesverband der Sächsischen
    Industrie
LVSA, see Landesvereinigung der
    Arbeitgeber- und Wirtschaftsverbände
    Sachsen-Anhalt

machine building industry, 57–8, 156,
    157
Magdeburg, 162
MAOSZ, see National Confederation of
    Hungarian Employers
Marburgerbund,
    establishment in eastern Germany, 48
    membership, 94
    membership composition, 67–9
    membership incentives, 122
    organization, 67–9, 94
    salaried staff, 131
market transition,
    east-central Europe, 9–10, 13, 18, 29,
        36–7, 52–6, 99, 137, 166–7, 177
    Germany, 25, 51, 71, 87, 111, 113–15,
        124, 172
Mecklenburg-Vorpommern, 41, 47, 131,
    150, 156, 159
medical associations, 26, 46–8, 50–1,
    67–9, 86, 131, 169
    see also individual associations
membership, 8, 40, 49, 77–8, 82, 83,
    86–95, 97, 107–8, 109–10, 116–17,
    130, 170, 174
membership participation, 112–14, 127–9,
    132–3, 135
MGYOSZ, see Association of Hungarian
    Manufacturing Industry
mining industry, 156–7
mixed economy, 54
MSZOSZ, see National Confederation of
    Hungarian Labour Councils

National Alliance of Workers' Councils
    (Hungary), 35, 75
National Association of Entrepreneurs
    (Hungary) (VOSZ), 36, 76, 127
National Confederation of Hungarian
    Employers (MAOSZ), 76
National Confederation of Hungarian
    Labour Councils (MSZOSZ), 35, 75,
    77
National Council of Hungarian Trade
    Unions (SZOT), 35
NAV, see Verband der Niedergelassenen
    Ärzte
New Forum (GDR), 29, 33–4, 38, 46
nomenklatura bourgeoisie, 10, 24, 36, 55,
    108, 124, 166, 174
Nordmetall, 41–2, 81, 143–5, 161, 163

Offe, C., 6, 7, 9, 52–3
Olson, M., 12, 16, 70, 125, 175
Opel, 60, 118
OPZZ, see All-Poland Alliance of Trade
    Unions
organizational design, 26, 55
organizational resources, 15–17, 26,
    107–9, 116–22
ÖTV, see Gewerkschaft Öffentlichen
    Dienste, Transport und Verkehr

Parsons, T., 5, 178
Partei des Demokratischen Sozialismus
    (PDS), 162–3
participation, 11–19, 26, 109–22, 127–9,
    176–7
    and civic culture, 13–15, 105–7, 113–15
    and incentive structures, 15–17, 107–9,
        116–22
    and political efficacy, 12–13, 100–5,
        110–13
    unconventional, 109
PDS, see Partei des Demokratischen
    Sozialismus
People Against Violence (Slovakia), 33–4
pluralism, 1–6, 7–9, 15–16, 19–20, 26–7,
    28–9, 70, 96, 124, 126, 136, 166, 169,
    175, 178
Podkrepa, see Independent Federation of
    Labour (Bulgaria)
    anti-communist opposition, 5, 28–37
    business groups, 55, 76–7
    democratic transformation, 23–4, 32–7,
        166
    market transition, 9, 54–6, 166
    participation, 100, 101–4, 123
    social capital in, 104–7

Poland (*cont.*)
  trade unions, 35, 74, 77
  tripartism, 139–41
political development theory, 23–4
political efficacy, 12–14, 100–5, 111–12,
  172
political entrepreneurs, 126
political parties, 20–1, 34, 36, 114, 127,
  140, 161–3
post-Fordism, 8, 62, 137–8
post-materialism, 12
post-modernism, 17–18, 176, 177, 178
post-socialist differentiation, 53
privatization,
  east-central Europe, 9–10, 36, 53–5, 108
  Germany, 39, 58–61, 70–1, 93, 110–11,
    120, 141–2, 166–7
professional groups,
  establishment in eastern Germany, 46–8
  interview research in, 26
  membership, 86, 94–5
  membership incentives, 122, 175
  membership participation, 127, 135
  organization, 86–7, 95
  organizational cohesion/fragmentation,
    67–70, 71
  and political parties, 162
  salaried staff, 95, 135
  social foundations, 67–72
  see also individual groups
Putnam, R., 14

rational choice theory, 2–3, 12, 15–19, 26,
  99–100, 116–17, 120, 124, 173–5
regime change, 28–30, 34
  see also individual countries
regional economic development, 151–3
retail sector, 79
Romania,
  market transition, 54
  participation, 101–4
  social capital in, 104–7
Rose, R., 15, 100, 103, 105, 107, 110,
  111, 128
Rostock, 150, 168
RUIE, *see* Russian Union of Industrialists
  and Entrepreneurs
Russia,
  business groups, 36, 55, 76–7, 127
  democratic transformation, 24
  market transition, 9
  participation, 101–4, 105
  social capital in, 104–7
  trade unions, 35–6, 75, 77
  tripartism, 139–41

Russian Union of Industrialists and
  Entrepreneurs (RUIE), 36, 76, 127

Sachsen, 147–8, 151–2, 156–9
Sachsen-Anhalt, 40, 134, 156, 159–60
salaried staff, 95, 129, 130, 132–5, 148,
  160
Scandinavian model, 61, 137
Schmitter, P., 5, 6, 8, 10, 11, 20, 22, 142,
  164
self-organization, 33
service industry, 59, 79, 168
ship-building industry, 150–1, 156, 168
Siemens, 128
Simmel, G., 5
Slovakia,
  anti-communist opposition, 31–5
  business groups, 76
  democratic transformation, 23, 31–5
  market transition, 9
  participation, 100, 101–4
  social capital in, 104–7
  trade unions, 35, 74
  tripartism, 139–41
Slovenia,
  anti-communist opposition, 5
  business groups, 77
  democratic transformation, 23
  market transition, 9
  trade unions, 78
small and medium-sized enterprises
  (SMEs), 60–2, 71, 76–9, 89–90, 93–4,
  108–9, 125, 146
  and collective bargaining, 117–19
  and trade unions, 120, 168
SMEs, *see* small and medium-sized
  enterprises
social capital, 2, 12, 13–15, 26, 98, 104–7,
  123, 172–3
social movements, 17–18, 31–5, 159
social psychology, 2, 11, 26, 98, 100–1,
  111–13, 122, 172, 177
social structure, 20, 26, 137–9
  east-central Europe, 1–2, 6–10, 16–17,
    29, 53–6, 107
  Germany, 56–7, 69–70, 71–2
social trust, 105, 114, 124, 173
Solidarity (Poland), 28, 32–7, 74, 77
Solidarity Pact (Germany), 142, 154–6,
  159, 164
Soviet Union,
  anti-communist opposition, 5, 32–7
  democratic transformation, 28–9, 32–7
  market transition, 9
  trade unions, 35–6

Sozialdemokratische Partei Deutschlands
  (SPD), 46, 152, 155, 159–60,
  162–3
SPD, *see* Sozialdemokratische Partei
  Deutschlands
state,
  communist, 28–9, 30–2, 37
  and organized interests, 78–9, 142–4
  and public policy, 19–23, 51, 138–9,
    148–9
  and society, 1–5, 173
Streeck, W., 7, 8, 118
SZOT, *see* National Council of Hungarian
  Trade Unions
Sztompka, P., 13, 14, 105, 107

Thüringen, 40, 60, 159
Tocqueville, A. de, 4–5, 11, 18, 178
trade unions,
  and collective identity, 117
  under communism, 34
  and corporatist exchange, 160–1
  elected officials, 129
  establishment in eastern Germany, 30,
    43–6
  industrial relations, 20, 52–3, 57–8,
    61–5, 120, 128, 148, 162, 169
  interests, 142
  jurisdictional conflicts, 85–6, 139–40
  and labour markets, 7, 65–7, 168
  and macro-corporatism, 153–6
  membership, east/central Europe, 77–8,
    97
  membership, eastern Germany, 87–9,
    97, 107–8, 109–10, 117, 170, 174
  membership incentives, 99–100, 108–9,
    116–22, 124–5, 130
  membership participation, 127–9, 133,
    135
  and meso-corporatism, 156–60
  organization, east/central Europe, 23,
    24, 74–7, 170
  organization, Germany, 55, 79, 83–6,
    96–7, 169, 170
  organizational cohesion/fragmentation,
    55, 75–7, 107–8, 117, 142, 148, 168
  and political parties, 140–1, 155, 158–9,
    161–3
  post-communist, 171–2
  reform in east/central Europe, 34–6
and regional government, 157–61
  salaried staff, 129, 133–5, 160
  and social learning, 114
  and the state, 142–4
  trust in, 121–2

and wage-bargaining, 63–5, 117–22,
    144–8
  see also individual trade unions
Treuhand, 56–9, 90–1, 120, 143, 144,
  146, 150, 151, 153, 154
tripartism, 23, 139–41, 164

Union for the Protection of the
  Environment (Slovakia), 31–2
Union of Democratic Forces (Bulgaria),
  33–4
United Kingdom, 137
Unternehmerverbände (UVs),
  competition with BDA, 42, 60, 170
  membership, 40, 93–4
  membership incentives, 125, 171
  membership participation, 112, 129
  organization, 60–1, 83
  salaried staff, 129–30
UVB, *see* Vereinigung der
  Unternehmerverbände in Berlin und
  Brandenburg
UVs, *see* Unternehmerverbände

VB, *see* Virchow-Bund
VDI, *see* Verein Deutscher Ingenieure
VDMA, *see* Verband Deutscher
  Maschinen- und Anlagenbau
Verba, S., 12–13, 98, 105–7, 123, 173
Verband der Chemischen Industrie,
  81–2
Verband der Metall- und Elektroindustrie
  (VME),
  and BDA, 81
  elected officials, 80
  establishment in eastern Germany, 40–1
  membership, 91–3
  organization, 58, 80–1, 130
  salaried staff, 130, 132–3, 134
  and wage-bargaining, 144–5
Verband der Niedergelassenen Ärzte
  (NAV),
  competition, 68–9
  establishment in eastern Germany, 48
  membership, 94
  membership composition, 67–9
  membership expectations, 121
  membership incentives, 68–9, 86
  membership participation, 112
  organization, 68–9, 86
  salaried staff, 131
Verband der Sächsischen Metall- und
  Elektroindustrie (VSME), 91–3, 114
Verband der Wirtschaft Thüringen
  (VWT), 116, 127

Verband Deutscher Maschinen- und
    Anlagenbau (VDMA),
  establishment in eastern Germany, 41
  membership, 90–1
  organization, 82
Verein Deutscher Ingenieure (VDI),
  establishment in eastern Germany, 49
  membership, 95
  membership incentives, 70, 175
  organization, 87
  salaried staff, 131
Vereinigung der Unternehmerverbände in
    Berlin und Brandenburg (UVB), 41,
    132
Vertrauensleute (shop stewards), 64, 128–9
Virchow-Bund (VB), 47, 68
VME, *see* Verband der Metall- und

Elektroindustrie
VOSZ, *see* National Association of
    Entrepreneurs (Hungary)
VSME, *see* Verband der Sächsischen
    Metall- und Elektroindustrie
VWT, *see* Verband der Wirtschaft
    Thüringen

wage-bargaining, 63–5, 117–22, 144–8
wage differentiation, 63
Waller, M., 29, 33, 77, 140, 143
Wiesenthal, H., 6, 8, 19, 39, 50, 111,
    139
works councils, 57–8, 62–4, 120, 128, 148,
    162, 169